DARRYL ON THE METS:

"I was looking at my option year with the Mets as a prison sentence. It had all been downhill from the World Series in 1986, when Davey Johnson pulled me out of game six at the end. The whole team had been celebrating and whooping it up, but I felt just like a fool."

"It seemed to me that the Mets had fewer blacks on their team than most of the other Major League teams and that they had signed precious few black players. Was I so much trouble to the Mets that they didn't want to deal with other blacks because of the example I was setting?"

"Frank Cashen never realized that I really did love the Mets, New York, and baseball after all. He never figured that out. He had his calculator out, of course."

DARRYL ON HIS TROUBLED MARRIAGE:

"There was no backing off and no backing down as Lisa and I kept on fighting. I could feel the violence rising inside me like the howling of so many demons. I was out of control."

DARRYL ON DARRYL:

"While at Smithers I finally understood that I had, over the years, become purely a creation of the media. The real Darryl Strawberry . . . simply did not exist. He had been erased by the media from the moment someone wrote that he was the 'black Ted Williams.' "

"[My father's leaving created] a well of anger so deep that even today it seems utterly bottomless. It's like a gaping chasm in my life that I'm afraid to look into, fearing that it will suck me in and I'll never escape alive. I can't fill that chasm, although I've certainly tried. I've thrown my own talents into that pit, tossed in people I've loved—friends, teammates, family, everything."

DARRYL

DARRYL STRAWBERRY
WITH ART RUST, JR.

BANTAM BOOKS
New York · Toronto · London · Sydney · Auckland

DARRYL

A Bantam Book

PUBLISHING HISTORY
Bantam hardcover edition published April 1992
Bantam paperback edition /April 1993

ISBN 0-553-56138-3

Published simultaneously in the United States and Canada

Bantam Books are published by Bantam Books, a division of Bantam Doubleday Dell
Publishing Group, Inc. Its trademark, consisting of the words "Bantam Books" and the
portrayal of a rooster, is Registered in U.S. Patent and Trademark Office and in other
countries. Marca Registrada. Bantam Books, 666 Fifth Avenue, New York, New York
10103.

PRINTED IN THE UNITED STATES OF AMERICA

RAD   0 9 8 7 6 5 4 3 2 1

ACKNOWLEDGMENTS

I'd like to thank my mother, Ruby Strawberry, as well as my brothers and sisters for their help and support. Thanks also to Michele Wolder at Darryl Strawberry Enterprises for steering this project in the right direction. And finally, to my wife, Lisa, and my two children, Darryl, Jr., and Diamond Nicole, thank you for the happiness you bring me.

—DARRYL STRAWBERRY

Thanks to my wife, Patty, for her help and support, and to all of my friends in the New York press and in Houston for helping me research facts and events.

—ART RUST, JR.

We also acknowledge the support and patience of our editor, Thomas Dyja, who sought out and inspired this book, and our literary agent, Bill Birnes, who helped make it a reality.

CONTENTS

FOREWORD

by Dwight Gooden

Baseball, like the rest of life, is about relationships. No one's in this alone. You develop special relationships with your teammates that sometimes turn into friendships. You learn each other's moves and share hopes and fears. You let yourself open up in ways you never thought you could. You stand up for each other when you can, and your problems become your friend's problems. Then, sometimes, for reasons you can't control, your friend goes to another team.

You were once on the same side, but now you have to face each other as opponents. You're a professional and you know that that's the way big-league baseball is supposed to be played. So you take a friendship and let it become a friendly rivalry. You will compete against each other one-on-one and you will try your hardest to come out on top even though you want nothing but success and good fortune for your friend. Who knows? Someday you may even be on the same team again.

That's the kind of relationship I have with Darryl Strawberry. He was a person I came to rely on as a friend when I was brought up to the Mets after he'd been there for about a year. Darryl stood up for me during my difficult periods and stormed out on the field to help me when he thought that I was outnumbered in a fight in a game against Philadelphia back in 1990. Afterward he told the press that he saw someone trying to hit me from behind and it just blew his fuse. He got his butt tossed out of the game for doing it, too. That's what friends do for friends.

When Darryl walked into the clubhouse after he had agreed to join the Dodgers, all I could do was look up at him and keep repeating "You're gone" because it hadn't even sunk into my own mind yet. I hadn't even thought about the possibility that he and I might someday be on opposing sides. I saw what Darryl had to go through during his years with the Mets, and I knew how he felt. Now I had to hope that whatever he could not find on the Mets, he would be able to find with the Dodgers. He was going home.

But when I faced Darryl Strawberry at Shea Stadium last season, it was with a kind of fire that you can whip up only when you're going up against a friend. He knew that I would give him some of my best stuff and I knew that he was trying to take me out of the park. Darryl rose to the occasion and had a good series against the Mets even though the fans that were booing him should have been cheering him. I was glad he got a hit off me and I was glad I struck him out. And that really was a full swing he took; I don't care how much he walked around laughing afterward. I saw it, he saw it, the ump saw it, America saw it.

Darryl is now walking in a different light where I know he will find the inner peace and satisfaction he's been seeking for years. Darryl has faced the issues of his past, and now he is ready to face the issues of his future. Writers can say whatever they want about Darryl now, but it won't matter. He's a man who has a secure sense of his own mission and his own purpose.

Part of his purpose is to write his own story about the issues of his past and his hopes for the future. Now he's done that, and I can tell you that this book really is the Darryl Strawberry I have come to know and respect over the years. It's more than just a baseball story or an autobiography. It's about personal growth, discovery, and revelation. The guy knows how to laugh at himself, too. Not many people can do that nowadays.

I'm happy for everyone who reads this book that they can now meet the Darryl Strawberry I know—the *real* Darryl.

1

HITTING BOTTOM

Where would you begin writing your life story if your life had two beginnings instead of one and was like a roller coaster in between? Would you go back in time to when you were most happy, like when you were drafted number one by the New York Mets and knew you would live your dream? Or go back to when you were most sad, like when you were watching from the dugout while your Mets violated all the laws of physics to pull off the biggest once-in-a-lifetime miracle in World Series history: MOOO-KIE, MOOO-KIE, MOOO-KIE. *"Duh, look down, Buckner, like it's between your legs."* Only you weren't playing because your manager from Mars had glued your butt to a bench. How about starting with your biggest mistake, like consenting to a blood test when you *know* that it was your National League All-Star sperm that beat out all the other sperm to reach the golden egg first? *"That's Strawberry breaking for second . . . Mike Scioscia with the throw . . . and he's SAFE!"* And you do this while rows of reporters from all the media are standing there at attention with their cellular phones on their ears, antennas cocked and ready. *"Darryl Strawberry fathers illegitimate child . . . at eleven."* Let's go to the videotape.

The road to my life's second beginning began in California on January 26, 1990, in the lonely hours before dawn when my wife, Lisa, and I had squared off for a fight in our bedroom. It seemed as if we'd been fighting for years. Actually, we had been. We'd been separated and reconciled so often I needed a scorecard to tell me whether I should go home or not. But this night was different from all the other nights because on this night all my mistakes came to a head.

Ten years worth of drinking, club hopping, fighting, and screwing around finally brought us to that early morning where those years would be suddenly topped by a moment of total stupidity. We'd always fought about my fooling around. We'd fought about my wife's staying out late at night with her friends. During the periods when we were separated and she'd move back to California while I stayed at my house in New York, I'd spent my time with some very lovely women. I met women in the scores of baseball cities around the country at night after the games, too. I didn't even remember their names, though they surely remembered mine.

I tell myself now, when I think about the emotions I had back then, that it was the demons who blinded me, the wild spirits who had run amok in my life for the past ten years. They had shown me some wild times and taken me on strange adventures. I was living on their credit—the Gold Card of Sin. But at three in the morning on January 26, 1990, they handed me the bill. In a sudden and violent explosion, my life began to change that very night.

Lisa and I had been fighting a marathon on and off for two days. That morning, when she walked in just after three after having been out with friends, we drew on our deepest reserves to pick up the battle where we'd left off. Neither one of us would give an inch, and we traded abuse until both of us were bloody.

Exactly what names we called each other in the winter darkness doesn't matter too much now. I only remember that the scene was ugly. I was angry at all women that night, but I directed my anger straight at Lisa. She brought it right back to me and fought like a cat. What did it matter, I said to myself, that I was a millionaire a few times over, that I had brought her and our children to the nicest seven-figure house in the West Valley (5 bdrms, fplc, cent. A/C, So. Blvd), that I'd bought my mother the house of her dreams, too, that I had all the success in the world? What did any of it matter as we kept on fighting up and down the stairs?

I saw in Lisa's eyes that I was a failure as both a husband and a father. It was the same look I had seen in my mother's eyes when she fought with my father about his gambling on another terrible night almost fifteen years earlier. We were living in a little bungalow of a house on Seventh Avenue in Los Angeles's Crenshaw Boulevard district. I was thirteen years old then. Now I was light-years away from that bungalow: twenty-seven, a father myself, and out of control just like my own daddy. Two days earlier, court-ordered blood tests had come back positive from a St. Louis laboratory. A woman I'd been intimate with who was also named Lisa, Lisa Clayton, had declared that little Eugene Michael Strawberry, a child she had given birth to eighteen months earlier, was mine. In order to settle it quietly, I paid her child support for a while, but then I stopped. She filed a paternity suit against me.

At first I had denied everything to the court, to my family, to myself, and even to little Eugene. But the blood tests spoke for themselves. Now the New York press had gotten hold of it, and they were eating me alive like a school of piranhas.

What had been a long-simmering argument between Lisa and me over my drinking and fornicating broke out into open warfare. She blamed me and I blamed her. Spirits were all around us when she finally came home that night, a houseful of demons feasting on what was left of our marriage. I felt that a pit had opened up in the world and was swallowing me whole.

I don't remember exactly what my wife said before the violence began because I was deaf and blind with fury. Maybe I should have listened more closely. But whatever it was, she said it again, only this time loud enough for half the block to hear. Suddenly I was out of control and I cracked Lisa across the top of her head with a thudding punch that echoed through the whole house. She fell over backward and then slowly got to her feet. We stood there, a deep silence between us, rage and fear welling up in her; shame and guilt welling up in me. The demons around us danced with joy.

Lisa had been humiliated in public by the press. Now she

had been belted by her husband, the cause of her humiliation. Her quivering lower lip was puffy where I'd caught her with the heel of my hand as it came down. I'd hit her before, but this time she intended to fight back. She grabbed a metal rod from somewhere and whipped it with full force toward my rib cage as if she were swinging a bat. I tried to block it with my hands, but the metal cracked across my wrists and sliced into my side. I doubled up at first, unable to catch my breath and afraid that she might have done some real damage. She started swinging it again, swiping at the air as she came toward me. Then my own temper erupted, and before I could stop myself I ran to the closet where I kept my .25-caliber semiautomatic pistol. She ran after me, still swinging the rod, and tried to force me to stay in the closet by jamming the rod into my chest. But I pulled my gun out of the closet and pointed it in her face as her mother, who had run up to the bedroom, started screaming.

My brain was on fire with evil voices. What did I say as she stood there ready to whack me again with that rod? "I'm going to kill you, bitch"? "I'm going to blow your brains out"? "Go ahead, make my day"? Did I scream more of the profanities we had been hurling at each other most of the night? Whatever it was I said, it was enough for Lisa's mother to call 911 and in so doing open up the trapdoor at the very bottom of the pit. In I slid, down the long chute. Down and around the circles I whirled while what looked like a squadron of black-and-whites from the Los Angeles Police Department wheeled around the corner of Ventura Boulevard and made a beeline for my driveway.

I heard a screeching of brakes and a loud banging on my front door before I even realized they'd been called. "Open up! Police!" they bellowed. They were already leaping and scrambling across my front yard and around the back of the house when I opened the door. Then they were right in my eyeballs, hands on their guns, batons at the ready, polite but relentless.

"Does this handgun belong to you?" one of the officers asked, holding up my automatic with the tips of his fingers on the trigger guard like it was a piece of garbage. "May I see the permit and registration for this handgun, please?"

They were oh so careful. One slip of procedure, one small comma out of place, and they would loose their grip on the big eenie meanie miney toe they so firmly held in triumph. But I wasn't about to holler, not me.

"Mr. Strawberry, you are under arrest for the possession of a handgun," one of them said, his glare riveting through my eye sockets and into my brain. He was right and I was wrong. I knew it and he knew it, but I still couldn't believe it. This wasn't happening to me! Hey, where's that little black-and-white dude in the three-button suit holding a cigarette who always walks into the frame at moments like this, squints, and says: *"Portrittt of a buh-lack superstar [beat] trapped in the corner of a nightmare."*

But this wasn't a movie, this was the real thing, and I was going down on a gun charge big-time. The demons were screaming in victory; this was the culmination of a thousand mistakes.

"You have the right to remain silent," the officer continued. "Anything you say can and will be used against you in a court of law. You have the right to talk to a lawyer and have him present with you while you are being questioned." He was holding a card that he was reading from right under his nose, but somehow he managed to keep staring at me. "If you cannot afford to hire a lawyer"—did I detect a small smile creeping around the edges of his mouth?—"one will be appointed to represent you before any questioning, if you wish. You can decide at any time to exercise these rights and not answer any questions or make any statements. Do you understand these rights?"

I think I nodded. It had been two days of attack and counterattack and now I was sagging under the weight of everything that had happened. I only wanted to surrender. There was no more I could have done, no more any human being could have done under those circumstances. *"Do not touch your dial. There is nothing wrong with your life. We are controlling the signal."* My personal demons, the earthly spirits I had been fighting with, had me pinned to the mat, and no matter how deep I dug that night, there was nothing I could dredge up to help me.

The police began to explain that gun possession is a serious crime in California. Sure, they said, they wanted to write it off as a simple "domestic." But they and I knew that it wasn't going to be that easy, not in California, not in Los Angeles County.

"We all have our problems, Straw," they said. "But no can do. Someone called in a weapon and it's already on the tape. We gotta make a report, homes, you know?"

Yo yo, check it out, homes, I thought to myself. I dig! I dug that I was in deep. I was caught butt-naked in a paternity suit; I had whupped my wife upside the head, waved an unregistered handgun square in her face and threatened her life with it, and was about to be hauled down to the West Valley Division of the LAPD like a common felon. No, this wasn't happening to me; it was the other guy!

The whole thing was unfolding like a play before my eyes. I was getting arrested, even though the sheriff's officers were trying to be human about what they had to do. They knew that this was a story that was going to explode all over me, but they didn't want to take any chances. They also knew that whatever happened to me would depend largely upon whether Lisa filed a criminal complaint against me and how I acted during my arrest. They had read the stories in the newspaper about the paternity suit and the blood test and were gracious enough not to make matters worse. But I still felt ashamed and humiliated, as if I didn't have a right to exist. If I could have found a rock I would have crawled under it and made everybody's life just a little bit simpler.

The police made a routine eyeball sweep of the house, took information from Lisa for their report, and then announced that I would have to accompany them to the station where I would be formally charged. Would I go quietly? I just kind of nodded. Then, after I assured them that I would have an attorney representing me, they simply escorted me to the back of the car and asked me to sit inside. I was still in a daze because I knew that I was no longer in control of anything. I believed my life had been taken out of my hands and I winced from the pain in my ribs where Lisa had whacked me with that metal rod. I remember being especially thankful that the deputies hadn't turned on their lightbars to play reds and blues through every bedroom window on the street or left their radio PAs on to blare police calls into the darkness. It would all be done as quietly as possible, or so I thought.

To be frank, much of what happened after I was taken down to the station and put in the lockup is still a blur. Whether I've blocked it out or whether I was still too much in shock to take it all in, I don't know. I was numbed from the events that had been going on for the past couple of days. I remember riding in the back of the black-and-white to the station worrying that half the world's press would be waiting for me there, ready to gobble me up. But it didn't happen.

I remember waiting, waiting to make phone calls to my lawyer, phone calls to my agent, Eric Goldschmidt, and to the Mets' team psychiatrist, Dr. Alan Lans. I was aware that there were a lot of discussions going on around me. Lots of conferencing among the officers and people I didn't know. There was back-and-forth and more back-and-forth. Was Lisa going to press criminal charges? Would I have a marriage left? Would I even have a life left when the dust settled from all of this? I kept asking myself how far down would I go? Was there any way to break this fall, to pull myself up? I didn't get involved; I had already said and done too much that night.

It hurt to close my eyes because too many memories flooded my mind. I remembered my father, Henry, fighting with all of us on one of the last nights he was ever in the house and how scared and angry I felt. I didn't even know who to blame at that time. I remember not understanding why he wasn't there anymore in the mornings or at night and how I wanted to bust someone's lip when my friends from school told me that they had watched him playing ball in the park. My friends watched him, but I never saw him at home anymore. Was that when the demons started? Was his fate going to be mine? Were my children going to ask the same questions about me when their own lives were in ruins twenty years from now? I had to exert some control, take some action to show that I was still in charge of my life. But I simply didn't know what to do except let the events going on around me play themselves out. Maybe if I kept on retreating I'd find a safe place to take up a defensive position. That didn't sound very creative, but at the time it was the best I could do.

The whole thing only took about an hour, but it felt like it went on all morning. I was formally charged with possession of an unregistered, unlicensed handgun. It was also clear from what Lisa was saying and how she was looking at me that she wasn't going to file criminal charges. The police weren't considering me a threat either. They were noting the incident as a "domestic," and everybody seemed to be winking at one another when the question of Strawberry's "drinking problem" came up. Just be glad, I remember saying to myself as I tried to find something positive in this whole mess, that you aren't involved in drugs. It's okay to be an alcoholic. Something noble about it when you have lots of money. But these were excuses, evil spirits jiving inside my brain, telling me what they'd been telling me since I'd gotten on the down escalator. They were liars and I'd been too willing to believe what they were saying. I was promising myself, as I sat there in the sheriff's station, that I had to find some good out of all this bad.

I posted twelve thousand dollars bail and was released. But more important, how serious had I been about the gun? It was loaded, you know. Would I have actually pulled the trigger? I had gotten too close to the edge, I told myself, and was hanging right over the cliff. I was sick; I was tired; but I was also very angry. The angrier I became about what had happened, the more I felt myself being sucked under against my will and despite my struggles into the deepest dungeon of despair that anyone could imagine.

When I got back home from the police station, I realized just how vulnerable I was. Nobody was responding to requests for interviews from the press, the Mets' management was concerned, and I was still facing possible criminal charges that easily could have kept me out of the 1990 season. There was also the problem of the paternity suit that I was about to lose. I was going to get socked with past due and monthly child support. I was bleeding money. And on top of all that, my marriage was in complete disarray. All my dirty laundry was hung out to dry in full view of the New York press. No wonder I was feeling like a walking bull's-eye.

Fortunately for me, the Mets had put Dr. Lans on a West Coast flight as soon as they got the news that I'd been arrested. I assumed I'd be talking to him anyway after the news of the blood test broke. I'd spoken to him on and off during the previous year and even had a picture of him in my locker at Shea Stadium, but I was embarrassed about talking to him and joked around with the other team members about it. I knew I needed help even back in '88 and '89—especially '89—but I was too busy trying to be one of the guys who played hard baseball, drank hard liquor, and screwed around as if they had more life than they needed. But I was only fooling myself, and Dr. Lans knew it. He came to the house later on the day I returned from the police station and we got to talking immediately. Dr. Lans said that he wanted to help, to intervene medically in my life, but that whatever we did, it had to be my decision.

"I can't force you to do anything," I remember him saying. "You should stop drinking right here and now. But it has to be your decision or nothing will take."

He assured me that we were talking about a medical problem and that whatever the public fallout was, he knew that I had problems that would respond to medical treatment. He kept saying that over and over, as if he were trying to convince me not to give in to the force of gravity dragging me down.

"You're *not* going to get worse," he said. "Things will only get better if you let them. I'm here to make sure they do."

You have no idea how much that advice helped in the hours after the crisis. I felt like I had nowhere to turn. I had estranged myself so much from my wife, Lisa, over the years that I had too much shame to ask her for help. How can you go back to someone whom you've just threatened and beg them for help? Forgiveness, yes, but help? That was another matter. Again it was Dr. Lans who urged me to talk to Lisa.

"Things won't start getting better unless you go right to where you feel the most guilty right now," he said.

So I confronted my wife. This time, however, I told my ego to walk away, to chill out in another room and get out from in between my wife and me. It was my ego, I understood, that had gotten in the way, my pride, the worst of sins. I had relied on pride when I was younger, pride in what I was and how I performed on a baseball field. Pride kept me going in the minors when I was lonely and under siege from the media. Pride was standing with me in the batter's box when I faced Cincinnati's Mario Soto back in 1983 the first night I came up to the majors. I whiffed that night, but pride told me it was okay to keep on going. Pride and I had gotten to be good friends over the years, but now pride had grown too big.

I realized as I faced Lisa in our living room the afternoon after our fight that I had relied too much on pride. It had gotten me into aggressive fights with other people over the years and had kept me from seeing the truth about myself even when that truth was staring me in the face. Now pride had gotten the better of me. I was fed up with my life, I told Lisa. Fed up to the point of needing to make a major change. I was a drunk, I said to her: a drunk and an adulterer.

I finally broke down and cried, letting all the bad attitude and hatefulness that had been stored up in me gush right out. It wasn't easy. I had to admit a lot of guilt that I had been hiding over the years. I had to talk about an evil part of myself that I was ashamed of. But I also knew that unless I stopped living in denial about what I was doing, I would never change. And in those moments on that day, I wanted nothing more than to change my life for the better. I knew I was going down on the road to hell.

I confessed to Lisa that when I woke up on certain mornings I was so filled with boozing and stuffing myself during my nights of club hopping that I was sick. Baseball had been my career for almost ten years. It was supposed to be fun, but now I was also sick of the circus that accompanied me wherever I went. I knew that part of it was my own making. I may have started off as a kid who'd just graduated from high school into the world of professional sports, but I hadn't adjusted well at all. I had let other people and alcohol take control of my life. Now it was time for me to take it back.

I couldn't stop crying. It was as if a kid inside me who'd been lost for all these years was finally calling out for help.

"Dr. Lans and I are going to hole up for a few days," I said to Lisa. "And we're gonna sort this out."

She asked me if I were going to leave her. I said that Dr. Lans and I were going to talk until there was no more talking left to do.

"I've got to get some rehabilitation or something," I said to her. "Drinking is going to kill me. I can feel it eating away at me right now. Eating away at us and our kids. In the end it's gonna destroy everything that's important."

Lisa was in shock because she'd never heard me open up and talk about myself this way. When we'd argue about something, we'd either have huge fights in which we'd blame each other for what was wrong and then become defensive, or I'd clam up in front of the TV or go out with friends. We hadn't spoken honestly to each other for years. I guess we were both pretty young when we got married and I already had my career and more money than I needed. I'd met Lisa in 1983 at a Lakers game at the Forum when I was the local hero, a rookie big-leaguer. I told the friends I was with when I saw her in the crowd that I thought she was a knockout. We were introduced, began dating, and got married in 1985. Inside of a year, we'd had Darryl, Jr., but I'd already begun to let the pressures of being a baseball player get in the way of our marriage. I had been taking our relationship for granted and didn't want domestic issues to get in the way of my career. And I was drinking. Lisa and I had been separated and reconciled twice, and during one of the most recent reconciliations we'd had little Diamond Nicole. But the stories about our marital disputes, the divorce filings, and how my drinking was affecting my marriage had been front-page headlines for years. Now, I hoped, if I had to go into rehab all that would change and we would have a chance to become the family where problems are talked out instead of fought out.

"If I have to go to the hospital," I said, "then I'm gonna go. Dr. Lans will check me in." He had been on staff at Smithers, where he'd dealt almost exclusively with substance abuse, before coming to the Mets.

She said she was worried about me, and then she started to cry also. We sat there crying and rubbing our eyes until they were red and swollen. There was nothing in anything we said that would resolve the big question mark that was our future.

"Why do you have to go away?" she kept asking. "What are they going to do to you in the hospital?"

"Dr. Lans says it's not what anybody's gonna do to me that's important," I tried to explain, but I was as worried as she was. "It's something I have to do. I have to leave the world in order to get back into it the right way."

Lisa also understood that we were only a few days away from the beginning of spring training. I didn't want to go to Florida and that had created a lot of the anxiety in the first place. I was looking at my option year with the Mets as a prison sentence. It had all been downhill from the World Series in 1986, when Davey Johnson pulled me out of game six at the end. The whole team had been celebrating and whooping it up, but I felt just like a fool. The drinking, womanizing, fornicating, and hatefulness since then were all part of being where I didn't want to be. But I didn't really understand it then, not the way I do now. And Lisa didn't understand it either. We just knew that something was terribly, terribly wrong, and there was nothing we could do about it. I could only stare at the hopeless prison that was my future, both as a member of the Mets and—a frightening alternative—as an inmate in the Los Angeles County jail.

. . .

Dr. Lans and I checked into one of the hotels near Sepulveda Boulevard at the Los Angeles International Airport complex that afternoon where we began talking in a way that let me say exactly what I had been feeling for the past five years. He listened to me. I felt in that conversation—as I had felt in earlier meetings with him—that I wasn't just an asset, a piece of property owned by the Mets and managed by Frank Cashen. I felt worthwhile, an experience I had not had in a while. Dr. Lans told me that what I was experiencing was a long-term reaction. The drinking may have been only a symptom of something else, he said. But I would have to recognize and admit that I was an alcoholic.

At first I was surprised. I didn't really know what an alcoholic was. I felt pretty ashamed, guilty, and humiliated. But Dr. Lans turned that aside for the moment. Those were normal feelings, he said, and most alcoholics experience them. We would have to deal with them at some point, he assured me, but the important thing was to address the medical issues first. He said that my entire body was like a toxic waste dump. Alcohol is a poison and I had been contaminating myself physically as well as mentally over the years.

I explained to him how sick I felt and how I hated looking at myself in the morning each and every day. I was drinking, I told him, so that I wouldn't be angry anymore and wouldn't beat up on myself so much. But the more I drank, the more night spots I went to and the faster I lived, the angrier I became. Now I was tired, I said. And he asked me if I was sick and tired of being sick and tired. Somehow that made sense, and then he asked me if I wanted to make a real commitment to stop drinking.

"First you have to get sober," he said. But he reminded me that it was nothing he could order me to do or prescribe. He suggested that I needed a break from the pressure that was building up around me again, even before spring training started. He said that I needed to get away from the world, from all the things in my life that had helped create this drinking spiral that had entrapped me so completely. I was out of control, he told me, so out of control that I needed to say "Stop" and apply the brakes. All alcoholics are out of control, because we don't understand that a chemical has taken control of our lives from us. I had to take the first step. I had to get clean and sober.

"What do I do?" I asked him.

"A rehab—Smithers," he answered.

We started a conversation that lasted for three whole days. We talked about the Mets, my life, my drinking, my family, and my father. We talked about the pressures that surround professional athletes, the pressures of working in New York, and the ways the media can get to you. We talked about rehabilitation. He tried to ease my fears and told me some of the crazy stories other celebrities (always anonymous) had told him.

"You're not alone in what you're feeling," he said.

He explained that when someone drinks to make himself forget that his problems circle around drinking, he's under the influence of a chemical substance. I needed a power greater than myself, Dr. Lans said, to get that control back. Otherwise no matter how many times I vowed to stop drinking, I wouldn't be addressing the problem. I was an addict. I had a disease. And I needed medical help.

Going to Smithers, Dr. Lans suggested, would also be a way for me to get a fresh look at life. "You have to learn about yourself and the disease you have," he said. "It isn't like getting over a cold. You're going to be an alcoholic for the rest of your life. Whether you're sober, dry, or drunk depends on what you do."

It was my call whether to go to Smithers. Alan Lans helped me see things in ways that made sense, but he left the actual decision up to me. The Mets' management stood behind Dr. Lans. My lawyer spoke to the court who would be handling the weapons charges against me and informed them that I was an alcoholic and would be checking into Smithers in New York for rehabilitative medical treatment. The court came back to us with an offer to drop the weapons charges if I successfully completed the program. Lisa was not going to press criminal assault and weapons charges. The whole matter was simply going to go away. Why was I so lucky? I asked myself.

In those series of discussions with Dr. Lans, I began to get the sense that I was being looked out for, protected. It was only a feeling at that stage, nothing I could really pin down for a fact. I didn't know why I deserved any special attention. In fact I felt pretty down on myself, guilty for what I had done and filled with remorse about how I'd led my life. But because I'd said that I wanted to change my life, it was as if something had happened to say, "Yes, you can." Was I special? Was all this happening because I was the great Darryl Strawberry of the New York Mets? One year later I would "get it." It would be revealed to me that what changed my life, or rather, *who* changed my life, was standing ready to change the life of anyone who came forward to ask. Asking was the key, and being ready to accept the changes. I didn't know it back in January 1990, and it would take another roller coaster ride to get me to see it.

People who knew me said they could see the signs of alcoholism way before Dr. Lans explained them to me. One-time Major League pitcher Sam McDowell, who himself was an alcoholic and later became a substance abuse counselor, was quoted as saying that he could see my problems from the newspaper stories that were written about me. I read those same stories and all I could see was bias and distortion. Maybe McDowell was reading between the lines.

I knew I was drinking heavily. I had even complained about it to my family, especially to my mother, Ruby. She started asking me about all the stories she was reading about me in the newspapers. I answered that you don't know what it's like when you've got fifty thousand people booing you from all sides of Shea Stadium. It does wonders for your self-esteem. She understood. She knew that adjusting to public opinion, which can be as fickle as the weather, puts a lot of pressure on you. Remember, I was the only Met getting boos in the 1986 World Series. When I was switched to cleanup in mid-1987 and my stats picked up to where I was kissing .300, the boos changed to *Darrrrryls*. I even got *Darrrrryls* when I went to Madison Square Garden for Knicks games. Go figure!

Drinking started to become a problem for me when I got to the majors and realized that this was "business." When I opened my mouth, some distorted version of my words wound up in the newspapers the next day. If I didn't perform with the bat or missed a ball in the outfield, I was hooted whenever I popped my head out of the dugout. But my drinking really started to get worse after the 1986 World Series when I blew up at Davey Johnson for taking me out of game six. His managing decisions on the field at times seemed to come from outer space and not from the situation in the game. They were unique, but rarely logical. I was still mad a couple of years later when I blasted Davey in an *Esquire* interview. Unfortunately I also blasted Kid Carter and Mex Hernandez, and in between more than a few brewskies, some other players. We would have won the pennant, I said, had their heads not been so totally up their asses. You can imagine the general reaction to that. The interview made so many waves that you could feel the effects in the newspapers for months after, like aftershocks from an L.A. earthquake.

I was still only twenty-five years old when I found myself overwhelmed by the pressure to perform and work miracles on the field. I would reach for booze the first chance I got. And I became angry, nasty, and selfish. I was mean to Lisa, mean to my friends, mean to my teammates, and quick to react when I thought someone was encroaching on me. That was why I said what I did back in 1988. I was an uglier SOB the more I drank, lapsing into gluttony and sloth. Worse, I kept drinking to make myself feel better about being so wrathful, as if, somehow, drinking itself would relieve the pressure I was under. But drinking simply created more pressure. It got to the point where it was an endless cycle. Some mornings I was so hung over, I literally had to be dragged over to Shea or to practice. Or if I didn't hear my wake-up call from the hotel desk on our road trips, I would sleep right through the beginning of practice. Being out the night before at clubs until four A.M. or at recording studios playing "Chocolate Strawberry" instead of at the ballpark didn't help either (though I still feel there's another side to that whole story). My performance had clearly started to suffer, and the New York press documented every breathtaking moment of it. Know what I did about all of it? I had another drink, and then another drink to forget about the drink I'd just had. That's what happens when you're an alcoholic.

I drank my rum until I would fall asleep and forget that I was a drunk. Then I started blaming my family. I told myself that Lisa held the key to my problems, that maybe it was her fault, or my brother Ronnie's, or even my brother Michael's. My father! Blame him. That's the ticket! The fault was never mine. My fuse got shorter and shorter. No one could tell me anything. Then I started turning violent—alcohol does that to you—and I aimed that violence directly at Lisa. That was what lay behind our fight on January 26, 1990.

After Dr. Lans and I came out of our virtual seclusion, hashing and rehashing the problems I was dealing with, I flew with him to New York to check straight into Smithers for rehabilitation. There were other reasons for this decision, which would have made some sort of isolation necessary in any event. First and foremost was the need to sort things out in privacy. Then there was the media pressure surrounding the incident on January 26. There was nowhere on the face of this planet I could have sorted anything out with the press hounding my every step. The story was even covered in *Time* magazine. I would have had to go to a bungalow colony on the moon to be alone. Smithers guaranteed a reasonable level of privacy, so it offered the best chance of stepping off the merry-go-round for a few weeks to do some quiet thinking about getting better.

Next was Smithers' national reputation. I knew that most of the therapists at Smithers had helped other alcoholics and substance abusers who were high-profile professional athletes deal with the pressure of being a sports celebrity. I believed they could help me. Because Smithers was a recognized recovery hospital, I also knew that I wouldn't have to explain my whereabouts to anyone. My going to Smithers was also a decision that the court would understand and accept. I didn't have to stay in California to await the outcome of whatever decision the prosecutor made; I could check into a hospital for medical treatment. When the prosecutor agreed to dismiss all charges against me, it then meant that I could go straight from Smithers to Port St. Lucie and begin spring training. Unfortunately, life wasn't as simple as that.

On February 3, 1990, I was officially in recovery. Recovery is like never having to say you're sorry, at least until step five. Recovery is, however, always having to say you're an alcoholic. I learned that one spends the rest of one's life healing from addiction because once an alcoholic, always an alcoholic. It's a disease, not a behavior, so you don't just get cured and walk away. You get sober by not drinking one day at a time and learn what it means to stay sober each day of the rest of your life. You learn what it means to live with the disease of alcoholism by relying on a higher power to help you resist the chemical craving to drink. You are also taught that you should take positive steps to remove yourself from the outside pressures that encouraged you to drink. For me that wasn't so easy.

Rehab began with the attitude of "easy does it" and "one day at a time." You're taught that you're not going to solve all of your problems by yourself and certainly not all at the same time. You're taught that you have a life-threatening disease that affects not only you but also your family and anyone with whom you've come into contact. That's why, the twelve-step program says, you have to not only take a "searching moral inventory" of your own life, but understand and accept where you've damaged the lives of others as well. At some point in your recovery, you're asked to go back to the people you've hurt and make some sort of restitution. That's when you say, "I'm sorry."

I learned that you can't resolve the issues of alcoholism in your life if you're still trying to dodge the incoming artillery shells. Part of my first discovery at Smithers was that once I was behind those walls, the sounds of exploding shells stopped waking me up at nights. I stopped worrying about who was saying what about me on the sports pages of the *Daily News* or on Page Six of the *Post*. And I didn't have to read any of the tabloids. That alone—the wonderful peace of seclusion—was a blessed relief. It told me that part of my problem was the pressure of being in a New York environment. Maybe that added to my eventual decision to leave New York City once and for all: it had become dangerous to my health and my sanity.

The recovery process also teaches you to accept honestly and without fear the person you are. I learned that part of my problem was that I denied the anger that had been building up inside of me over the years. I was angry at the Mets, angry at having to play in New York, angry at being the butt of so many derisive and untrue stories in the newspapers, and angry, in general, about being the whipping boy for an entire baseball club. Maybe my reaction to the anger I was feeling hadn't always been one hundred percent mature, but it was okay for me to be angry. It's true I was making lots of money, but no human being should have to endure the ugliness of the criticisms that I had endured.

While at Smithers I finally understood that I had, over the years, become purely a creation of the media. The real Darryl Strawberry, a person who had feelings, wants, needs, aspirations, and all the failings of a human being, simply did not exist. He had been erased by the media from the moment someone wrote that he was the "black Ted Williams." I was never the black Ted Williams, the black Joe DiMaggio, or a young Willie Mays. If you're a black outfielder who hits a long ball, you get to be a young Willie Mays by default. I had become so many creations of the media that at one point someone should have asked, "Will the real Darryl Strawberry please stand up." No one would have gotten up, not even me.

I had, during my decade in the Mets organization, become an invisible man. When you're black, being invisible to whites is a way of life. Most white people look right through black people as if they aren't there. Take a walk down Fifth Avenue by Fifty-seventh Street at noon on a weekday and see what I mean. When they need you to be there, they simply create a version of you that fits their mold. You're a superstar; you're invincible; you're the savior; you're a "gentleman"; you have an "attitude"; you don't live up to your potential; you're a "bad ass." But in reality, black athletes are simply robots. Nobody sees you; they only see what they want to see. You conveniently disappear.

I was no different, even though I didn't understand it in 1980. At the time I joined the team, they said that I had the potential to become the greatest baseball player of all time. Believe it or not, that made me sick to my stomach. It's one thing for a John Mosely or a Brooks Hurst—two baseball coaches from my childhood in Los Angeles—to tell you privately and during moments of doubt and frustration that you shouldn't give up because you have great potential. It's quite another for the sportswriters of the world to write about your potential as if they, not you, had all the rights to your future. My career had become their property. Even the Mets had gotten into the act. As a result, the Darryl Strawberry who was the human being had simply, but not at all quietly, ceased to exist. I was eighteen years old, and although I didn't understand it, I knew that I had been violated as if someone had reached right down inside of me and yanked out my heart and soul. I was more than mad now; I was totally pissed off.

At least now I knew part of the problem. There was a much deeper problem that I would come to grips with later that year. But for the present I only guessed at the signs whenever they appeared. However, I talked to Dr. Lans about what I was thinking about in Smithers and he encouraged me to work on that. I expected, hoped, in fact, that knowing what had happened to me over the past ten years, even though it steamed me up just to think about it, would at least toughen me for the future. I knew the Mets' front office had always given me a hard time about my living up to their expectations, but if I could console myself by saying those were *their* expectations and not *my* expectations, it might make a difference during the year. Was I ever wrong!

I walked out of Smithers believing that at least the Mets were behind me, and into a firestorm of negative press. I held a press conference and said, in effect, don't beat me up because I'm not really a bad guy. I explained that I didn't know how to handle all the pressure of playing in New York and that I was a sick guy who was getting better. I had hoped they would accept that. I admitted to making mistakes and wanted to make a fresh start in New York even though I knew that I was in the last year of my contract—my option year—and that free agency loomed ahead if the Mets decided not to negotiate an extension.

Maybe, I figured as the team got ready for the season, just maybe I'd be able to play ball as I used to play it—for fun. I was no longer a drunk. I was in recovery. At least I had *begun* to understand part of the nature of the seething anger that had been burning inside me for the past ten years. I had joined Alcoholics Anonymous and was attending meetings. People there were speaking to me as if I were a human being and not some robot who played baseball. Maybe I could just play ball, keep my mouth shut, and not get into trouble anymore.

This year, I promised myself, I would simply say "No comment" to the gentlemen from the press who shoved microphones in my face every time I walked into the locker room. I would politely decline to be interviewed every time somebody made a crack about Strawberry's not living up to his potential or letting the team down. Hey, the white players were allowed to walk out of the locker room wearing the "Aw, shucks!" grin of a Mr. Potato Head, and the press would eat it up. I would do the same thing. Show 'em teeth, Straw! I promised myself I would let my bat do the talking.

I figured it would be natural for me to be a better player once I was healthy. I made a determined decision: I would make 1990 work. I would be the best and most productive

New York Met you ever saw. I'd make them proud to have Darryl Strawberry on the team. I would carry the team into the World Series on my back if I had to. Nothing would matter except baseball. The Mets would like me. They would appreciate me. I would turn my life around and write a new chapter in my history. I didn't know it then, but my optimism regarding the Mets, like most of my other attitudes about the Mets, was just another mistake.

The Mets, you see, apparently had made other plans.

2

ROBOMET, 1990

There are moments during a baseball season when you are in the flow of success; when the world moves around you in slo-mo and you glide in between the seconds at will, seeing objects from two and three sides all at once. At moments like that, when a Mike Scott fastball comes spinning toward you from the mound like a comet swinging out from behind the sun, your eyes capture it and slow it down to where you can see it breaking ever so slightly down and away. You measure the angle even before the ball itself moves. You can count the number of spins it will make before you clobber it. Suddenly the fans grow silent and all you hear is the whooshing of the wind as it swirls over your bat. You're the only person on the face of the planet. You and the ball. You bring your bat around to meet the ball where it's supposed to cross the plate and you feel the contact all the way down to your ankles. As you bring your bat up and through the ball, you can feel it lift, launched in a trajectory that will take it somewhere far away into the upper deck. When you finally hear the fans roar, you realize that the entire incident—the pitch, the swing, the contact—all took place in cold silence, as if you were in another universe. By the time the volume returns, you're already rounding second and heading for third. That's the way to play baseball.

Sometimes at night, when I was a kid playing in Little League, I used to dream about being in the flow. I used to imagine how the ball would come in and how I could set up for it, waggling my bat high over my head to build the torque in my back, rearing up on my left leg for power, and connecting with a swing that echoed through the entire stadium. I could visualize every second of that swing, the perfect stroke on a perfect spring day in Los Angeles when something inside tells you daddy's coming home after all and you can do no wrong.

Every year, every hitter on every team dreams of the magic swing when the ball cracks sweetly off the bat and time stops. The fans stop and everybody stands to see how far the ball travels. You don't even bother to run it out because from the feel of the bat in your hand and the sound of the crack, you know it's gone. The fans know it's gone too, but they watch to see how far it will go. By the time you've tossed the bat away and begin jogging toward first, the ball's already in the upper deck, disappearing in the thousands of hands reaching up to snag it. Those are the home runs every hitter dreams of. Those were the hits I was dreaming of as I tried to set my life straight at the end of my stay at Smithers.

Whatever exhilaration I was feeling when I was released from rehab quickly dissipated when I returned home to Los Angeles. I started thinking about the crushing weight of the Mets like a rush-hour headache on a muggy, hundred-degree afternoon on a New York Monday in August. At the close of the disastrous 1989 season, Frank Cashen had decided that he would not reopen negotiations on my contract until the contract expired. No midterm extensions, he ruled. I was pissed off, but I decided to play out my option year and let the Mets sit at the table with any other team that was interested. But just as spring training began, Eric Goldschmidt told me the Mets had changed the rules and decided that they did want to reopen negotiations after all. Within twenty-four hours of returning home, my attitude did a one-eighty. I was elated. I was back on the roller coaster again. It looked as though my decision to quit drinking and straighten my life out and the Mets' decision to go back to the bargaining table were somehow related. Maybe the Mets had decided to make the kind of long-term commitment that would keep me at Shea for what I knew would be the prime of my career. Maybe I was naive, but "you gotta believe," and a part of me wanted to believe in the Mets. I felt that we could have won all the marbles in 1988 and 1989, but we short-circuited ourselves. This year I wasn't going to let it happen. If the Mets were planning to take me seriously, I remember saying to Eric Goldschmidt, then I could be the motivator for the entire team even though I didn't want the total responsibility to "carry" the team all by myself. It's not fair to expect one person to shoulder that kind of pressure, especially someone who'd been going through what I had.

I didn't expect that negotiations would go smoothly. The Mets knew that I was looking for a five-year contract, something in the neighborhood of what Don Mattingly was looking for and what Reggie Jackson was saying Jose Canseco should be getting from Oakland. I felt I deserved it. If you looked only at the numbers, my stats were on a par overall with Mattingly's and Canseco's. They had higher batting averages, sure, but I had hit more home runs over the past five years than Canseco had and also gotten more total bases. I believed I was a better fielder overall than both Mattingly and Canseco and had a more powerful throwing arm.

Will Clark of the Giants was the top-paid player in baseball when the Mets and I reopened our negotiations in early March. But in April on the very first day or so of the new season, Don Mattingly, who was coming up on his option year, signed a five-year $19 million pact with the Yankees and re-wrote baseball contract negotiations. Mattingly was a George Steinbrenner issue because everyone knew the Yankees didn't want to test the free agent market. Despite what people said about the Steinbrenner trades, George was still a more clever negotiator than Frank Cashen because George understood the simple arithmetic of free agency. If he gambled on letting Mattingly file his free agency papers at the end of the year, he would be gambling against his own team's prospects. Say what you want to about Steinbrenner, but he wasn't a baseball executive who played the odds against his own team's chances.

The Yankees' logic was clear: if they let Mattingly go the entire year without a contract, they'd have to be betting that his value to the team would *not* bring him an "unofficial" tender from another team even before the season was over. Although other teams were not allowed to tamper with a player before the fifteen-day exclusive negotiation period between the player and his original team expires, it's common knowledge—although certainly not first-hand knowledge from me—that other teams send out feelers. They could have traded him, of course, but you're asking other teams to trade players for a man in the option year of his free agency. No percentage in that. So George must have figured that by the time Mattingly and the Yankees were staring at each other across the table in October, Mattingly had better not have had a good year because his value would have increased. Other teams would already have put money ideas into his agent's head, and he would be weighing those when he sat down with George. If the Yankees wanted to play chicken, they could wind up not only losing Mattingly but losing the players they would have gotten by trading Mattingly at the start of the season. But by signing Mattingly before the season, they had to make a judgment that Don would have a super year and would bring people into the stadium. In other words, they'd have to bet on their own team's prospects. George made the right call. He went with a winner, signed Don Mattingly early, and knew that because he'd committed to Don, Don would play his heart out for the Yankees. It set the tone for contract negotiations for the entire year, even though Mattingly's back went out early in the season and he hardly played. Too bad Cashen didn't think like Steinbrenner until the following year when he had to deal with Doc.

Through the early phase of negotiations, we tried to get the Mets' front office to see things our way. I believed my home runs, total bases, and RBIs were on a par with Mattingly's, so I stuck to my position that I should have more than a simple two- or three-year contract. It was becoming apparent though that the Mets wanted to lowball us. That was okay too. If they wanted to lowball, we'd play along, knowing that at some point in the season they would have to improve their offer or see me go the route of free agency. Half of me was secretly hoping at that time, however, that the Mets would let me go. After 1989 and the bruising I took from management and from the press and the years of anger I had admitted to myself, my optimism about the Mets was dampened. I was ready to get my butt out of New York if I had to. Enough was enough.

Even with all of this happening, I got off to a good start in spring training. I was confident even though some of the coaches and all of the press were doubting me. Sportswriters said, "His bat's slow," "Strawberry's not going to do it this year," "He's going to dog it because of his contract." I laughed. Why would I dog it the year when I would be going into free agency in the fall if the Mets didn't give me a new contract? Besides, the other half of me still wanted to stay in New York. The Mets *had* been decent about Smithers, and New York had become a second home. I was pretty conflicted about that, and it was becoming obvious to everyone who knew me.

Even the Mets' coaches were more confused than usual. At first, some spread the word around the clubhouse that I would be traded before midyear. Then they said, Well, let's see what happens by the break and if he's not doing what we feel he should, then we'll have to trade him. Trade me? Trade me halfway through the season of my option year? What were they going to get for me—two pizzas and a six-pack? Just be glad the Mets' coaching staff never had to make any decisions about national security.

The season started very slowly for us. As usual, I started off on the wrong foot in the eyes of the press and the fans, but I refused to take the bait. If Cashen was going to fire salvos at me through the newspapers, more power to him. I would answer everything on the field with my bat. Unfortunately I hadn't figured on Davey Johnson's getting mixed signals from up front and then dropping what seemed to be all the blame for the team's early stumbling right on my shoulders. Wasn't it Davey who once said that when Darryl's hitting the whole team comes to life and when Darryl's bat is quiet, the team becomes lethargic. Hey, I was willing to carry my share of the burden; at times I even said I'd carry more than my share of the burden. But there was no way I could be the entire team. When Davey said he wanted me to *be* the entire team, I wanted to say to him, "Good, just figure out how to get me three at-bats each and every inning and pay me everybody else's salary." You can imagine how that would have flown if I'd said that to the reporters in the locker room. But I tried to let Davey know that I didn't appreciate carrying the burden for the entire team. I said to him, "How can I do it all? It's impossible." I didn't carry the team in 1986 when we won the World Series—in fact I had a mediocre Series—and when I led the team in hitting in 1988 and hit the ball all over the place during our National League playoffs against the Dodgers, the team still lost. "These are facts, Davey," I told him. I could be a home run specialist, but I couldn't be the whole team. But Davey just shrugged his shoulders. It was like a Davey clone was running the club, because he sure wasn't the guy I'd known before 1990.

It was one thing for the fickle fingers of most of the Mets fans in New York to point at me and say that because I wasn't hitting .350, the team was going down the drain, but for Davey to do it too wasn't fair. I had just walked out of rehab a few months earlier and was trying to follow Dr. Lans's advice and let the pressure pass over me. Yet, almost on signal, the Mets turned up the pressure. Was I being paid back for my comments in 1987 and '88 about how we blew our chances because the rest of the team didn't pitch in? And I was getting pretty pissed off at the way I was being made the scapegoat. There were other guys on the Mets who were contributing absolutely nothing to the team's performance.

In fact, the team was in such a mess under Johnson's lack of leadership that guys were getting away with murder. But if I did one thing amiss, had one late practice, for example, he would fine me and make it a public hanging. This seemed even worse to me than the pushing and shoving that Davey and I had back in 1987 because it seemed to have an edge to it. It was weird. No matter what happened to the team, I was the target. If I had been paranoid, I would have thought he was doing it on orders from Cashen to reduce my value to the team to make it easier to deal with me in negotiations. Would Frank Cashen sacrifice a National League pennant just to get a better deal with Darryl Strawberry? I'd put money on it.

Later in the season, I came to believe that Davey had been getting his signals directly from the front office. He had been my friend once in the minor leagues, and I was happy when the Mets brought him up in 1984. Back in '84, I thought he would be the perfect manager. But he, too, it seems, gave way under the pressure of the big leagues. In game six of the World Series, I still think he made a particularly stupid decision that didn't help the team by taking me out, and that it was personally directed at me. But there were times, even after 1986, when I considered him to be a friend. There were also times that we fought with each other in public. However, in the early months of the 1990 season, it was as if he were deliberately looking for a way to cripple my performance. There was no other reason for the kinds of statements he was making before and after each game. Things were bad enough on the ball club without Davey's reign of terror. Then when he turned to the press and invited them to chime in, it was like I was getting leg irons snapped on whenever I came to Shea. I began looking forward to every game in Dodger Stadium because at least there I knew I had some friends.

The team played as if it were in a fog during the early part of the year. Our opener against Pittsburgh was a 12-3 disaster in which not only was Doc buried, but everything else went wrong. I forgot which end of the bat to use and the rest of the team looked like the Keystone Kops. I told the mob of reporters that we still had a lot of rust in the pipes and couldn't capitalize on the few opportunities we did have during the game. That was putting it mildly, but what was I supposed to say, "We suck and don't give me a new contract"?

METS NOT READY, STRAW SEZ. I ate crow for that headline.

Whenever Frank Viola pitched, we won. Throughout April, Viola's pitching was the reason for our .500 ball. He got us by Pittsburgh, Chicago, Montreal, Houston, Cincinnati, and Los Angeles. Viola's stats were incredible. He single-handedly stopped two separate losing streaks, one of which had gone on for four games, and was the only bright spot in our rotation. In fact we had no rotation at first. It was as if Frank saw his mission as supporting the entire team until Doc exerted his control, found the strike zone, and began throwing his patented speed-of-light fastball. By mid-May, right before we began our drive out of fourth place, Viola had a 7-0 record, an 0.87 ERA, and 52 strikeouts. He was enjoying the best start of any National League pitcher, but the team that should have been supporting him with their bats and their fielding was simply in another world.

My own personal highlight came at the beginning of May when Reggie Jackson announced that he had taken on Oakland's Jose Canseco as his personal project. I guessed that Reggie was reacting to the Mattingly deal, as were all of us playing out our option years. While Eric Goldschmidt and the Mets were still playing telephone tag between coasts, Reggie came right back and said that Canseco needed to lose his negative image, quiet down, and talk only with his bat. Sounded like smart advice to me. I was particularly impressed with Reggie's estimate of Jose's market value and the worth of his contract were he ever to file for free agency. Maybe Reggie was stung by the praise being heaped on Mattingly—after all, Jackson *was* the Yankees during their glorious 1976 season when he shone as "Mr. October." Who knows? But he said that Canseco was probably one of the most charismatic players in baseball and was looking for and deserved a similar five-year contract with even higher numbers than Mattingly had gotten. That raised my eyebrows because I knew that my stats and Canseco's were just about the same, but I had hit more home runs than he had and had a higher number of total bases. Then my eyebrows went all the way over the top of my head and down to my backbone when Reggie said there were no other players in Canseco's class except for one: Darryl Strawberry. REG-GIE, REG-GIE, REG-GIE. I'll vote for that. Thank you, Reggie!

Clearly Mr. Jackson's interview couldn't have made Frank Cashen and his bow tie very happy, but it certainly got the New York press to sit up and take notice. Suddenly Darryl's being in his option year took on greater import, as did the fortunes of the stumbling-bumbling Mets. Is Darryl dogging it? Are the Mets completely incapable of sustaining any drive? Why is it that every game the Mets blow early leads through errors and ineptness? We were mad at the fans, mad at the press, but especially mad at ourselves. We were so hapless that we tripped ourselves up in almost every game. In one particularly embarrassing incident, poor frustrated Dave Cone got so mad at the first base ump over a call, while two runners were standing on base, that he stomped over to argue with the umpire without calling a time-out, and Dale Murphy skipped home from second. The umpire, Charlie Williams, was in shock, the fans hooted and howled, and Davey Johnson just sighed in disgust. When Williams suggested to Cone that he might want to think about the other runner still on base, Dave became so furious that he argued even harder. Meanwhile the second runner danced home. Part of me simply wanted to shoot Dave Cone on the spot to put him out of his misery. It was getting downright scary. The next night Ron Darling gave up four home runs to the Braves in what could only be termed a rout. The Iraqi air force would have put up more of a fight than we did.

On May 2, Frank Viola momentarily put a stop to the humiliation by shutting down Cincinnati and striking out eleven Reds. But after HoJo's three errors the next night, even the home fans were screaming *"Davey must go"* from the stands. Not even our sweep of a doubleheader from the Astros on May 6 quieted the hometown rumblings, nor my home runs, nor Frank Viola's dismemberment of Houston the next day. When we beat San Francisco the following day for our fourth victory in a row, some people began saying that the turnaround had begun. I must admit that I was feeling pretty confident when Rick Reuschel's pitching broke down against us. He walked me out of sheer fright after what I'd done to the Astros the week before. After Rick loaded the bases by putting me on first, he backed down from challenging Kevin McReynolds over the plate, walked him, and in so doing walked in a run. Things were looking up as we were just shy of second place in the East.

I was only hitting .231, however, and on May 14, in San Francisco, Davey dropped me to fifth in the order. I let him know that I felt insulted, but now I realize that again Davey must have been operating on orders from the front office. Why slap your potentially leading hitter right in the face just after it looks like he's coming out of a slump? Makes no sense unless you're playing hardball with his contract instead of with a baseball. By the time we lost to the Giants on May 16 after having gone ahead 3-0 behind Doc's pitching, a feeling of gloom had settled over the dugout again because we had so thoroughly blown a solid lead. Davey's response was to stand there looking dejected and separated from everything going on around him. I could tell that he had been mentally defeated, but I couldn't help thinking—call me paranoid—that the front office was as much his enemy as anything else. It looked like management was sabotaging its own team. I had the sneaking suspicion that Frank had been after Davey's scalp for two years and that now he saw his chance to get it. I was sure my scalp was next, but I didn't know yet how he had planned to take it.

I knew what was in the wind when the press began saying

that I was behind the fall of the Mets. Hey, forget the fact that
Dave Cone stood there bellowing at Charlie Williams while
two runs pirouetted home—tlink, tlink—it's Darryl's fault.
Forget Davey Johnson's Ralph Kramden "Gee, Alice" expression as HoJo groped for balls sailing over his head. And forget
that we had to trot a guide dog out to the mound during
warmups to show Ron Darling where the plate was; it's all
Darryl's fault. You see, according to Dave Anderson in the
Times, Darryl was getting special treatment from one and all
because he'd slapped around his wife, pointed a gun at her
head, told her to go ahead and make his day, gotten hauled off
to the pokey, and then "took the cure." Was this the new front
office party line that was showing up in Anderson's column?

"Stop coddling the 'new' Strawberry!" Dave Anderson ordered. Anderson's prescription, let the Straw man know—and
"bluntly" at that—he's "still more sluggish than slugger."
What a nice turn of phrase! But wait, there's more. I was "a
sad excuse for a cleanup hitter" who was—and get this—"being paid to *carry the team*" (italics mine). What happened to
the eight other guys? What are we, the New York Strawberries?

Anderson really spelled it out for the Mets—or were the
Mets spelling out their negotiating position for him because
Davey Johnson was already effectively brain dead?—that
Strawberry was not only not worth the $3 million a year he
would probably be asking for, but not worth the $1.8 million
he was currently getting. Did the voice of Frank Cashen have
any more brilliant and original insights? He sure did! Get me
going or trade me away. I wasn't nearly as valuable as Jose
Canseco—"Take that, Reg-gie"—or even Bo Jackson; even Bo
knows that. Did a building have to fall on my head or what?
Dave Anderson had spoken. So let it be written, so let it be
done! *"Earth to Strawberry. Frank's made his decision. Only he
doesn't have the guts to sit down and talk to you about it."* That's
what I believed. Also, there were so few black players on the
team as it was, I felt as if I were playing baseball at Dred Scott
Memorial Park in glorious downtown Johannesburg instead of
in the middle of New York City.

Now that Dave Anderson had told the rest of the team that
they didn't have to hit the ball because I was carrying all of
them, things went from bad to worse. That Saturday when the
Keystone Mets played the Padres, glassy-eyed Davey watched
the entire game as if he'd just stumbled out of a three-rounder

with Iron Mike Tyson, while our "catcher" Mackey Sasser was
so wrapped up in the debacle unfolding before him on the field
that he plopped open his metal chair right on Doc's middle toe
and sat on it. Oops! "Clubhouse accident," the press called it.
The way things were going, if I had sat on his toe they would
have called it an assassination attempt. Fortunately, the injury
wasn't serious, and Doc didn't miss a turn.

We lurched forward into the latter part of May. Things were
so bad when we hit Los Angeles that Bobby Ojeda and HoJo
suggested we bar the press and Davey from our locker room
and have a team meeting. This was a crucial time for us because we were still hovering close enough to first place to take
it away from Pittsburgh whenever we decided to make our run
for the top. Our meeting was just for the players. We looked at
one another and decided that we had to come together as a
team. We had to play as if we were in this game for keeps. I
know that many of them felt that I wasn't holding up my end
of things. But we spoke to one another like human beings who
shared a common goal. "We look like fools out there," I said.
"I'm not sloughing off any of the blame; we're all in this together." Other voices piped in. You could hear the commitment building among the players. Then I said to the guys on
the bench that they had to get into the game also. They were
too quiet. They just sat there like a bunch of stiffs. "You guys
got to be more lively," I challenged them. "Give us something
to cheer about," Tim Teufel said right to my face. "You want it,
you got it," one of the starters said, and I just went crazy with
the desire to win. "I'll break my back for you guys," I promised.
"I mean it. I'll hit the ball so far they'll never find it. You guys
just get on base. The rest of you guys just cheer. Let them
know we mean business. Don't worry about what I do. Just
worry about what you do."

It worked! We blew the Dodgers out of the stadium 12-3
with an eight-run third inning that had people rolling their
eyes in disbelief. Was this the same team that couldn't even sit
down without getting hurt two nights ago? I homered into the
bleachers, as did Kevin McReynolds—a grand slam for K-Mac
—and Daryl Boston. We belted Mike Morgan so bad, we
thought they'd have to carry him off the field on a stretcher.
Doc got up on his injured toe and all and threw strikes so fast
that the radar guns couldn't even measure them. What about
Davey Johnson? Ron Darling put it best when he said in an

interview afterward that the situation between Davey and Frank Cashen was not really our issue. "We can't be worrying about Davey," Ron was quoted by *The New York Times* as having said. "What we have to do is play better."

The magic wore off two days later when we laid down and died like dogs against the Padres. The hometown newspapers hooted and hollered at us as if we were losing deliberately. "Have more team meetings," reporters suggested, as if the team meeting itself was a supernatural event. The real reasons for our erratic performance not only had to do with Davey's having lost control of the team, they also resulted from the disastrous trades Mets' management had made over the past few years. We'd lost three important members of our powerhouse lineup: Ray Knight, Lenny Dykstra, and Roger McDowell. Then we traded away Juan Samuel to Los Angeles. Samuel was one of the National League's leading hitters in the first part of this year (1991). All of these players are now invaluable to the teams we traded them to, and the Mets paid dearly for their loss. It was one thing for Al Harazin or Frank Cashen to minimize our losing these players, but quite another for the fans to overlook that the Mets had traded away part of the nucleus of their 1986 World Series victory. While all this was happening, Davey was still using his new sleepwalking management style. Maybe he thought that we'd magically come together.

Then on May 29, the thunder and lightning struck. Frank Cashen actually spoke to us and called us a bunch of underachievers. His physically speaking to us was in itself a kind of event. I brought a camera. He said we didn't have any fire in our bellies. Actually, most of us had heartburn from what we'd been through the past six weeks. You knew your team was in trouble when you could picture Ron Darling chewing Rolaids instead of chewing tobacco on the mound. I myself had given up booze for Mylanta. Then Cashen said our problems of the past were now over because we were getting a new manager. He had dismissed Davey Johnson, who was the winningest manager we'd ever had, and replaced him with third base coach Buddy Harrelson. Frank had finally had his revenge on Davey. Frank, it was said, had had it in for Johnson even during the early years in 1984 and '85. I had heard from sportswriters, although it was only a rumor, that Frank Cashen thought Davey was too arrogant, even though he won more than he lost. I had even heard that Frank and Davey had had

run-ins as far back as the time they were on the Baltimore
Orioles together. But rumors were flying all over the clubhouse
at the time Davey was fired and Buddy was moved up, and
nobody knew anything for sure except that we had to start
winning. We *assumed* that Frank had used the team's stumbling as an excuse to get rid of Davey. Yet we knew that even
though Davey had his problems, Cashen had taken the team
away from him through all the disastrous trades. Now Davey
was taking the fall, not only for the entire team but for management as well.

Ironically, after Davey left, it seemed as though a pall had
been lifted from the entire club. At first, I thought that maybe
we needed a change in leadership to shake things up on the
field and put a little life in the ball club. Then I realized that
the front office had lost confidence in Davey's field stewardship
in 1989, long before they moved Harrelson up. Had the team
started off strong, maybe Davey would have stayed. But the
front office began the season by making Davey's managing
decisions for him. It wasn't Davey's team anymore the way it
had been in 1987. Gradually, the front office had usurped Davey's authority because the New York media began putting too
much pressure on management.

The Mets had always had a strange relationship with the
media. It was as if Frank Cashen believed that the sportswriters
knew best how to run the team and surrendered his judgment
to them. If they criticized me, then Frank criticized me in print
the next day just to keep the columnists on his side. If the
press thought Davey was making poor decisions on the field
(confidentially, after 1986 I thought so, too), then Davey bore
the brunt of Cashen's anger. Suddenly people stopped talking
about "Darryl" for a few minutes and began talking about "Davey." In articles in *The New York Times* and other papers, columnists wrote about the need for a managerial change on the
Mets because the team's play seemed aimless and because
the Mets needed to be motivated. Other columnists wrote that
the Mets simply needed a change in leadership to shake things
up. Still others wrote that the players themselves had gotten
too complacent and needed a new manager to bounce them
out of their lethargy. I wasn't being criticized, but I couldn't
help feeling that some of the "complacency" and "lethargy"
stuff were messages to Buddy Harrelson about me. Just paranoid, I guess. But then . . .

One player who didn't mince any words about Davey's departure was pitcher Ron Darling. Ron was bitter that other teams in the league were pushing us around, throwing balls at us to brush us back, confident that we weren't going to do anything about it. Ron and a few others of us felt that the Mets teams of '86, '87, and '88 wouldn't have taken this bullshit from some of the second-raters who thought they could throw at us and get away with it. Maybe we were entering our death throes under Davey, but a few of us went out to start fights when we saw other teams trying to take advantage. We had a few bench-clearers in the final days of Davey's tenure, and Ron went public by criticizing Davey for not giving our pitchers permission to throw at opposing batters after one of ours was hit by a pitch. This started another controversy, but you have to give Ron credit for not backing down. He knew how to throw a punch and had no misgivings about mixing it up if he thought it might generate some team spirit. Ron is smart and loyal and doesn't like to get pushed.

I could easily have been as conflicted about Davey Johnson as I was about the Mets. One side of me said that I wasn't angry *that* Davey was fired but at *the way* it was done. After all the things he and I had been through together, and despite our public disputes, I had through it all come to rely on him as a friend. Part of me said, "Total bull," and that I should stop being conflicted about stuff. Davey was burying me in 1990 just like he'd been doing in 1987, and I should deal with my anger instead of feeling guilty about it and making excuses.

On the other hand, as it became more obvious that he was no longer in control of the team, I started to sympathize with his position because I understood what he was going through; maybe it was kind of a love-hate relationship. I said to myself in moments of guilt about my own anger that Davey kicked me around because he was looking for me to explode into a hitting streak to keep his butt from getting fired. It was self-preservation, maybe; although it wasn't self-preservation in 1987, that's for sure. He always said to us that year that he knew we would eventually come together and dominate the league. He only hoped, he said, that he would be the manager when it happened. As it turned out, we did explode into a streak, but Davey wasn't around to enjoy it.

The Mets have a brutal way of getting rid of you when they don't want you anymore. I would soon find that brutality di-

rected at me. I was bitter at the meeting when I heard
Cashen's announcement and said that it pretty much solidified
my belief that I wouldn't be back after the 1990 season. Other
players were saying the same thing. They believed that Davey,
although he sometimes made some strange decisions, was able
to instill confidence in his ballplayers. You have to rely on a
manager for team spirit sometimes, and Davey had a way of
getting everyone involved. But when management turned him
into just a shell before blaming him for the decisions that they
had made themselves, it convinced the players that Davey
Johnson had gotten a raw deal. The front office was making
the press happy and the press was running the ball club. Once
that happened, Davey couldn't rely on his team. When management saw that he couldn't rely on his team, they got rid of
him and blamed him for the whole thing.

I wasn't too sure about the prospects for the team at the end
of May, and I was angry about the way Davey had mistreated
us and had been mistreated by Cashen. I was never really
concerned about my own game because I knew from the way
things were going at batting practice that I was getting my
brain on the ball, so to speak, and I'd be lighting up scoreboards across the National League any day. I was so confident
that when stories began turning up in the New York papers
about Davey's being fired because of "Strawberry's problems," I
knew it was all baloney. Davey was fired because of front office
problems at the Mets, pure and simple. Maybe if everyone on
the Mets had stopped worrying about a "Darryl problem,"
there would have been no problem.

Suddenly, in early June, the wind shifted just like I knew it
would. I had settled comfortably into my stance and that was
the most important thing I had to do to hit the ball consistently. People have commented about my stance as if it's
something mysterious, but I've refined it over the years. It
comes from my being very tall and from having to get a lot of
my body across the plate quickly to control where I'm going to
send the ball. It's a stance that I developed for long-ball hitting. I have a very high kick when I rear back to set up for my
cut as the pitcher delivers. Some coaches have said that it
doesn't give me enough time to bring the bat around, but
they're wrong. It helps me get the bat around faster and with

more control. I also like to waggle the bat as the pitcher is going into his windup because it gives me a better sense of position.

The key for me is coordinating when I pick up my right leg and when I use my back and upper body to turn into the ball. That's where my real power comes from. Also, when my leg, back, and arms are all working together, my head will move naturally through the swing and I won't lose sight of the ball. When I try to rush it, or if I hesitate, I'll take my eyes off the ball and that's when I head into slumps. Part of the secret of batting is to learn how to follow the ball with your eyes from the pitcher's hand to the catcher's glove. Practice hitting the ball mentally. When everything is in sync, I *know* where my bat has to be at any given point from the delivery to the contact. Once I'm at that point, there is not a pitcher any-where in the Major Leagues—even Nolan Ryan—that I can't consistently take out of the park.

During the exhibition season, most pitchers are still wild after their winter layoffs and need to get their control back before they work on position. That's why they'll feed straight-on fastballs or slow curves that are more like practice pitches than game pitches. I take these downtown all during the preseason. I can hit these kinds of balls blindfolded and still get distance. But during the very early part of the season, there's a time when pitchers are getting their control and throwing game pitches while I'm still trying to coordinate my stance. That's when you'll see my stats nosedive. By the time June rolls around, though, I've usually made the adjustments I have to make and I'm hitting to the game situation as well as for the long ball.

Buddy Harrelson and I used to have this game when he was third base coach. He would lob pitches in with increasing speed and I would see how many balls I could send out of the park. As I got more and more comfortable with my stance, I would put more balls into space. In May 1990, I was getting into my groove. Even the reporters hanging around Shea for a story were impressed with the games Bud and I were playing at batting practice. The results began to show up on the field. That's why when Davey Johnson was fired, I was at first happy that Harrelson was taking his place.

By June, I was hitting safely in most of our games and real-ized that I was on the upward swing of a curve. I was entering the flow and walking on air. The Mets and I had started our winning streaks. You could hear the groundswell start to build. We were seven or so games out of first but matching Pittsburgh win for win.

First Dave Anderson piped up with his official assessment of my "value" as trade bait. He thought the Mets had already passed the point of no return as far as swapping me for other players was concerned. The season was too far gone, the streak had already started up, and the Mets had already played out the hand they'd been dealt. Whatever Cashen's grand scheme was, and I would not learn it for another six weeks, trading me away during the season was not it. Then, as if answering Dave's column, Joe McIlvaine stated that any rumors about my being traded to the Yankees were complete speculation. "It's entirely a media creation," he said. Then, which I took as a personal message, Joe announced, "All we're saying to Darryl is: 'Look, show us we should keep you. If we're going to pay you zillions of dollars, show us.' " When I read that quote in the *Times* on June 7, my heart just about leaped out of my chest. "Yes, yes," I said. "Joe, you asked for it; you got it. Tell me more about the zillions of dollars."

I remember waking up early on Saturday morning in my house on Long Island on June 9 and pinching myself. Did I dream that last night Sid Fernandez pitched two-hit baseball against the Pirates for seven innings and that I had belted two home runs? Joe Durso was right when he said "The magic was back." I sat up in bed, savoring the taste of a walloping victory. The sweetness was still on my tongue. Glory! I felt like I could take on the entire world. I could hardly wait to get suited up and into the batter's box. My arms, my legs, they were tingling with power. I wondered if the other guys were feeling the same as I was.

I had my answer later that afternoon when I got to Shea. The whole team was suddenly alive. "Yes!" we yelled at each other. "Let's eat 'em up!" Which is just what we did that evening. I hit—did I say "hit"? I mean, I "pounded" my third home run in two days. That ball soared off my bat. I told the reporters shoving their tape recorders in my face after the game: "This is it! I'm in the groove." And my groove continued the next day, Sunday, as I hit another homer and we beat the Pirates 8-3.

The next night we were on the road at Wrigley, where the

Cubs edged us. But we came back the next day and stomped Chicago 19-8, and then the next day swept the Cubs in a doubleheader 15-10 and 9-6. Then we went to Pittsburgh while the New York papers crowed about us. You could see that the entire team had caught fire. Other teams in the National League were becoming so scared of us that pitchers were losing control instead of challenging us. You could see it in their eyes as they shook off signal after signal. We had become the new threats in the league.

There was a downside to this too. It was like the Mets refused to play division-winning ball until I started hitting. They had to wait for me to start before they came together as a team. Okay, I'd said in the past that I shouldn't have to carry the whole team. I'd said in the past that I didn't like it because it put too much pressure on me. I also said that it made me the scapegoat when the team lost. Every word of that is true, true, true, and I was still worried about those things. But *this time* I thought I was ready to accept the responsibility when it came because it meant two related things, both of which were purely business. First, we had a shot at the pennant after all and I believed that I could show the way. Second, Frank Cashen would have to realize that I was the driving force behind the team, whether I was the leader or not. He'd have to see that, even if he had a blindspot where I was concerned. He proved to be far less blind than I thought, however. Shortsighted, yes, but blind, no.

I began ripping the ball into the outfield even when I didn't hit home runs. There were shots that I hit that were too hot to handle even when the fielders got a glove on the ball. And when the ball flew, it flew into the upper deck so hard that you could hear the crack of the shot all the way out in the parking lot. I wanted the straphangers on the number 7 train, the one you take to Shea, to know every time I hit a home run and to feel good about it. I had another agenda as well. I figured that if the Mets wouldn't negotiate seriously, then I would literally hit myself out of the Mets and onto another ball club. I was still pretty conflicted, but remember, we're talking about professional baseball and I couldn't just clean out my desk and go to another company across town. I had to go through a whole process of negotiation, filing for free agency, waiting for the Mets to make a final offer, and then opening up negotiations with other clubs. But I still had to go through the entire season and play baseball with an eye to either having the Mets meet our contract demands or making myself valuable to another club should the Mets decide not to meet them. It's not at all as straightforward as it seemed. In either event, I would go out strong, I told myself, even as I tried to show the Mets that I could still contribute to the ball club. But even as my hitting streak was reaching its peak, I noticed that the Mets were trying to put a damper on everything by stepping up their criticisms of me.

We were seven games back after our doubleheader sweep at Wrigley, so the series with Pittsburgh was crucial. On the night of our first game against the Pirates, Dave Magadan stormed down to Buddy's office and pounded on the door. He was furious because Bud Harrelson had benched him for Teufel, who was coming back to the lineup off the disabled list. He later said to the press that he'd told Harrelson to his face that he shouldn't be benched. Bench anyone else, he said, but his bat was so hot the Mets couldn't afford to have him sitting on his can. Buddy tried to explain that he was using his left-handed and right-handed hitters strategically, but Magadan told him to stuff it.

"You play your hitters," Dave said. "And I can hit anybody! You put me in and you'll see what I can do," he boasted to Harrelson.

I told Dave that I could relate to his being benched because Davey had done it to me during the World Series and I remembered how bad I felt about it. Magadan evidently made his point because the next night, Bud had him in the lineup and he went four for four. He hit shots all over the field as the Mets blew the Pirates right out of Pittsburgh. That was an especially rewarding game for me because I was sure I saw fear eating away at pitcher Walt Terrell's spirit. It was in his eyes. I bet he was thankful for the rainout the night before because he was throwing such garbage, he must have needed a rest.

But he was still throwing garbage when I saw him on the mound. You could tell that he was in trouble by the pitches he was giving me. He got way behind on me my first time up. With the count at 3-1, he had to play it safe and floated a pitch over the plate that had absolutely nothing on it. I saw it drifting in frame by frame as if it were a series of slides. I could see the exact spot in the upper deck where it would land and brought the bat around with such smoothness that the ball was in the upper stands before I even heard the crack. I think it was my longest shot of the year to date.

The Pirates came back to beat us on June 16, but any euphoria they felt was short-lived because we took it away from them in the next game, on Sunday. We were contenders again, playing the way we had in 1986 and '87, making situations happen, and stealing what they wouldn't give up. We were playing like the first-division ball club we were, and we kept looking at the box scores every day as we lopped off the games that separated us from the Pirates. Soon they'd be ours.

By the time we blew by the Cardinals behind Dave Cone and Sid Fernandez, we were only four games out of first. There were still a few days left in June, and the Pirates had begun to stumble. Now was the time to make our move, and we did it against the unfortunate Phillies and our nemesis, Lenny Dykstra. Lenny had the hottest bat in the league in June 1990, and wanted nothing more than to be the spoiler. Philadelphia had given him the opportunity he wanted, to play every day and hit consistently. His predictions had come true. He had told Davey Johnson that if he were given the chance to play every game, he would generate more runs than anyone else on the Mets. Davey apparently didn't believe him and wanted to trade him to end his misery. Frank Cashen was looking for power hitting and power pitching and wanted to trade him for players who could give him that. Both men thought that trading Lenny was a good idea. Thus the consistent, fiery, ever-dependable Lenny Dykstra figured in one of the ruinous trades that unraveled our championship team.

Too-brash Lenny more than met his match when he faced Frank Viola, though. Dykstra was shut down except for a measly little single. By the end of the day, we were only three games out of first and on the march. The next night I belted a 430-foot home run off the billboard in right center and we were only two and a half games out. A day or so later, the other shoe I was waiting for finally dropped in the business of professional baseball. Jose Canseco made history.

On June 27, right in the middle of my eighteen-game, .400 hitting streak and the Mets' climb into first place, Jose Canseco got a $23.5 million five-year contract from Oakland. My appetite was whetted. How long would Frank Cashen try to hold out? Didn't he realize that once the Mets climbed into first place—and get there we would; it was inevitable—he'd look like a piker if he tried to play it on the cheap? If the newspapers kept writing that Strawberry was instrumental in the Mets' success, Cashen would only look worse the more he stalled. But Frank knew how to play the columnists like the keys on a piano.

Stories suddenly started turning up in the newspapers that I was being unreasonable in my negotiations and that I was ungrateful for all the effort the Mets had put into my career. Ungrateful? I was hitting over .400 in my current streak and propelling the Mets toward first place. We were only a game out and unstoppable. Then management said that I was less interested in playing for the Mets than I was in playing for myself. That was also untrue because by then even I had become caught up in "Mets fever" 1990. I remember walking around the clubhouse in early July and saying, "Wow, I like what I see here. I want to be a part of this team!" This was a Mets club that in the beginning of July was more of a championship team than at any point since the magic 1986 season. It was a winning Mets team that I wanted and the rest of the players wanted to keep together for years to come. There was a camaraderie, a clubhouse spirit that was so intense, it was infecting all of us. This is what I was looking for and what I wanted to preserve. You gotta believe, we kept saying to ourselves, the magic is back. Talk about the boys from New York City. Weeeee're back! It's the Amazin's all over again, and did it ever feel good.

On June 29, two days after Canseco's contract with the A's, we belted our way into first place in the National League East by beating the Reds while the Pirates walked the plank. I put the kibosh on Sweet Lou's little Redlegs by bouncing a 450-foot corker of a shot off the BALL sign on the Shea scoreboard. Of course, Uncle Lou would go on to win the World Series that year, but at the time the home run was a real honey and we had our eyes on the prize.

Before the game, I remember saying to Bobby Ojeda, the starter, that we would both have a big game that night. "You set the trim on the mound and I'll set it with the bat," Bobby quoted me to the press in interviews after the game. It was funny, but the more I hit and the more the team succeeded, the more unsatisfied the press became. It was inevitable, they said, that the streak would end. It was inevitable that when the streak ended, the fortunes of the Mets would sag as well.

That was a lot of pressure. When I was released from Smithers I told everybody that the one thing I got out of rehab was a deeper understanding of the nature of pressure. I had spent my life in a pressure cooker in New York. Now I was just learning to understand it. The front office was pressuring me to cave in to their refusal to treat me on the same level with Jose Canseco and Don Mattingly. The New York sportswriters were waiting like vultures for me to collapse and bring the entire team down with me. And I even sensed that the team was nervous. If Straw doesn't hit, then we're lost. Nothing I could do, even at our peak, could break this team's codependency. It's one thing to be a clutch player, but it's another to be the only player.

Shortly after Buddy became the manager at the end of May, I had a talk with him about what my role should be. I was really in conflict. I was pissed off about my contract negotiations, of course, but there was a spirit inside me that wanted to go out strong. I was still worried about assuming the role of team leader. How was I supposed to settle the feelings, which were clearly opposite: I'm a member of the Mets family; I'm a leader in the Mets family, but I don't think the Mets want me —and so I don't want them. Sound confusing? That's how I felt. The "family" part of me wanted to run out on the field and whip up enthusiasm. But Harrelson said that real leadership means teaching by example. "Show them how to win on the field," he told me. "You're the natural leader of this team. They will follow you if you perform well."

When I was talking to the players about turning this season around, Buddy pulled me aside again. He asked me what was holding me back and what was keeping me from showing instead of telling the other guys how to win. We talked about Smithers and about the sense of inner security that rehab gives you.

"What do they tell you to do with your feelings?" Buddy asked.

"They help you understand them," I answered.

"And what are you feeling toward the pitchers who are making you hit grounders and strike out?" he asked again.

"I'm angry at the pitcher," I told him. "But I'm holding it in and I don't know why."

"Don't hold it in anymore," he said. "Get intense. Get mad. But get mad at the other guy instead of at yourself for holding it in." I stopped and thought about that. The next night I became the worst nightmare of National League pitchers.

Davey Johnson never had the courage to talk to me that way directly. He seemed to know that at some point in the season I would turn on, and the rest of the team would follow. But Buddy said it straight up, and I think it might have made a difference. Unfortunately, that same conversation with Harrelson also showed me that Buddy could deal with my concerns as a human being when he wanted to. Months later, when things fell apart and I was looking to him for advice and guidance, he turned his back on me. That showed me exactly what he thought of me as a human being and hardened my decision not to stay in New York.

But by the end of the first week of July, I felt I had Buddy Harrelson on my side. Maybe I was falling into the Cashen trap, but I felt too good to worry about it. I was among the top ten batters in the National League, I had the highest ratio of RBIs to games played of any point in my career, and I was hitting pitchers all over the field. I was positively ripping the ball apart. I was determined, seething at pitchers who tried to take chances away from me, and completely focused on baseball. The free-agent contract negotiations were just another arena in which to compete, and I wanted to come out on top. I felt that was even more likely during the week of July 12 when we became locked in a hand-to-hand struggle with Cincinnati, who were leading the Western Division. This was the kind of brawl that I liked best of all. The games were filled with flying dust, crashing bats, balls screaming into the outfield, and collisions at the plate. This was barefisted baseball, the Mets against the Reds, and I wanted to come out on top in both.

"Hello, Straw?"

"Yeah! Eric? Whuzz up? You know what time it is?"

"You'll read about it this morning in the papers."

"Read what?"

"The Mets broke off negotiations."

"I'm hitting .415; the whole club's come alive. What are they, crazy?"

"They won't go above nine and a half and won't agree to anything beyond a three-year contract. At least not now."

"They've screwed me around the whole year. Now what am I supposed to do?"

"Just what you've been doin'. They're playing chicken. They're betting you won't file for free agency because you're afraid of what's going to happen when you don't get offers from other teams."

"!/¶#%&!&*@•*!™²©!!!"

"I said the same thing. Just don't get too pissed off when you read today's papers," Eric said before he hung up.

And that's how we ended up losing that series to the Reds.

3

FREE AGENT AT LAST

HE AIN'T WORTH IT!

Did you ever see a quote like that about you staring you right in the face on an otherwise miserable New York summer morning? Kind of gets right down to the nitty gritty of life, so to speak, don't you think? What would you do if you saw that on the company bulletin board, say, right above the old coffee machine, at 8:45 in the A.M.

Worse, what if your boss pasted that up for all to see during the very week when you were trying to land your very biggest account, the coup that would for sure put you and your company right up there for all the world to see in *The Wall Street Journal*? Pretty dumb, right? Or pretty savvy, depending upon which way you look at it. If getting you at a good price is more important than getting the pennant (or that big account) at any price, then your boss is showing the world he knows how to "manage" people.

Other writers were slightly more creative. They went further
with what Cashen & Co. said and compared me to other, let's
call them "high-profile," ballplayers:

NO WAY LIKE JOSE

The theme was basically the same—Frank Cashen's heat-
seeking missile aimed at my bat—but the sportswriters went
into some detail with Frank about my comparable worth as a
big-league hitter. I "pouted"; I "sulked"; I was "spoiled"; I was
a "crybaby"; I would "never" fulfill my "potential"; I would
always be "simply mediocre." Frank, though, didn't budge from
his original position: I simply wasn't worth it. Interpret that
anyway you want to, boys, he said. Oh, he restated it corpo-
rately, of course, slamming the door shut on future negotiations during the remainder of the season, but holding out the
possibility of a resumption after I had formally filed my free
agency papers at the end of the season. He covered his position by holding open the door just a crack so he wouldn't
automatically waive his fifteen-day exclusivity period after I
officially became a free agent. That, he must have assumed,
would keep everybody away while he watched me twist slowly
in the wind. It was nothing less than a public hanging to check
off Eric Goldschmidt and put me in a weakened position for
the rest of the season.

I was very bitter about it then. Although I'm in a different
place now and can look upon that day with a different spirit, I
was full of rage at the time. I knew that everything I had done
for the Mets over the previous ten years had in one press
announcement been turned absolutely into nothing. There
were fifty ways the Mets could have gracefully closed down
negotiations without humiliating me and without compromis-
ing our position in the National League pennant race. But I
believe they chose the most inflammatory way so as to under-
mine me and my position on the ball club. In so doing, I'm
convinced the Mets deliberately sought to hurt my ability to
play baseball in order to reduce my marketability in the free
agent selection period. It was a personal affront which hurt me
deeper than most people will ever understand. I may forgive
them, but I can never make believe I wasn't hurt. It was as if a
parent I believed in had turned his back on me by telling me

that I was just another foster kid paid for by the county. The day the checks stopped coming in was the day that I was out in the street. Do you think I'm overdramatizing this? Maybe I take loyalty and team spirit a little more seriously than the New York Mets. I was willing to be loyal. I'm not just a robot.

I put down the newspapers with a feeling of letdown and relief. At last the waiting and tension were over. At least I knew where I stood. I think I cried a little, too, because I knew that a ten-year relationship with my adopted city was over. We still had about half the baseball season left to play and were just about tied with Pittsburgh for first place. I tried as hard as I could to whip up enthusiasm for getting back in that batter's box that afternoon and swinging for the fences. I tried not to feel like a big dumb stupid fool who was the laughingstock of the whole country, not to mention New York City.

Suddenly the baseball season and our pennant race didn't seem fun anymore. It seemed like just another job. Just another day at the office, a shift on the assembly line. I felt abandoned and bewildered and wanted to be anywhere except where I was. I wanted to go home. I had to get out and go for a walk.

"Jo, Estrah, que pasa?" the cabdriver screamed at me as he drove by. He was almost leaning out of the window as he pulled up close to the curb and wagged a finger into the warm July morning. "Mira, joo tell Frankie I say oon*gatts*!" He thrust the middle fingers of both hands out the window as he swerved out into the early morning traffic and somehow avoided hitting a couple of bright-eyed pinstripes who recoiled in horror at the taxi barreling toward them through the intersection.

I had tried to be as inconspicuous as possible when people passed me on the street, looked up, then, embarrassed, looked away. But when you're six-six and walking along Queens Boulevard in Forest Hills, it's hard to hide. And it's especially difficult when all eight million who live in New York City had been told by every broadcaster from Warner Wolf, bouncing up and down on his cushion, to the network anchors on the evening news that I'd been slapped right in the face, publicly humiliated. I felt that if I turned on my TV I'd hear: "Is Darryl

Strawberry really not worth it? I'm Ted Koppel and this is
Nightline."

"Frank says you're not worth it, Darryl. What do you say?"
"Does this come as a surprise?"
"Is this what you expected?"
"How much *were* you asking for?"
"Do you think you'll have a new contract with the Mets in
November?"
"Do you take this as a personal attack?"
"What effect will this have on the pennant race?"
"Do you feel the Mets strung you along?"
"Have any teams contacted you?"
"Do you feel you're more valuable than Jose Canseco?"
"Will you be leaving New York?"
"Who will you play for next year?"
"What do you think of Frank Cashen?"
Bang! Zoom! To da moon, Alice!
I put up with the reporters for close to a week. I was bitter
and hostile, as you might expect, but I tried to hold my feel-
ings in check. The papers were looking for signs that the Mets'
race to the pennant would fade; signs, they would say, of my
failing to sustain the Mets' drive. The reporters got what they
wanted, but not in the way they expected. Frank's announcement was so downright mean that it took the entire team by
surprise. Even people who were not my bosom buddies on the
club stuck out their hands and said, "Tough break, Straw," or
"The guy's a jerk; you always knew that." I looked to Buddy
Harrelson for support, for understanding. He would talk to me
about it, I thought. But Buddy Harrelson, my friend, seemed to
be avoiding me. My imagination? When he seemed to turn
away as I entered the clubhouse on the afternoon of July 14, as
if he were embarrassed about something, I felt like the ground
had shifted under me. And being from Los Angeles, I was used
to the earthquakes.

If I had learned one thing from living and playing in New
York for ten years it was that New Yorkers do have an "attitude" about dealing with personal adversity that most other
places don't have. The highest praise a native New Yorker will
give to someone who reacted well to a setback or an under-

handed blow is, "He was a *mensch* about it!" or even, "She was a *mensch* about it!" which I can't figure out, but then I'm from L.A. Anyway, I tried to be a *mensch* about it for the next few days. That meant I tried to do my job despite the blow, go out on the baseball field to hit the ball, and pretend that the Mets "family" I was really feeling I belonged to again had not just thrown me out in the alley like yesterday's lunch. I tried to be careful in my quotes, tried not to bad-mouth the team, Cashen, or Harrelson, and generally kept my answers to questions to either one or two grunts. However, even my grunts were subject to interpretation. Until it all hit the fan the following week.

We started a tough series with Atlanta at Shea on July 19 and were still holding our own in the race with the Pirates when someone from the New York *Daily News* asked me to speculate about where I would be in the '91 season. He asked me whether I wanted to stay in New York.

"Sure," I remember saying. "I'd like to stay in New York."

"What if the Mets don't come back with the offer you want?"

"Well," I said, "I still wouldn't turn down an offer to play in New York just because the Mets didn't give me the contract I'm looking for."

"Does that mean you'd play for the Yankees?"

CUT TO:

INT. NIGHT

The New York Mets locker room.

TILT DOWN TO DARRYL STRAWBERRY, who is being backed against his locker by a horde of swarming reporters, each trying to get his microphone down the beleaguered ballplayer's throat. Darryl is trying to wave them off, but he's trapped as the other players, seeing his plight, leave him alone to face the mob.

DARRYL

(opening mouth and inserting foot all the way in up to the ankle): Sure I'd play for the Yankees. I'd have serious interest in the Yankees. Or the Mets, for that matter, if they came back with an offer. I wouldn't turn down New York teams. New York's my home and I like it here.

FAY VINCENT (VO)

Say what?

FRANK CASHEN (VO)

Now this puts him over da barrel. Chortle, chortle!

Yes, I could see the headlines even as the camera lights were turned off:

STRAW SOLICITS YANKS!

STRAW TO YANKS: TAKE ME!

I'D PLAY FOR YANKS, STRAW SEZ

What was my response?

STRAWBERRY HITS 24TH

METS NIP BRAVES BY TWO

The blast brought me up to 61 RBIs for the season and let Cashen & Co. know that I wasn't going into a tailspin just because they wanted me to. I wasn't going to cave in. I wanted them to know that I could keep the Mets in contention for as long as the rest of the team kept up with me. Management may have let me down, but this team could *win* and I wanted to win no matter what, hurt feelings and all.

We stayed in contention right through the end of July, now a game out, now half a game up, now tied. The papers were saying it was simply too close to call. When we'd drop a series, the Pirates would drop a series. When they'd lose a squeaker, we'd lose one. We were tied going up and tied going down and New York fans were getting frustrated. When would we either break away from the Pirates or fade out of the pennant race altogether?

I believe I displayed my most honorable behavior on August 1 when we went into extra innings against the Expos in Montreal. As pissed off as I was about my contract, Cashen's behavior, and Buddy Harrelson's aloofness, I was still a loyal team member. That's why when Buddy ran out to first to protest umpire Bob Davidson's call, I backed him up. Buddy screamed at Davidson until the ump told him to shut it down and walk away. From where I was, that's just what Buddy did. He turned his back and walked back to the dugout. But right then, Davidson threw him out of the game.

Hey, what's goin' on here? Throw a man out when his back is turned on you? No one does that to a Met, at least not while I'm still on the team. I stormed in from right field and put my mouth right in Davidson's face (I had to kneel all the way down to do it, too) and cursed him out right down into the ground.

"That was a load of garbage," I hollered at him. "Don't you throw out my manager when his back is turned." This is baseball, right?

"Get your butt back out in right, Strawberry!" Davidson howled. "I'm not taking this from you."

I put my jaw right up against his and called him every name I could think of. Then he jerked his thumb toward the dugout, kicked at the dirt, and screamed, "Yerroouudaheah!"

Then I looked down and saw a giant wad of slimy gum all over his shoe and burst out laughing in his face before I walked off the field.

"Strawberry!" he screamed after me, but I just kept on walking and laughing.

When I got back to the dugout, Buddy, who was already on his way to the locker room, told me that just before he turned his back on Davidson, he opened his mouth and spit a full hocker of chewing gum all over his shoe. I couldn't see any of this, of course, from out in right. By the time I realized what had happened, I was on my way to the showers, too. At least I showed that I was loyal to the team, and we eventually won the game anyway. The next day, just to show there were no hard feelings, Bob Davidson sent Buddy Harrelson a whole pack of chewing gum.

Two nights later we beat the Cards in St. Louis by staging a rally in the top of the ninth. We had gone ahead of the Cardinals on Dave Cone's pitching, but then he started to get shaky around the seventh. Buddy sent Bobby O in to relieve, but he took a quick beating and the Cards came back to lead 4-2 after eight innings. Our batters pounded St. Louis in the ninth for three runs and a 5-4 lead, and then we shut them down in their last at-bat. We were ahead of the Pirates by one game and playing frantic do-or-die baseball. Nobody was giving up even though the tension was beginning to tell on all of us.

I was enjoying myself even though my heart was breaking. The part of me that wanted to be on the Mets was still hoping for a way to remain in New York. That was the man playing late that summer. That part of me still believed that I could be in the Mets "family," even with everything that had happened. Despite our early-season insanity and our amateurish play, we had managed to come together as a team. I clowned around with Ron Darling, Dave Cone, and even with Mackey Sasser a lot about wild pitches, wild throws, and the errors on the field we all made. They even clowned with me about my "moodiness" when things didn't break my way. The intensity of the race for the championship had turned us into friends playing baseball together on a team that had the potential of going all the way. If only management had believed in us as much as we believed in ourselves. But we were fighting our own leadership, and we knew it.

Eventually, gravity caught us and we began to drift back to earth after our incredible rise. Following that comeback win in St. Louis, we dropped the next three in succession to the Cards, and it became evident to all that we were only playing .500 baseball again: just where we were in May before we began our run at first place. Fortunately, Pittsburgh was still in the tail end of a slump, so we stayed relatively close to each other for another few weeks. But some local sportswriters could see what was happening. My hitting had fallen off again as the negative press about me began to take its toll. Other sportswriters were encouraging, urging the team to keep fighting and telling me that I was too valuable for New York to lose. But the frustration was evident.

We had a near riot on August 9 when Philadelphia pitcher Pat Combs hit Doc Gooden square in the knee. Doc had earlier hit Tommy Herr and Dickie Thon completely by accident, but Combs's pitch looked too deliberate to be ignored. There had been bad blood between us and the Phillies ever since last season when Roger McDowell kept baiting Gregg Jefferies. We didn't like them—who in his right mind can like anything about Philadelphia anyway—and Doc simply blew up after Combs deliberately hit him. He threw the bat down and took off after Combs, who began to cover up. Catcher Darren Daulton tackled Doc and began to punch him from behind. I went berserk. Nobody swings on my friend Doc and walks away. I ran out of the dugout like a maniac and would have taken Daulton's head right off, but Von Hayes tackled me from behind and was lying on top of me. "I'm trying to keep you out of this for your own good, Straw," he said. The fight lasted for eight minutes, and the game didn't resume for another twenty. By the time the umpire threw me, Doc, and Timmy Teufel out of the game we were pretty well wiped out. Also tossed out of the game were Daulton, Combs, Dennis Cook, and Phillies coach Mike Ryan.

As August wound down, the Pirates led by two games and then three, but we caught them again early in September. By the middle of September, things were still very close, when the sports columnists picked up the tune that I was dogging it because I was "pouting" in the clubhouse. More bull! On the very same night that they were plugging away on their typewriters that I should be killing myself to prove that I'm worth $5 million instead of demonstrating that I'm not worth $5 million, I was blasting a two-run homer that helped us knock off the Cards behind Frank Viola's flawless pitching. As one sports columnist put it, the stars that emerged for us in 1986, who were not going to reemerge in 1990, were Lenny Dykstra, Kevin Mitchell, Ray Knight, and Mookie Wilson. They were all gone and could not help us anymore. It was Frank's own trades that forced the team to rely solely on my bat down the stretch. Then it was Frank who threatened to take the steam out of my hitting by denigrating me not only as a ballplayer, but as a human being.

On September 12 and 13 at Shea, I absolutely dragged the Mets kicking and screaming back into contention when we swept a series from the Pirates. In the second game of the series, before the biggest crowd of screaming fans at Shea in over two years, Doc and I buried Pittsburgh. "Strawberry saved the Mets"—that's what the papers said. In the fourth inning, with the Pirates up by two, I cut down a runner at home with a rifle-shot line-drive throw from deep in right. Yes! I held back the Pirates with my bare hands and then in the bottom of that same inning I took pitcher Doug Drabek so deep they'll never recover the ball. It was a monumental blast for a three-run homer, my thirty-fourth and my hundredth RBI, that put us into the lead and put us within one and a half of first. "If this is the end," I told the papers, "if my days in New York are going to end here, then I want it to be big. I want to be remembered as the guy who didn't give up on his team, who remained the leader and kept on bringing the team forward to the very end of the season."

George Vecsey of *The New York Times* said it best, I think. He said that in the middle of September the Mets were my team, mine all mine. He said it, I didn't. I knew I would rise to the occasion in September. I believed in myself, believed that after taking the knock that I took in July, I would be able to regain my balance and work my way back. I wasn't putting on a show for the fans just to justify my contract demands. Vecsey saw that. I was simply saying that I wanted the pennant, wanted it more than I wanted anything else that September. Poor, dumb Frank Cashen never realized that I really did love the Mets, New York, and baseball after all. He never figured that out. He had his calculator out, of course. He figured he would undercut me, good businessman that he is. But he never realized that there are moments in baseball when you go beyond what's around you and rise to a higher level. You even stop trying to showcase yourself; making sacrifices, instead, for the greater good of the team. That's what happened to me in September 1990.

Sure we had a lot to overcome. We had lost the meat of our lineup. We had to rely on a rookie manager who still made serious mistakes whenever we went on the road. He tended to change his mind a lot and blew hot and cold toward the players. But we had to rise above all of that. We had to go up against the National League's strongest teams, teams that were out to injure us physically if they couldn't beat us in the game, and knock them on their asses. And we did it! We did it by relying on certain players one night and other players on other nights. We stayed right in the race even though management undermined us at every turn. And when the Mets needed a key swat when the going got rough, I put the ball away. Frank never figured on that. He never realized that people could rise above their squabbles to put out for a team. Poor Frank Cashen.

The rest of the season is history. No, we didn't win our division. Pittsburgh went on to win. Los Angeles didn't win the West, either. Cincinnati went on to win. In an unbelievable World Series, Sweet Lou, banished from New York by George Steinbrenner, managed his Reds to a total domination of the Oakland A's with a four-game sweep. The World Series will go into the books. The Mets' might-have-been-glorious 1990 season went into the books too.

'Round about the end of October the Mets did what they had to do: they made me their offer. Frank was a little bit kinder this time. He said that he never meant to insult me personally when he said that I wasn't worth $5 million. He said that he felt no player, not even Jose Canseco, was worth $5 million. Maybe if he'd said that in July, things might have been different. If he had only taken fifteen minutes out of his otherwise busy and hectic schedule to sit down for a talk with me. He could have called me into his office, dropped by the locker room, called me up on the phone for a lunch or something. He could have done anything just to tell me that I wasn't only the houseboy for the New York Mets.

The Mets tendered an offer of about $15 million to Eric Goldschmidt, which did not extend to five years. Frank Cashen told Eric that in order to save time and put the bad feelings behind us, this would be the only offer he would tender. Don't even bother to counter, he said. This is it. If you reject it, Darryl's gone. We rejected it.

Then Fred Claire from the Dodgers began talking to Eric in Los Angeles about a five-year package. It was happening! The dream that I might go home to play baseball was becoming a reality. Eric and Fred talked a few more times; then I got a late-night phone call that they had agreed to a five-year package for more than $20 million.

Before I left for good, I saw Doc in the Mets clubhouse.

"You're gone!" Doc said. There was a sadness in his voice and both of us were teary. He was my closest friend on the Mets, and I will always love Dwight Gooden. "From the way they treated you," he told me, "I don't know how you put up with it." We hugged. I left. It was over.

I flew to Los Angeles where I put on my Dodger uniform for the first time for the press and announced that I would play in Los Angeles for the 1991 season. Glory! I had been brought home. I would play in the stadium that I had thought about and dreamt about from the first time that I heard the word "baseball."

A year of absolute madness was over. The New York sportswriters kicked up a lot of dust after I left. They predicted the Mets would be a better team without Strawberry. Frank Cashen said that he was glad that I was gone because the Mets had relied on me too much. Everybody said, in effect, good riddance to Darryl Strawberry, and the bitterness in New York welled up into some of the nastiest articles I've ever read. But for me it was over. The eight-year nightmare was over. Almost magically the bitterness that had been welling up in my own soul seemed quieted as well. I became more than thankful, I actually began to understand that there must be a pattern to all of this, a higher logic behind the craziness that had marked my life. I could see it now. I could actually see meaning forming up around me.

I was home now, and I was ready for a new discovery that awaited me with the coming of the new year.

4

CRENSHAW BOULEVARD

In sports, especially professional sports, your accomplishments only stand up on their own when you retire. While you're playing, what you do one day wipes out what you did the day or the week before. Seems unfair, but things change. Before the All-Star break in 1991, I felt myself on the way back from a shoulder injury. I was hitting balls, pounding home runs, and throwing base runners out from deep in right field. But right after, my bat was quiet, as if it had a life of its own, and already some people were wondering whether my honeymoon with the Dodgers was over.

I wanted to get angry, get mad at opposing pitchers and the team we were playing. I wanted to feel my old edge when I stepped up to the plate because it helped me focus on the ball better. But at the same time I understood that anger was what was eating me up from the inside. The demons and crazy spirits that had eaten me up in the past might have given me an edge, but they also demanded my soul as payment. Where is the line between consuming yourself and consuming the oppo-

sition professionally? I know I found it after I was released from
Smithers and Buddy Harrelson finally told me to stop holding
it back. I went on an eighteen-game hitting spree after that.

Last year, Brett Butler told me the same thing during a game
with the Montreal Expos. He walked out to right field during a
pitching change and told me I had to start getting mean. I
realized what I hadn't been doing since the start of the season
and how it was affecting the rest of the team. What had started
the incident was a Marquis Grissom single that bounced into
right field. I had my eye on the ball instead of on Delino
DeShields, who was the runner at first base, and by the time I
scooped up the ball and threw it to the cutoff man, Juan Samuel, at second, DeShields was already around third and streak-
ing for the plate. DeShields scored ahead of Samuel's throw,
which wouldn't have been necessary if I had thrown directly to
our catcher, Carlos Hernandez, at home plate. Was I so blind
that I couldn't see DeShields?

Did it hurt to hear that from Brett Butler? You bet it did.
The next night, against Philadelphia, Lenny Dykstra, and my
sparring partner Darren Daulton, I got a couple of hits and
drove in a run, but we still lost. I knew, as I watched Orel
Hershiser struggling on the mound to get his speed and power
back, and as I saw our relievers trying to cover up what the
starting rotation couldn't do, that we were in trouble those
days. But I also knew that you don't get into first place in the
West on a magic carpet. The Dodgers needed my bat to produce runs. I know now what happens when I turn on, become
electric, and drive the team.

I know it sometimes seems as if I'm looking at the game
going on around me through a thick fog, but it's not of my own
making, and I'd be lying if I said I wasn't concerned about it.
Even Oil Can Boyd, who we demolished on the mound in the
'86 Series when he was pitching for the Boston Red Sox, told
the papers that I seemed more laid-back. I'd lost my edge, he
said, and went on to say that he'd noticed the same thing in
other players who'd talked about being born again. Gary
Carter agreed with Oil Can. He told the *Los Angeles Times* that
he no longer sees the "anger" in my swing. Maybe he's right.
Maybe I still have to get used to the inner peace that I'm
experiencing these days. I can't let that affect the Dodgers or
my career. Somehow, however, I know everything will work

out fine. I just know it. But sometimes it feels like I still have too many people to satisfy.

Reggie Jackson told me very early in the 1991 season that the most important person you have to satisfy is yourself. He called me when I was in the middle of a terrible slump. Reggie said that you can't let other people, especially sportswriters or fans, set your goals or evaluate your achievements for you. You'll fall into slumps, he said. And there are times when you'll look for all the world like you're not the athlete people thought you were. The same fans who turn on you when you're in a slump will cheer for you like crazy if you can hit three home runs in a World Series game. And sportswriters, sportswriters are paid to give their opinions just like you're paid to play baseball. But if you can keep listening to your own voice, Reggie said, and be honest with what you want to do, eventually you'll pull out of your slump and get into the flow. Just don't quit, Reggie told me. Never, never, never, never, never, never, never quit!

What Reggie explained about my starting with the Dodgers as a $20 million outfielder also applied to my starting with the Mets over ten years earlier with my $200,000 signing bonus. It was advice I tried to give myself then, but events, immaturity, and the pressure to perform in New York kept me from hearing my own voice. But Reggie's advice, the advice of a former New Yorker who had come back to California, started me thinking. I, too, wasn't a New Yorker anymore. I was an Angelino and was happy to be back, even though it meant going through more readjustment than I realized at first.

I had spent the previous ten years getting used to an insanity I had actually learned to like: life in New York City. A New York life-style is difficult, but once you adjust to it, being out of it a long time can give you a case of the emotional "bends." I know that my "depressurization" was a reason for the violence on the night of January 26 when I was arrested. There is a kill-or-be-killed attitude in New York that is unnerving to anybody who hasn't learned to deal with it. Spend an afternoon riding the number 1 or the A train; change lines at Times Square some rush hour; or else be a commuter for a day and ride the Metro North. You'll see what I mean. Worse, try to catch a taxi in midtown Manhattan at 12:30 in the afternoon and stay a civilized human being afterward. These are all parts of living in New York that I had actually gotten to know and love.

I had grown up in Los Angeles but had become a New Yorker. New York and Los Angeles are as different as any two American cities can be. In New York, people live up, not out. Apartment buildings stretch to twenty-five, thirty-five, fifty, seventy stories, with high-speed express elevators and rooftop athletic clubs. You can live in a penthouse so high above Manhattan that on certain days in October and November you can barely see the street through the fog and drizzle. Just getting to the first floor on certain mornings may add fifteen minutes to your commute to work. And New York is always, always, always crowded and wet, and dark, and you learn to live with all of it and to wish you were back when you're not there.

That's not Los Angeles! Where New York goes up, Los Angeles spreads out. But there's definitely one similarity. Like New York, Los Angeles is a city of ethnic neighborhoods marked by delicate cultural balances and the red lines on a real estate agent's "Thomas Guide." If you're black or Latino you get to know those red lines real well. You think maybe someday you'll break into the public light and the red lines will disappear for you. But they won't for your parents or your friends; just for you because you're special. You can hit a baseball so far that no one can see where it falls. When you were ten or eleven someone said that someday you'd be a professional athlete and at the very least you'd make more money in a single season than most of the people in your neighborhood would see in a lifetime. And that made you special. It put a responsibility on your shoulders that whatever you accomplished, you accomplished for everybody else, as well as for yourself. The red lines would disappear for you someday, but there would still be a set of invisible lines as thick as prison bars. No one would see them but you. No one would acknowledge them, not even you. But they'd be there all the same between you and the rest of the world. And all of this—the promise, the responsibility, and the pressure to represent your entire neighborhood—would happen when you were only ten.

Now I was back in Los Angeles and I could see the red lines and feel the prison bars. I could see my past laid out on a map every time I drove along the Mulholland Overlook and peered down the mountain to the city of Los Angeles spread out below me. As you wind along the Mulholland ridge you cross the canyon roads that take you from the valley to the basin. And if you head east from the ocean, you'll eventually come to my old Crenshaw Boulevard neighborhood on the western edge of downtown Los Angeles. The signs still say CRENSHAW DISTRICT as you drive south and east into the heart of the neighborhood along Martin Luther King, Jr., Boulevard.

We lived in a tiny green stucco house right on Seventh Avenue near where the Harbor Freeway cuts east from the Pacific Coast Highway in Santa Monica to downtown Los Angeles. The freeway, Interstate 10, keeps going right across the bottom of the United States and dumps into the Atlantic Ocean in Florida. It was like a railroad, but all we knew of it was the small stretch that bounded the little dirt baseball fields in our neighborhood where my father sometimes played baseball. I learned to play ball in those fields by watching my father and older brothers play. When I was nine and ten, those fields were more my home than the house itself. Sometimes on Saturday mornings, our father would take my brothers Michael and Ronnie, and me, with him to Manchester Park where we would play in the local baseball league.

Even though I like to call those days the most peaceful years of my life, I know that there were seeds of anger and unhappiness planted even then. Even when you're ten years old, you don't really know for sure what your parents are up to, but you can tell if the ground under your feet is stable or not. Hell, even animals in the forest can tell if an earthquake's coming or if a fire is raging somewhere. That's how it was with us.

Our father, Henry, worked for the Post Office, played for the Post Office in the league, and was a popular local athletic figure. He was a good-looking guy, tall and thin, and he would hit a ball farther than anybody else on his ball team. He was a softball pitcher who could whip the ball across the plate so fast you wouldn't know where to start your swing. Nobody hit my father when he was on the mound. Nobody. I'd watch him with my jaw dropped wide open as he brought his windmill delivery over his shoulder and around his back and straight out in an openhanded pitch that would corkscrew the ball right past the batter's knees. Sometimes he'd have so much English on the ball that it kind of dipped and rose as it crossed the plate and hitters would either look with total amazement as it skidded by or they would try to golf it away.

When he was in control, he'd have hitters squirting the ball along the ground and looking like fools or whiffing while people on the benches hooted and hollered. Then when he'd step up to the plate you could feel the silence come over the entire field. People playing on other diamonds would kind of stop and look over his way just to see him hit. My father's stance spread over the whole plate, like he was challenging pitchers to come at him. He knew he was good. And when he brought his bat around he'd send the ball way over the heads of the outfielders. He'd hit the long ball over and over again, every time he came to bat. Fielders would play him so far out that when he chose to hit into the outfield instead of over it, he'd always be able to pick up extra bases and drive the runners home. Henry was on his way to becoming a legendary baseball player, not only in the neighborhood but in Los Angeles itself.

He was also a football player, a quarterback who could not only thread the needle to his receivers through tight coverage, but run the ball full out off a keeper, get up after a brutal hit, and throw a pass on the very next play. Just watching him run was like watching an artist at work. He was fast, of course, but he was also a very tricky runner to take an angle on. Like all great backs, Henry had a way of looking one way and cutting another so smoothly that even when tacklers got a hand on him, he'd shake them like a snake twisting out of its skin. And when he twisted out of our lives, he shook us just like a skin, too. We tried to wrap ourselves around the emptiness of where our father had been, but there was nowhere to grab. He was there and then he was gone, and we had only the memories to mark the place he'd occupied. He was on to other things and we were left to fill in the empty space.

Maybe I felt it more. Maybe I was more impressionable. I'll never really know, but it seemed as if his leaving had the greatest impact on me. I think my little sisters might have been too young to feel the blows. Michael, my oldest brother, seemed to step into the role of father in my life. Ronnie and I seemed to pair off, and I followed him wherever he went. But I remember being left with a well of anger so deep that even today it seems utterly bottomless. It's like a gaping chasm in my life that I'm afraid to look into, fearing that it will suck me in and I'll never escape alive.

I can't fill that chasm, although I've certainly tried. I've thrown my own talents into that pit, tossed in people I've loved—friends, teammates, family, everything. But it is all-consuming. Nothing fills it up. I've thrown liquor into the pit, using it to fill the void, drinking until I was so sick I couldn't stand up without help. I've screwed myself silly to fill the emptiness, but that didn't work either. Then I threw in love, sacrificing it, tossing in anybody who ever lent me a helping hand. As soon as they pulled back those hands, even to scratch their own heads, I took it as a sign of disloyalty and they went into the pit. Davey Johnson was in the pit; Buddy Harrelson was in the pit. By sacrificing them, part of me hoped, maybe it would ease the pain of my father's sacrificing me. Or did I sacrifice him? But that didn't work either. Nothing worked, and the pit is still there, still as bottomless and destructive as it ever was.

Daddy was a gambler. It wasn't pretty, and there was nothing romantic about it, especially because nobody ever taught him when to hold 'em or when to fold 'em. He just bet because when he was betting he thought he was alive. Addicts aren't "characters" or eccentrics, they're downright ugly. I'm an alcoholic and I know. When you have an addict in the household, the entire family tends to form up around him and make sacrifices to support his needs. My daddy's needs were all about money. Somehow, the harder everybody worked for it, the more it was gone, and the less the family had. There were five of us in the house and we always had to worry about there not being enough food to go around when Daddy was on a gambling binge. Worse, my mother, Ruby, worked for Pacific Bell, where she made a good salary, but we were always wanting for money because Daddy was always betting the farm every time he had a farm to bet. He was completely out of control and would have sucked the entire family under had we not eventually run our own intervention on him by default.

My daddy wasn't much of a companion even when he was around. I know I'm angry about that to this very day. You might say, if you came from one of those "normal," happy, caring, young Caucasian families that march across your screen every night on Nickelodeon, arching their eyebrows just so, saying meaningful things like, "Would you pass me the Hollandaise sauce and my golf club, dear?" Or, "How were things at the stock exchange today, dear?" or, "Jemima, I'll have just a smidgen of your wonderful apple pandowdy and another splash of coffee, thank you," or, "Uretha, how's your no-account husband doing? Did he ever take that job that I got him sweeping up late nights in the asbestos factory? And I'll have just a smidgen of your wonderful angel food cake and another splash of coffee, thank you"—you might say, "Just get over it,

Darryl! You got twenty million dollars. Ain't that enough to take care of all the daddyin' you didn't get?" And I'd say, "Not by a long shot."

When one of your parents is an addict, you don't get the complete parent package. They take something out at the factory. There's always a part of that person more committed to the addiction than committed to taking care of you. It's like being in a conversation with someone who's not really there. You look at him and he looks over your shoulder at whoever else is in the room. When you're a little kid and your sense of self is still dependent upon what your parent puts in you, you tend to believe you're not important or you don't really exist. And that makes you mad because you know you do exist. Why won't your father acknowledge it? Why won't he look at you and just tell you that you're important in his life? Why can't he spend just some of the time with you that he's spending at the track, or at a card game, or at a baseball game, or with his friends?

Sure, sure, your father will tell you, he loves you. Always will. Maybe. But at some point you want the man to put up or shut up. You need discipline. You need guidance. You need your parent to put a hand firmly on your shoulder, turn you around, and say, "Go this way" or "Do it this way." You want your parent to know you as totally as any human being can know another. You don't want your father stumbling into the kitchen on a Tuesday morning when you're on your way to school, kind of looking at you like maybe he knows you from somewhere, cocking his head like the pit bull in the junkyard down the street, and in a gravelly voice, saying: "Sump'in 'bout you looks familiar. You live here?" It's not the best way to go through life.

My father began spending very little time with the family after I turned eleven, even though he still lived in the house. He would take us to his ball games on the weekends, but there was always a lot of tension in the house. My parents were constantly fighting about not having any money.

"But you make good money," my mother would say to my father at night. "Why do your kids have to want?" My father would have no answer. It was as if he would reach down inside himself for an explanation and nothing would come out. He tried to think, but nothing happened. He was an addict. Addicts can never tell you why they do something; they can only stand there helplessly with no reason for anything. The more you confront them with the pain their lives are causing everyone around them, the more they seem to blank out. Then they get defensive and find places to hide emotionally. You think they're lying, they're abnormally stupid, or they're simply as deadly as snakes in the grass. You never think they're sick because they act so normal in other areas of their lives. With my father it was money. He was always handing it over to someone else while we had to worry about putting food on the table. Whatever my mother made was fair game for my father too.

The worst part of all of it was that he could be so all-fired mean and ugly that we often walked in terror when he came home. I could hear Ruby and Henry fighting at night after I'd gone to bed, their voices carrying not only through the house but through most of the neighborhood as well. He'd be drunk lots of times and would not even know what he was saying. He'd be abusive and menacing, threatening her, threatening us, threatening the way we lived. Henry was chewing through money as fast as he got it. The more you gave him, the more he blew. Ruby had to call a stop to it. She'd lived with it long enough, but it was coming to a choice between keeping her family in their house and keeping Henry in betting money.

You could hear him screaming that he worked for it, he could spend it. And you could hear her saying that any man who'd let his children want for food and the good things in life just to bet on a horse or whatever else was less than a man. Henry couldn't take being called less than a man, even though he knew he was less than a father. It was this family, he kept saying, this family that was keeping him from realizing his dream. What was his dream, winning a trifecta? His own family was keeping him in chains, he said, locking him up in responsibility. Think how wonderful it feels to hear that at night as you're drifting off to sleep. It makes a Frank Cashen press release sound like the opening of *Mr. Rogers' Neighborhood,* or " 'hood" may be more like it.

On one particularly hateful night, I remember, Henry had come home very late and very drunk and started complaining about his family. "Family?" my mother shot back. "What do you mean family?" She'd be really mad that he never spent time with us or with her. He was always out, always gambling, always drinking. When weekends came, he'd look for excuses not to be with us or to pretend we weren't really his family. Ronnie, Michael, and I would be playing ball over at the park and we'd see my father drinking with his friends and he wouldn't even acknowledge us. What kind of father is that? This is what my mother told him time after time, and on this one night, she must have gotten to him. Why do I think I'm playing a broken record?

Maybe Henry said that he wanted to kill all of us. At least that's what I think it sounded like. Children tend to block out those kinds of threats, especially when they're made by someone who's never seemed too thrilled that you're alive in the first place. Ruby answered him, but we could hear fear in her voice. I say "we" because I knew my older brother Michael, who was fifteen, was already in the kitchen. We all got up. I remember thinking this wasn't like one of the hundreds of other fights they had. This one was dangerous. I was afraid because it had the sounds of the kind of thing that could rip out whatever pilings kept your life from tumbling down into oblivion.

As rocky as it was, my life was still held together by two parents, both of whom worked, and both of whom were together in the house some, if not all, of the time. Besides, when you're a kid, you know when a parent is truly turning on you as if you were an alien. Maybe that's what makes it hurt so much. You can put up with the neglect because you lie to yourself and say that the parent really loves you way down deep. You can put up with the abuse because (a) the parent will eventually get tired and go on to something else, (b) you develop calluses and scar tissue in all the right places, (c) it always feels better when it stops hurting, (d) at least you've got a parent who gets involved enough to be abusive, and (e) all of the above. Next, using your number 2 pencil, blacken the letter preceding the *most appropriate* description, completely obliterating the letter. If you blacken all the letters you'll know how I felt as the fight between my parents grew increasingly life-shattering.

As my father drew ever closer to my mother and hissed at the rest of us with greater and greater anger, we could smell the alcohol on his breath. He was spraying us with a superfine mist of it with his cursssssesss. He was a fearsome sight, all liquored up and mean like he hated us. But he was also hating himself. I can understand that now after having gone through that experience myself. He was weaving, kind of staggering, but all the more menacing because you knew he was speaking a version of the real truth, even though it was "potentiated," shall we say, by the liquor.

It was when he said that he would start hurting us that my brother Michael stepped in. Henry had threatened us in the past, but we'd learned to duck and the threats just passed over our heads. This time, however, his threats carried weight and Michael had decided not to take them anymore. "Who was he to come in here drunk and start threatening us anyway?" Michael would say later. But at the time, I saw my whole family splitting like so many parts of an atom in *Mr. Wizard*, and there seemed to be no force keeping us together. Michael spoke back and you could see my father turning in his direction and raising one of his very dangerous eyebrows. I didn't like this.

"Whazz!" he kind of half spit and half said.

"I said stay away," Michael ordered. I didn't actually know how much of it was empty bravado and how much was his own confidence that he could hold his ground against his father. My knees were knocking because this was bigger than anything I had ever seen. Things were spinning out of control and the confrontation was drilling through the bedrock of my life. Somebody, anybody, *help*!

My father took a few steps toward his oldest son, glaring down at him not just as an opponent but as someone challenging *his* leadership of the tribe. The two of them began squaring off for what I could only assume would be a fight to the death, and my mouth became dry and I wanted to pee real bad. Michael puffed up his chest and you could feel the electricity between them. It all felt like the crack of doom and part of me huddled in terror.

"You get out," Michael bellowed in a voice so artificially bass you could feel the vibrations all the way along the fault line to San Dimas. "You get out of our lives."

I was in shock. Michael was throwing his father, *my* father, out of the house. Hey, wait a minute!

"Say, what?" my father said, balling up his fists as if the whole kitchen were going to explode into violence all over Michael.

"You leave us alone," Michael screamed. He was trying to be a man, but he was only fifteen and there were tears in his eyes as well as in his voice. I don't care who you are, you'd rather roll over and die than inflict pain on your own father, even if you hated his guts. "Just get out."

But my father didn't seem to have the same reservations about hurting Michael as he moved toward him as if he weren't his son but just another person he wanted to beat up. He wasn't a father at that point, he was an assailant. That scared me. This was no dream.

My fourteen-year-old brother, Ronnie, was scared too, but he couldn't stand back and let Michael get beaten up. He challenged my father also, telling him that he would protect his brother. I broke out into a cold sweat, for sure, and I think my tongue was actually stuck to the top of my mouth.

"M-m-m-m-e, too," I think I said as I stepped up behind my brother Ronnie. I could feel the blood pounding behind my eyes and right below the base of my skull. I could feel my throat close up all the way down to my lungs. I couldn't breathe. I couldn't swallow. I couldn't think. I was almost paralyzed by fear. But it wasn't a fear of my father that was wrenching through my muscles like an electric current, it was a fear of myself, a fear that every support frame of my entire being had just been kicked away. I was alone, fearfully alone, atop a too-high precipice, and I couldn't climb down.

My father himself almost disappeared behind a veil of terror I had drawn around me. I was cutting myself off, challenging my father on a violent, physical, primal level of combat that was leading straight into the unknown. Worse, I knew that I was crossing an invisible boundary; I was suddenly in a universe where I should not be. Your father, your blood, does not turn against you. Even Abraham had his moments of fear when God told him to slay Isaac. But at the very end, the Lord showed His countenance of mercy, stayed His sentence, and withdrew the hand of Abraham. I was not in that world. I was in a world where my father had turned his full violence on his eldest son and would have hurt all of us. It felt like he might have even killed us. It was just moments away.

But we stood firm.

Then he backed down.

What was worse? Being hurt and possibly severely injured by your father, hurting or injuring your own father, or forcing him to shrink away from you and surrender all the mystery of being a grown-up and *your* parent. Better to have been hurt, the voice still tells me, than to have challenged and upset the natural order of things as we did that night. We were right in the immediate scheme of things, but it was basically wrong to have driven off our father, driven him off, leaving us to be the men of the household. I felt the wrongness of the act pulse through my whole being. It was as if we had been forced into a breaking of some elementary law of the species. I felt profoundly sinful, as if nothing could go right for me until I undid the effects of that act.

Although I only stood there alongside my older brothers and protected my mother and sisters, I felt suddenly much older, as if I had eaten the fruit of the Tree of Knowledge. Whatever had been my childhood had been cut off. I felt "wrong," shameful, guilty, and have not been able to see things clearly since. But I didn't know any of this then. It only felt like a trembling somewhere deep inside of me. It knocked me off course, that I know for sure, and since that night I've been drifting in a way that I cannot stop.

As our father disappeared into the night, we still stood there in the kitchen, Michael puffing himself up at having successfully challenged the old man, Ronnie and I staring at each other wide-eyed, not knowing yet how serious things were. Maybe we managed to laugh from the relief of the tension afterward, but I don't think so. I think we were more afraid of what was about to happen than of what had just taken place.

We knew that we weren't the same family anymore and that all of us had been changed. But what did it mean? A couple of nights later, Henry returned and sat at the kitchen table with my mother. This time he was sober and we weren't allowed in the kitchen while they talked. Our mother was trying as best she could to set things to rights. To put us back in our places as children even though we might have saved her life a few nights earlier. She felt as bad about it as we did. "Bad" isn't even the right word—"sickened" is better.

My mother told him that whatever happened was directly the result of his gambling and drinking. He was destroying us, she said. He was destroying his children. If you don't want to have a family, then you won't have one, she said. She told him she wanted a divorce and that she would make sure he left us alone. When she finished explaining it to us after the fact, we closed ranks around her and against our father. He wasn't our father anymore after that. Moreover, in an awful realization, I understood that he had never been our father, not in the way fathers are supposed to be. He lived with us. He used us as his family, but he never did what fathers do for their families.

I no longer hate him for that night. I no longer have that fear of him that I had for all those years growing up, although the gut reactions are still there. However, I still miss whatever it was I never got from him. I miss not ever receiving the discipline from him that other boys got from their fathers. I miss the guidance that I should have gotten. I miss those moments—and I know they probably never really occur anyway —when you get from your father the sense that he has built your house on a rock and it will not be swept away by the flood of life. Until the natural order of things takes his physical power over you away and you strike out on your own, he is the person who guides you through life. Your mother may give you unqualified love, but I believe my father could have related to me on that wavelength that only runs between fathers and sons. There was a switch inside of me that he was supposed to have turned on. It's the switch that flips on the cruise control that takes you through life.

I tried to get it from my brother Michael, but he got married. I tried to find it in my brother Ronnie, but his is off too— short-circuited on the same night that mine was. My mother tried as hard as she could, but she didn't have the right PIN to get into the file. Not coach John Mosely, or coach Brooks Hurst, or manager Gene Dusan, or Davey Johnson, or Buddy Harrelson, or, unfortunately, Tommy Lasorda can turn on that switch. No one can, only my father, and he forgot.

Therefore, Tommy may have to tell me when he wants me to hit, or to catch, or to pick up the stupid ball that's rolling against my foot so the runners don't score and score and score. Juan Samuel better signal real hard that he's the cutoff man, and Gary Carter better walk directly out into right field and tell me straight into my face to shape *up*!

I'm in L.A. now. This is where I want to be. This is where it has to begin. This is where I have to make it work. And I will make it work. Just you wait and see.

5

"THAT 'C' MEANS HUSTLE"

My father was gone. You'd think I'd have been relieved about it. Maybe I should have been breathing a little bit easier because a threat to all of us had been removed. But that wasn't the way it was at all. My father may have been an addict and selfish in the ugly way that addicts are. He may have used everything we had to feed his addiction, but he was never a menace until the night we threw him out of the house. And after he was gone, I felt guilty. Not only had he said that his children were chains around his neck, it was his sons who drove him away. Now we had no father and there was a hole in my life as a result.

You adjust, of course; you have to. You learn denial. I learned it so well that I practiced it for about fifteen years, until I was arrested in 1990. By denying the pain I was feeling because my father had walked out on us, I closed off a part of myself. By denying the guilt that I felt because we physically challenged him, I allowed it to grow like an abscess. But my father had actually turned on his kids. That wasn't fair. We didn't have a choice in who our father was. It wasn't as if somebody came up to me floating along on a cloud somewhere and said I had a choice between being a "Strawberry," a "Kennedy," a "Murphy," or a "Hall." I didn't look down from some cloud floating over Los Angeles, see my father tearing up ticket stubs at Santa Anita, and say, "That's the man for me. Sign me up; I'm number forty-four." So, not having had a choice, there was no point in feeling like I'd let the guy down. He'd let me down. But because it was over I felt empty and angry.

That's where baseball came in. We still saw my father in league games after he left, but he made believe that he didn't see us or that we were invisible. Maybe that's where I first learned about becoming invisible. Anyway, if I couldn't "officially" watch my father play baseball, I could play baseball myself. I became fixated on the game. It was something I could do to kill the pain, to release the energy that was building up in me. And I was good at it. Boy, was I ever good at it.

I'd been playing ball at the park even before my father left. I was a kid, eleven or twelve, and like any kid, I played on pickup teams and finally in Little League. I remember one of my friends telling a Little League coach by the name of Willie West that I was a better player than some of the fifteen-year-old kids that were on his team. Mr. West didn't believe him, but my friend kept after him, kept bugging him, until Mr. West agreed to take a look at me. He asked me to hit a few balls out, play the field a little bit, and toss a couple of pitches. Then he watched me in a game during which I hit about three or four balls to the next diamond. He came up to me afterward and told me that he wanted me to show up for the Little League draft, but just to stand over on the side so people wouldn't notice me. My friend was laughing because he knew what Mr. West was up to.

On the Saturday morning of the draft, I did just what he told me, standing over on the side as if I were completely invisible, which I was getting particularly good at doing, and waited for all the bigger kids to get picked. Then Mr. West picked me and the rest of the coaches fell on the grass laughing so hard I thought they would bring up their morning chitlins and grits. "Him?" one of them said, pointing at me and holding his guts in as if they were going to explode all over the

field. "He so thin he looks just like a . . . a . . . Straw!"
And the rest is history.

THE END

Actually, the other coaches did laugh quite a bit, but Mr.
West managed to keep a straight expression on until we broke
into our teams. Then he told me he would have the last laugh
on them. But I was nervous about the whole thing, because
these kids were a lot bigger than I was. And they looked
stronger, too. But Mr. West just took me aside—he was starting a pattern that would stay for the rest of my playing days, it
seems—and told me not to worry about size.

"You're talented," he said. "Size is not as important as you
think it is. You got a good swing, a good arm, and you're quick.
By the time the season is under way, you'll have them eating
out of your hand."

He was right. As the season went on, I began making a
reputation for myself in the area, and other kids wanted me to
play for their teams, too. At that point, though, as much as I
might have dreamed of being a big-league ballplayer, those
dreams were only the dreams that every kid dreams. I thought
they were far, far away, but other people thought they were
much closer than that.

Baseball is a game of breaks, like life. My first break came
early, when I got to have Michael and Ronnie as my brothers.
Michael and Ronnie were already working with a coach
named John Mosely, who soon became one of the most important people in my life. Mr. Mosely was a neighbor of ours who
had once played pro ball back in the old Negro Leagues and
was a truck driver by profession. He was also the assistant
coach of the Compton College baseball team. He was really
interested in my older brothers, both of whom, he believed,
could have become Major League players. And he was right.
Michael, who is a cop in the Los Angeles Police Department,
was and still is a great athlete. He could play football and
baseball and had the basic physical strength you need to become a professional athlete. He was in Crenshaw High School
already, however, and had his own life. He was socially very
popular and a natural leader.

People say that I'm a natural leader, but I'm not. I may have
wanted to lead from time to time, and people like my former

manager Buddy Harrelson and Dodgers manager Tommy La-sorda have taught me *how* to lead, but Michael was the natural leader. As far as I'm concerned, he still is the leader. When I was thirteen and fourteen, I was simply a younger brother tagging along after Michael. He would tell me to get lost and stop following him, but I couldn't help myself. With our father out of the house, Michael was the only father I had.

My brother Ronnie was more familiar with my Little League games than Michael was at that point because Michael was becoming more interested in girls than he was in athletics. Ronnie had been talking to Mr. Mosely about me for months, even while the coach kept telling him that "The boy's too young." But Ronnie kept at it and finally said that I was playing against high-school teenagers who were twice my size and still dominating the game. That's what interested Mr. Mosely, Ronnie once told me. It was a chance for the coach to get his eye on a potential player at a young enough age where he could have some real effect.

"Just see him," Ronnie said. "Just watch him play at the diamond on Saturday and make your own decision."

"Okay, okay," Mr. Mosely finally said. "Let's see what he does."

I don't remember being watched, even though Ronnie had spent some time at my Little League games when I was pitching for the team. Mr. West said that I was one of the few ballplayers in Little League who had enough control over his throw to consistently deliver strikes. When Mr. Mosely saw me pitching inning after inning to kids twice my size and going one-on-one with seventeen-year-old hitters and striking them out, Ronnie told me, he just about had a fit.

"What's your brother doing pitching?" he asked Ronnie. "Is that boy crazy?"

Ronnie was only fourteen himself and didn't know what to make of what Mr. Mosely was saying.

"Boy's got too strong an arm to wreck it now trying to throw strikes," the coach said. "Put him at second base for now, put him in the outfield, but don't put this kid on the mound. I don't want him to be a pitcher."

Then the coach saw me get a hit on my first at-bat and clucked like he was a mother hen.

"If I could fix his swing, he could be a long-ball hitter,"

Ronnie told me he said. "And I know how the big leagues like long-ball hitters."

Of course, I didn't know any of this firsthand. Ronnie told me what had happened after the game and Mr. Mosely told me himself months later that when he saw me play that first day, he believed I could make it into the Major Leagues. He didn't tell me right away, he said, because he wanted to know if I was prepared to make the kinds of sacrifices you have to make to get into professional sports.

He told me you have to practice, you have to be dedicated, and you have to make yourself into a fanatic if you want to succeed. He said that he saw too many Little League players hit high school and start all the dating and partying you do at a neighborhood school like Crenshaw. A lot of good players lost sight of what they thought they wanted when they were younger.

"Don't be a fool," Mr. Mosely said. "Most people don't know what they're endowed with. When you got a talent that can take you places, you got something precious. You got to nurture it, bring it along, train it, hone it, aim it, so it can take you as far as possible. You have to make yourself a promise to play fair with yourself and not piss away what you've been given."

When I was a thirteen-year-old, that sounded good to me. Let's face it, he was the first person who ever told me I even had a future in front of me. The night my father left, I was trapped in such a state of panic, I thought I didn't even deserve to have a future. Mr. Mosely first opened the door a crack on what was to become an entirely new world. He was one of the first male adults outside of my brothers who actually took an interest in what I could do and what I thought about.

John Mosely was a short guy but very husky. He'd really built himself up over the years by hauling cargo around. He spoke with authority, too. He had the bark of a coach who's used to giving instructions just once and expecting that they'll be followed. But he was patient, too, like a teacher who knows that he has to explain things so that they make sense. Once he thought you were supposed to know something, though, you could see him change and become more of a coach or drill instructor and less of a teacher.

After Mr. Mosely had seen me play, he let me tag along after Michael and Ronnie when he was giving them baseball instruction. Years later, Mr. Mosely would tell Bill Nack of *Sports Illustrated* that "Darryl was never a guy to mess around with girls." Hmmm! "Baseball is all Darryl talked about. He was a baseball fanatic." That was then, and considering the trouble I've gotten myself into with women over the years, I should have thought more about what he said to Michael and Ronnie about not getting tangled up in relationships.

John Mosely took Michael, Ronnie, and me over to the Harvard diamond, a park in the neighborhood, to practice baseball fundamentals on weekends and whenever he could get free in the afternoons after his two jobs. He'd hit fly balls out to us all afternoon and then sit us down and explain what we did right and did wrong. After we'd run ourselves around the outfield until we thought we couldn't breathe anymore, he'd take us out for some food. In those dark days after our father had left, Mr. Mosely was a lifesaver. He was more like a father than the father that had left us. It was as if Mr. Mosely held the key that was able to unlock everything I had in my wishes and dreams. Mr. Mosely picked up the key from the moment he began talking to us. He had a way of making the person he was talking to feel as if he were the only person in the world. He reacted to what you said, and he pulled you up short if he thought you were slacking off. I came to rely on his way of instruction and explanation more than I realize, because even today, I don't believe that I can be left to my own devices too much. I'm afraid—and maybe I need to work on this more aggressively than I have in the past—afraid I may just screw up during the early part of the season to get someone to corner me in the locker room or trot out to right field during a change of pitchers and say, "Look, Straw, you got to get focused on what you have to do. We're all behind you because you're part of our family." Man, someone says that to me and I'll hit the ball all the way to Jupiter and beyond. There is no way that I'm not going to respond to that kind of talking to.

John Mosely became involved in our lives in other ways as well. He gave us emotional and spiritual support. He would lecture us—and I mean *lecture* us—about staying in school, applying ourselves to the books, keeping away from the type of gang violence on the streets that we could see happening all around us, and believing in our right to have a future.

Now I can see it a lot more clearly than I did even a year or two ago. Mr. Mosely didn't want us to give up on ourselves just because our father had left. He knew—and maybe it was only by instinct—that in our community so many families were breaking up that a generation of children could have been lost. And that's exactly what's been happening in black communities and neighborhoods across the country. Why do you think so many black young men are dying on the streets? What hope do they have in their lives? It breaks my heart just to think about it, but it has to be thought about. But for the absolute grace of God, I could have gone down toward the dead end of street violence; Michael could have gone, or Ronnie could have gone. Our lives were saved. Mr. Mosely stepped into our lives and told us we had futures that were valuable. Sure I'm an All-Star Major League baseball player today, but more important, I'm alive. And I know that part of that achievement belongs to Mr. Mosely because he believed that children in trouble were worth saving. We need more John Moselys in this world.

He used to talk me up all around the neighborhood. He believed, and now I can understand why he thought that way, that the more people know about your skills the more they will talk. The more people talk about your skills, the more they exaggerate the facts and begin making myth. Baseball scouts love myth because everybody believes in "the natural," the shoeless kid whose raw skills turn around ball clubs. It happens! It's the American myth. By saying to everyone who would listen, "I've got the best kid of all. He's going to be in the Major Leagues and he's going to dominate," John Mosely helped create an aura of success that permeated everything I did while I was at Crenshaw. In his own way, the man's a genius.

I had a natural ability to play baseball. I was aware of that, but I needed the insight John Mosely had to offer, and I was more than grateful to get it. He made me sharper. He was able to see what talents I did have and focus them in such a way that I began improving right before my very own eyes. By the time I was fourteen, I was hitting balls to the next diamond. He also taught me basic fundamentals that I needed to know in order to get the jump on the eighteen-year-olds I was playing against. Mr. Mosely was always encouraging me. He would put me in one-on-one situations against giant eighteen-year-olds who looked to me at the time more like radioactive mutants out of a Japanese monster flick than like human beings. He'd say, "Hit this guy's pitches," and I'd look up from the plate at some fifty-foot celery stalk from Krypton who'd deliver a ball with the speed of a bullet, relatively speaking.

"I can't play these guys," I'd cry.

And he'd say, "You get up there and hit 'cause that's just what you're gonna do. You're gonna play them no matter what." And he'd make me stand up to these guys and swing away at the best pitches they could throw. Then he'd say to me that someday I'd be in the Major Leagues and what I was learning now would stay with me for the rest of my life.

"You'll be one of the best," he'd say over and over.

This man's crazy, I would tell myself. But he would say it over and over again until I believed it too.

I remember, in particular, the days when I would hate to get up to go to the park for workouts. Sound familiar, Straw? On those days, Mr. Mosely would come over to the house to get me up.

"He's asleep," one of my younger sisters would tell him.

"Well, you go in there and wake him up," he'd say to her. "Tell him that I'm out here and I'm sitting here until he gets dressed and comes with me."

Many times my sister Michelle would come out and say that I was still sleeping and wouldn't get up. "That so?" he'd say. Then he'd walk into my room himself, check out my head under the blankets, walk into the bathroom, fill up a glass of water, walk back into my room, and dump said glass right over my head under the blanket. That got me up. I went out with him.

Mr. Mosely believed in accomplishment, self-reliance, plain dealing, and truthfulness. He was the perfect reinforcement to my mother, Ruby, who had the impossible task of raising five children while working full-time. Ruby Strawberry "made" us a family and held us together in the face of absolute disaster. When I think about how I've often screwed up my life and made a total ass of myself in front of millions of people, I'm more concerned for people like my mother and John Mosely than for myself. Now that I've "got it," and understand who has been intervening in my life from day one, I understand a little bit of what I have to be thankful for.

John gave me lots of TLC during the tough year or so after my father left. Then I went to Crenshaw High School, where my brother Michael was the team's center fielder. By now, what I had done in Little League had gotten the attention of some of the newspapers and lots of coaches. Some of the papers began calling me the hottest Major League prospect to come out of Los Angeles in years. Michael made sure I met the Crenshaw High School baseball coach, Brooks Hurst, who would become my next major influence and father figure. Mr. Hurst was a white man (in fact, he was so white he made *The Brady Bunch* look like *Boyz N the Hood*) running a team of black high-school ballplayers, and he was a real-life version of the seventies television show *White Shadow*.

Mr. Hurst had his hands full with me, I can tell you that. I was a moody adolescent, nervous about being in high school, distrustful of older male authority figures in general, and out to cause trouble. I'd follow my brothers around when they went to look for fun. I'd sneak out of my bedroom window at night after my mother put us to bed. I would catch up with Michael, who was seeing a steady girlfriend, and simply hang around. Or I'd go to the parties my brother Ronnie was going to. I was a pain in the ass, but on a dangerous path. Michael was about to leave the family because he was grown-up. Ronnie, though, had made friends with some of the less-than-perfect kids in the neighborhood. He was embarrassed about it and didn't want me tagging along after him. There were more than a few times he'd catch me sneaking after him, punch me around till it really hurt, and send me packing back to the house on the verge of tears. Ronnie kept me out of a heap of trouble when I was fifteen.

Mr. Hurst was not someone to put up with a moody kid driven more by attitude than by desire. He told me right up front that he wasn't about to put me out in right field to replace the right fielder he already had. I wasn't a hot dog on his team, he told me, until I proved myself during the season. But I had my own ideas and wanted to play right field, where I had played since Mr. Mosely had taken over my training. We're only talking about a couple or three years here, but to a fifteen-year-old kid, two or so years is a major chunk of his career.

I played a lot of positions, sometimes in the outfield, sometimes at third, but I kept moping around despite Mr. Hurst's yelling at me to move my butt around the field with more hustle. It got so that I became sick of the word "hustle." Yuk! But one day, something happened that would repeat itself years later with Davey Johnson. I simply ambled off the field at the end of an inning instead of running in. We lost the game that day and Mr. Hurst bore down on the entire team. Then he turned on me because I was the most lackadaisical of all the players.

"You're just out of tenth grade and you think you're a superstar already," he said. And he jabbed his finger right at the "C" on the chest of my uniform and bellowed, "That 'C' means *hustle*. When you wear it, you hustle."

I felt like a humiliated fool in front of the entire team. I took off my uniform right then and there, and threw it down. "Man, I don't even want to play anymore," I said.

"I can play baseball all I want in the summer," I told myself, but I was lying.

I went out for basketball and played under Joe Weekly, the Crenshaw coach. But to tell you the truth, basketball hurt my ankles, and as much as I liked the game, it was a real "no brainer." Not to insult anybody playing basketball, but I found that it took more intelligence to figure out baseball situations than to toss a ball at a basket. You run a lot in basketball, it's true, and you have to know your position, of course, but let's face it, folks, it's you and the basket, right? I mean, the Lakers are a great team and all and they make the game look more like ballet, but they say to this eight-foot Vlade Divac guy, "Hey, big dude, dunk this little ball in that hole," and he says, "Hokay, Merikanski," jumps up, and drops it down the hole like he's putting a dime in his pocket. "Scottie, beam me up!" Know what I mean?

I spent the whole summer that year after my fight with Mr. Hurst even more moody and difficult. Finally I swallowed my stupid pride and asked him if we could talk. We had a good talk. In trying to explain my feelings and troubles to him, I realized how much I really loved baseball, how much it was really a part of me, and how I couldn't live without playing it. There was no way I could hide from that, I told him. I wanted to play; I wanted to be on the team. And, I said, almost breaking into tears, I wanted to be on a great team because I *needed* to be on a great team. Mr. Hurst understood me. He explained that he felt the same way about the game.

"That's why," he said, and he made me feel like twenty million dollars, "I can't stand it when someone who's as good as you, as talented as you, and who's basically a good kid, screws up. You can do it all," he said. "And I want you to help me help you accomplish what I know you can do. I can show you exactly what you have to do to realize your dream."

What did he mean?

"There are certain things you have to learn in your life," he explained. "Certain things that apply not only to baseball but to life in general that can take you all the way. If you can make yourself a better person, you *will* be a better player as a result."

I was all ears. He talked about playing position and about doing the very best you could in one particular spot on the field. If you're in right field, then it's playing right field as well as you can. You have to hustle—there was that word again—everywhere on the field to let the other team know that you haven't been beaten. Winning is mental, he said. If you can get your mind on winning, everything else will be easier.

"Try it my way," he said. "Take the talents you have, but just apply yourself mentally and see what a difference it will make."

I did. I came back the following season and we had a championship year. Our team was so strong that the Major League draft picked up three seniors from the Crenshaw team. Mr. Hurst just looked at me in a very knowing way when the news broke in the papers, and I realized, just by the look in that man's eye, that I would be next. That was the first time I realized that I would have a real shot at breaking into the majors. I was thankful for Mr. Hurst's dedication to the school, to the team, and to the kids in our community.

Then, in my senior year, the attention of baseball scouts was turned on me. Our team was one of the most powerful teams in the entire country. They called us "the Lumber Company" after the mighty Pittsburgh Pirates. We had mashers all up and down the lineup, powerful hitters who consistently put the ball out of the park. And you could see that Mr. Hurst got a lot of pleasure out of coaching us. Reporters showed up to cover the games and asked Brooks Hurst about my prospects. Even my father called up Ronnie a few times to ask about what was going on, because the news about me was spreading through

Los Angeles. It pissed me off because Henry wouldn't talk to me, he would talk to Ronnie. What was I, invisible to the man?

Ronnie would tell him to show up at a game once in a while.

"Stop down and see Darryl," he said into the phone while I was standing right there. "You'll be amazed at what he can do."

So Henry began coming to some of the games. When the reporters and scouts realized that he was my father, a couple of them began asking for interviews, and more than a few scouts tendered offers through him to me. Hey, wait a minute, guys. You're talking to the wrong parent. Finally Ruby stepped in and Mr. Hurst routed all the "expressions of interest" to her.

My senior year at Crenshaw was magic all the way to the championship game. We played a powerhouse school called Grenada Hills in the city championship game at Dodger Stadium. Grenada Hills was a strong club with a hot young pitcher who was also the school's quarterback—he shoulda stayed in football! A Mr. John Elway started at third base and then came in to relieve. What an arm on that kid! I started in right field and then came in to relieve. The two of us dueled, but Grenada Hills came out on top in a heartbreaker of a game. I would have to wait for my revenge against John Elway for another six years, when the Mets beat Boston in the very same season that my New York Giants absolutely demolished John Elway and his Broncos in the Super Bowl.

Life was changing for me. Agents visited our kitchen, pushing cash into Ruby's hand and telling her they were giving me an advance bonus to sign with them. They would negotiate the contract they were sure I would get when the draft was held. Ruby was at first flattered but then offended. She saw that much of the attention was really pretty condescending. "They wanted to tell him about the big money," she told a reporter for *The New York Times* in 1980. "They feel that kids brought up in the ghetto—money excites them."

It was more than money exciting me in 1980, Momma; it was the world. It was big, beautiful, and wide open, and I believed I owned all of it. I believed that all of the problems of the past, all of the anger, the frustration, the bitterness over losing Daddy, the meanness that would sometimes rise right out of me and dominate everything I wanted to do, were all gone. That's what I thought as the reporters lined up on Seventh Avenue in Crenshaw just to get a photo op of the new Ted Williams.

But I was wrong!

6

THE MINORS

"Darryl Strawberry, come on *down!*"

It was June 1980. It was *The Price Is Right, Let's Make a Deal,* and *Jeopardy!* all rolled into one. Look great so they pick you, choose the right door, and make sure you have all the right questions. You're not supposed to have any answers yet because you're still too young. It *happened* for us.

The whole family came down in June 1980, when I graduated high school and entered the Major League baseball draft. It was an exciting time, especially for an eighteen-year-old and a very hungry family. For the past five years and then some we'd held our own against the economics of where we lived and what was happening to us. Before my father left, the family was bleeding money because of his gambling. After he left, my mother was able to make her salary stretch to take care of us until we got older and could earn our own incomes too. And always, during that five-year period, there was the promise, however far away, that one of the boys would make it to professional sports and turn the family into something else. Michael was already in the Dodger farm system and people had high hopes for him. Then it was my turn. For the past two years, as the sports magazines and newspapers focused on the baseball diamond at Crenshaw High School and profiled me as one of the best baseball prospects in the country, this draft had been our dream. Now the dream was coming true.

I had a backdoor plan just in case I wasn't picked in the Major League draft or if I couldn't come to terms with the team that had drafted me. Because I had played varsity basketball at Crenshaw as well as baseball, I knew that I could have gotten a basketball scholarship to college and eventually play pro basketball. I could have played baseball in college, too. The decision would be which college to go to and which draft to think about after finishing college.

So, as happy as we were as the draft came along and agents kept throwing offers through the window as they drove by, I knew that I had a back door to my future if baseball didn't pan out. But everything I could have hoped for in the draft happened. I was the number-one pick in the entire country, and the Mets, a last-place team in 1980, had that first pick. It was clear that I was going to New York to play ball if the Mets and I came to an agreement.

"You know anything about New York, Darryl?" my highschool friends asked me.

"Nah, just that they got snow," I would answer. "And, I hear, lots of rain." And that was it. That was all I knew. I used to watch *Kojak* all the time and knew there was a lot of traffic in New York. I saw the Mets' games on television and knew they played at Shea Stadium. But I didn't know how big New York was or how aggressive the New York sportswriting community was. In fact, I didn't even know *where* New York was or anything else about it, for that matter, but it didn't bother me a bit.

From the hordes of sports agents and law firm representatives that churned down Crenshaw Boulevard toward Seventh Avenue, we narrowed the list down to a few likely prospects. I say "we"; actually, it was my mother, with my father, Henry, putting in his two cents from time to time. Suddenly he discovered he had a family.

In reality, many reporters and scouts were talking to my father even before they were talking to my mother or me because they had spotted him at the games. It was a tricky situation for him as a person because he had to admit to himself that he'd walked away from his own family and now they weren't his family anymore. It must have been very painful for him. We've never seriously talked about it, although we've talked about other things. It will be one of the great confrontations he and I will eventually have to have at some point—step five, I suppose—during our respective recoveries. Neither of us is looking forward to it because it will be a gut-wrenching experience. But it has to be.

Picking an agent wasn't as tough a decision as you think, once you find out who represents whom, and what kinds of contracts they've negotiated; then you ask what each agent thinks you should be looking for in your first deal. My mother and I each had our own agendas as well. She was looking for some sort of assurances that I would be taken care of once I left home. I'd never lived away from home before, and this promised to be an especially challenging period of my life. I wanted to make sure that I got some assurances from the Mets that I would get into the majors within a couple or three years. I didn't demand that I suit up, choose my bat, and hit number three in the order the next week when the Mets came to Dodger Stadium, but I wanted to know that I wasn't going to spend the next five years of my life in the minors. If they said to give it at least four years, I'd open my back door, go to college on one of the athletic scholarships I was being offered, major in business, play varsity somethingball, and enter the pros after graduation.

Richman Bry told me that probably wouldn't be necessary because no Major League team would let a first-pick outfielder and potential long-ball hitter rot in the minor leagues for more than three years. "The money you'll be getting," he said, "would preclude your spending too much time in the minors. The team wants an electric player like you to drive in runs. You'll stay in the minors until you learn to hit the kinds of pitching you're not seeing now. Then they'll move you up as soon as they think you can hold your own against Major League pitching."

We liked the sound of what he said, so we hired him, and a few days later he'd negotiated my first Major League contract with the Mets. He presented us with a $200,000 signing bonus from the club, the largest they'd ever paid and certainly more money than we'd ever seen in our lives. I had one last "t" to cross before agreeing. I asked the Mets for that assurance that I'd be moved up to the majors inside of three years. They came back with a guarantee. One of the executives pulled me aside and said, "Listen, there's no way you're not going to be in the Major Leagues. You've got such unbelievable talent that you'll have to be up very soon. If you develop like we think you will during the course of your minor league career, you'll be at the Major League level before you know it." Then he added, "And the people watching you won't let us keep you down there too long, anyway."

What did he mean by that?

I made the decision to sign. Little did I know that I was putting myself into the clutches of the New York press, who would follow my every move, listen for my every breath, hand me toilet paper over the transom, rifle through my garbage, and basically be hiding under my bed for every moment of my life for the next ten years. But to me at that time, the world looked big, bright, and full of money and limitless opportunity. What did I know about life in the city of New York?

Willie Mays once said that playing in New York can transform any athlete. The press, he said, put an inordinate amount of pressure on professional athletes because they have the absolute power to make you or break you. If they're on your side and you live up to their expectations, you can do no wrong and your future—your marketing future—is secured. If they turn on you, and turn on you they will if you don't play their game, they can make life a living hell. Willie Mays was right. I got on the wrong side of the New York press very early, and they ate me up like fish food. But at the time, I expected none of that.

In June 1980, I was staring at the $200,000 bonus, taking the Mets' guarantee that I would make it up to the majors in three years, and planning what I would do with the money. Actually, I bought myself a Buick Riviera, the car I'd always wanted, and bought my mother a Datsun Z. Then I put the rest of the money in her hand and planned to take off.

Immediately after I had signed, the Mets went to Los Angeles to go up against the Dodgers. Frank Cashen, a formal, businesslike person but also very cordial to me and my family, invited me to come to the Mets' dugout to meet the players and be a part of the team in Los Angeles before I went down to join their rookie league farm club. The day I drove to the stadium to meet my new ball club was one of the proudest days I ever had. I was ushered into the dugout like I was already a superstar. That, too, can create an ego out of nothingness. I met the 1980 Mets, shook hands with all the players, and got a little razzing about what I would be facing down in the minors. Some of them looked at me as if I were dinner being brought to the table. I couldn't understand those stares at the time. Now maybe I would look at a new player with the same blank stare that I saw over ten years ago. But, again, it was a message that I didn't get. The meat grinder was waiting, and I was smiling as I slid along the conveyor belt.

Now, in the afterglow of my years with the Mets, I still like to remember those weeks of glory after the draft. It was a period of complete weightlessness when I had achieved escape velocity from my life as a high-school ballplayer by reaching the very highest pinnacle—the Major League draft—and just before I was trapped by the gravity of the New York Mets. I was in the zone between the planets, a blissful adolescent who could do no wrong because I still wore my innocence and naivete as righteously as I wore my cap and gown at Crenshaw graduation. But like all periods of weightlessness, this one was soon to end. Already, as those weeks wore on, I began feeling the pull of gravity. My happy smile was disappearing from the pages of national sports magazines, but I was quite happy beneath my "cloud of unknowing." I was just another bonus baby staring into my future in New York, ignorant of what was ahead but feeling the pull of the tide dragging me out and the undertow sucking me down.

If my mother was worried about what was lying in the trail ahead of me, she didn't spend time with me fretting about it. As I packed my bags for the trip to the world of minor league baseball, shoving little packages of beef jerky into the pockets of the suitcases, my mother just repeated her simple instructions: call every night so she'd know that I was okay.

"You've never been away from home before," she reminded me. "You're gonna have to expect you'll need to adjust." She didn't know how right she was. "Don't be too hard on yourself if you get lonely. We're just a phone call away even if it is across the country."

And that's when it hit me. It was the stuff about "across the country." I realized that I wasn't simply going on a school outing to Big Bear or to Knotts Berry Farm for the day. I would soon be flying across the entire continent. I'd be in the East and the world would be in the West. That's when I began getting really nervous. It must have become pretty obvious because my mother talked more and more about my calling home every night.

But that was only part of my worry. I also vaguely realized somewhere in the back of my ever-growing skull that I was going to be meeting other draft selections at the pinnacle of their success, too. I may have been number one, but number two would be hot on my trail and looking to knock me off without so much as a "pardon my spikes." This was not Little League or high-school baseball, and gradually but inevitably I began to feel the pressure of having to perform building up on my shoulders. Baseball, in my ever-expanding view of the world, would soon no longer be fun; it would be a requirement. Hitting would be something I'd be expected to do all the time, rather than when the spirit moved me. And even the daily game itself wasn't just entertainment to the fifty thousand screaming fans howling for the opposing team's blood, and for your blood if you fell out of their favor. This was becoming *worrrk!*

Shortly after signing all the papers, saying all the good-byes, and feeling generally great about myself and the future the world had opened up for me, I reported for work as a player at the New York Mets' rookie league farm team in Kingsport, Tennessee. It was like going to another planet at the very end of the universe. I hadn't heard yet of the firestorms roaring in New York about the desperate situation of the New York Mets and the pressure already building on Mets management to work me through the farm system. I was happy-go-lucky; that is, until I saw Kingsport.

Friends from California began asking me, on the phone after I arrived, "What do you do down there?"

"Ain't no there there," I answered.

It was true. Kingsport was so small that if they had had a traffic light, people would have stood out in the street to watch it change. But the Kingsporters loved their local baseball team and followed it with a loyalty and enthusiasm you can see only in the minors. If you've seen the film *Bull Durham*, then you will understand the kind of affection the locals had for the club. If all I learned from the minors was that type of relationship between fans and club, then my experience there was still worthwhile because it helped me understand baseball in a way that I couldn't in a Major League city like Los Angeles.

My arrival in Kingsport was the subject of a national press conference that put the entire team on display. I was the center of the conference not because of anything basic to myself but because of the New York press frenzy surrounding my selection in the draft. I was put on notice that New York sportswriters would be following my every move in the minors because they were tracking my development as a player. The more the Mets floundered, the more the press wanted to focus on me as the future of the team. That bothered me in a way that I couldn't put my finger on. It was like the rumble of distant guns.

The press was building up expectations for me, a set of objectives and achievements that they were going to use as benchmarks for my worth as a professional baseball player on the Mets. High on their list was the impact that I was supposed to make on the Mets once I arrived in the majors. You can't fault them for that. After all, from a purely business standpoint, baseball players represent investments. As a team owner, you give someone a contract worth a certain amount of money because you expect that that athlete will provide you with a return on that money. If you invest millions in a Reggie Jackson or a Dave Winfield, you expect not only that they will play million-dollar ball but that your team will see increased revenues from attendance. So Reggie becomes an "electric" player, "Mr. October," "Reggie at the bat."

But expectations can not only be self-fulfilling, they can also be self-enhancing. And that's where the trouble starts. I didn't know this at the time because I was drunk on the praise that I had been lapping up for the previous few months, but the more the expectations fed on expectations, the more they grew until they began to reach impossible proportions. It's one thing to be flattered by the press's calling you one of the most valuable additions to the Mets in years. It's quite another for the press to say that you represent "salvation" for the dismal Mets and that the sooner you are brought up and begin hitting .400 (my average in high school), the sooner the Mets will get back into the first division. I was Ted Williams; therefore, I was supposed to hit .400.

The press had picked up on a quote they got the year before

from Crenshaw baseball coach Brooks Hurst, who had once said to me that I could be another black Ted Williams. At the time, my baseball heroes were Dave Parker, the powerful former Pittsburgh Pirate and the present California Angels home run hitter, who was the first player to break the million-dollar contract barrier, back in the seventies, and the wonderful and unfairly maligned Pete Rose, Mr. Charlie Hustle. Coach Hurst raised an eyebrow when I sarcastically piped up with "who's Ted Williams?" The joke I was making was that the heroes for my generation were the Pete Roses, the Dave Parkers, the Dave Winfields, and the Reggie Jacksons. These were the clutch players who always came through in tight situations. I wanted to emulate these playing styles. Mr. Hurst told me that the way I swung the bat and the natural ability I should train to pull and jerk the ball to different fields made me seem more like Ted Williams. That's how the term "black Ted Williams" got created, more of a joke in the context of a conversation than an interview.

But hey, give the press the ball and they run with it. Suddenly, in June 1980, I became the "black Ted Williams," and the press followed me from whistle-stop to whistle-stop waiting for the black Ted Williams to emerge from within the protoplasm of a rookie league ballplayer. Imagine trying to start your own career by hefting the career of Ted Williams on your shoulders and throwing it out in front of you like an anchor every time you tried to accomplish something. That can turn you into all potential and no achievement. The expectations about your career multiply in proportion to your achievements. Sounds like a vicious cycle, right? Absolutely, because there's no way you can ever catch up with the runaway train of potential your commentators have created for you. Your career gets out of control and you are always playing catch-up.

This had begun for my career as early as the summer of 1980 when reporters started coming down to Kingsport to cover the games and monitor my development. Part of me was flattered. Part of me was becoming quite concerned. I had secretly wanted to become known as Mr. Hustle, the guy who plays his position and supports the team. However, I was becoming known as the future Ted Williams, the player who would someday be the personal savior of the entire Mets ball club. I didn't like the sound of what was happening. I didn't like the reporters yip-yip-yipping at me wherever I went. No, I told my manager, Chuck Hiller, I didn't like the sound of it at all. But I couldn't tell him why.

I was very fortunate to have had a manager like Chuck Hiller, who had played Major League ball with the San Francisco Giants, the New York Mets, the Philadelphia Phillies, and the Pittsburgh Pirates. He was amused by the activity surrounding my arrival, but he wasn't in awe of it. He told me that he had seen plenty of talented kids with lots of promise come through the system only to listen to their own press and never live up to their potential. He told me something valuable: "Don't worry about your potential; that's what someone else puts on you. Worry about what you do on the field every day, and the potential will take care of itself." I understood what he meant, but didn't really know how to do what he said to do. "Just be your own person," Chuck kept on telling me. "That forces people to take you on your terms instead of your having to take them on their terms."

Chuck was one of the rare baseball managers who didn't let reputation get in the way. I was an eighteen-year-old kid away from my family for the first time in my life when I entered his turf, and he treated me like the lonely tentative kid I was. He kept the press from making my life miserable and provided me with the closest thing I had to a family structure that entire year. He let me know that whatever he said to me was completely unconditional. He wanted nothing in return except a good performance on the field. He defined a good performance as something that while helping the team win was also something that I could be happy about. "You're professionals," he would tell us. "You've got to make a lot of people happy in your performance. But never lose sight of your need to be happy with your own performance, or else nothing you do for anybody else will carry any weight with you."

I know that making me feel comfortable was part of his job. But Chuck made it seem as if he were extending himself to you beyond the requirements of his job. He had a very rare ability to make his players feel as if they were important as human beings. This, too, taught me a valuable lesson. If you want to get the best performance out of your people, make them feel important. Make them feel that who they are as human beings and what they do count. Don't diminish them. When Buddy Harrelson turned against me in August 1990 after the Mets' management broke off negotiations, he told me, in effect: "I

don't care about Darryl Strawberry the human being." All that
mattered was what I could produce for the team. He cast me
off into the darkness when I had come to rely upon his friendship. I know now that my expectations were not unrealistic
because of the way Chuck Hiller treated all of us, especially
me. He wanted to keep the younger players happy. He understood what we were going through and what many kids just
out of high school go through in a strange town and in a
demanding situation where they have tremendous pressure on
them to carve out a career in one and only one spectacular
season in the minors.

Chuck was also quite adept at dealing with the press. He
knew they were getting to me with their interviews after each
game and their baiting me by saying, "Hey, Darryl, the Mets
played a disastrous game against the Phillies. What would you
have done against Steve Carlton?" Before I could get a chance
to stumble out an answer, Chuck would step in and take over.
He kept the press off me every time they would start hanging
around. He told me he wanted me to play ball, not sit down for
interviews. So when things got intense, Chuck would hold the
interviews, without me, and he would answer reporters' questions as if he were me.

My life in Kingsport was also brightened by a really interesting person—a character—whom I called "Starvin' Marvin"
and who just popped into my life one day at the ballfield. He
introduced himself to me and said that he knew I was in a
small town and that I probably missed my family and that he
could sympathize with my being at the center of so much
media attention. He called himself a "country critter," and his
casual attitude and willingness to be friendly when he didn't
know a thing about me was a surprise, to say the least. I didn't
know what to make of him at first.

Starvin' Marvin showed me the sights of Kingsport and took
me all around town. He told me he worked at the Post Office
—well, I felt good about that—loved baseball, and supported
his Kingsport team. Too bad he wasn't Susan Sarandon or,
better still, Whitney Houston, but then you can't have everything. He said he wanted me to feel at home and part of the
community. He was a friendly guy, and you can be sure that I
was glad for the companionship.

We were almost complete opposites, the two of us. He was
white, thirty-something, a contented civil servant, and short. I

was black, nineteen, only just out of high school, and a thin six-six. Folks passing by the local schoolyard used to stop to watch us play one-on-one basketball and would talk about our strange friendship. After a game of schoolyard ball, we'd maybe play some catch, have some dinner, and then go out to a movie. After the ball games he'd stop by to see if I needed anything, wanted to talk, or just wanted to grab some food. He really helped me adjust to being alone and away from home.

I left Kingsport at the end of the season. Marvin stayed. In fact, he still lives in Kingsport and still stops in at the ballpark to say hello whenever we play the Braves in Atlanta. Marv is a good guy who tried his best to cheer up a lonely teenager away from his mom, his older brothers, and his sisters for the very first time in his life. When I think about Marv in the context of all that has happened to me since 1980, I realize that there are lots of nice people in the world who'd like to relate to you as a human being instead of what your reputation says you're supposed to be.

In August 1980, I got word that I was being flown to New York to receive the Tanqueray Award as the amateur athlete of the year. This was my first real award for accomplishment outside of high school and I was more than a little overawed by it. First of all, they explained, they wanted my prestige as a number-one Mets draft choice who would eventually be an important player in the Major Leagues to invest the award with an increased stature. Wow! Talk about swallowing your own press. They were giving me an award because they believed that I would make the award more prestigious. I had a tough time trying to squish that down, I can tell you. I wanted to walk around town holding up the award, saying, "Hey, look, see this? I'm being awarded to it, not it to me." You tend to want to wallow just a bit in your own grandeur.

My time in Kingsport was divided into two parts for me. The first part I was trying hard, but I was moping around because I was lonely. By the second half of the season I had gotten used to the new situation and was hitting the pitching I was looking at. I was more aggressive during the latter part of the season. I wasn't letting myself get brushed back as much by the pitchers.

When I first came down, pitchers would throw the ball right at me and laugh as they were doing it. "Who's this hot dog who's making all this money while I'm stuck here yanking on my pump handle for fun," they'd say. Then they'd throw the flamer right at my head and I'd get brushed back right off the plate and into the dust. In the last game of the Kingsport 1980 season, I remember, we had two runners on base when I came up and this one pitcher seemed to take a real delight in throwing at my head. Every time I'd flinch or hit the dirt, he'd double over with laughter. Chuck Hiller told me to stand up to the guy. "Hit that SOB outta here," he said.

And that's just what I did. I got right up. I cleaned myself off. I stared right back at the guy and wouldn't let him escape my Muhammad Ali glare. I said to myself, "Hey, you be playing every day now against people who be doing this to you. You got to get tough." I stepped back into the batter's box and promised that I was going to let this guy have it. "I'm not afraid of any pitcher or anybody on this field, for that matter," I told myself. I waited for his next pitch and hit that sucker as hard as I could for a three-run homer. Boy, did that feel good to send the ball away. And the stupid bonehead pitcher just stood there and stared at it as it flew out of sight. "Check it out, homes," I said as I rounded second, looked him right in the eye, and showed him teeth. "Ball's in orbit." Years later, Chuck Hiller would always remind me of that day.

"Never let 'em get to you, Straw," he would say. "Just think about the pitcher who sent you right into the dirt and you got up and sent his next toss three hundred and fifty feet away."

I felt that was the game when I arrived professionally. It was the final game of the season when it all seemed to come together. I was happy that I would soon be going home, the press was there and I wanted to show them the improvement I had made, and the pitcher made it easy for me because he thought I was afraid of him. When I hit that home run, I convinced myself that this was what baseball is all about. You have to have an aggressive attitude and you have to show people that they're not going to push you around. I was pleased with my first season as a professional ballplayer. In forty-four games, I'd batted .268, hit five home runs, and batted in twenty runs.

I had my crack at the professional ranks again the following year when I was assigned to the Mets' A ball club in Lynchburg, Virginia. I got down on myself almost as soon as I arrived. Was it the small-town nature of minor league ball? Were Lynchburg and Kingsport too alike? Was I doomed to spend the first part of any season in a kind of perpetual gloom until something snapped me out of it? Was I just a big baby, as others on the Mets later so eagerly described me to the media?

Again, however, I was lucky to find a manager who befriended me in ways far beyond what would normally be required. His name was Gene Dusan, and he saw almost immediately that I was playing far below my professional abilities. The press had already descended on Virginia for their Strawberry feast because the Mets had begun another disastrous season. "So how's the Messiah doing this year?" they would ask. "Hey, Messiah, you ready for the big boys?" a couple of them said to me, all in good fun of course. Of course!

My roommate, Lloyd McClendon, told *Sports Illustrated*'s Bill Nack that I went into a shell and tried to deal with my problems on my own. "He was troubled," Lloyd said. "There were times when he talked about going home. I told him, 'Hang in there. Keep your head on right.' He was young, he didn't have good work habits. In this game, it's easy to stay in bed all day, especially on the road. What Darryl didn't understand is that you have to get your body regulated. You've got to get up early, walk around and do things—go to the mall, take in a movie. It's very easy to lie around and grab a bite and go play. But you're not getting yourself ready either physically or mentally to play the game."

Lloyd was right. I was in a funk. I didn't know if I wanted to keep on listening to the press ask if I was ever going to pan out as a real ballplayer or not. When I was supposed to be concentrating on playing, I was paying attention to the press. They never really got off my back and even seemed to enjoy the fun of seeing me screw up after they'd done a number on me the night before. Maybe, I thought to myself, I should just pack it in, go home, pick up on a basketball scholarship, and return to the draft in the future when I would have more of an ability to deal with the pressures.

One day shortly after this thought had crept into my mind, I simply didn't show up for a game. I just stayed home and said to myself it was all over. "Forget about it," I told myself. "Just forget about it."

The next day there was a story in the paper that I had left Lynchburg, gone back home, and didn't want to play baseball anymore. It wasn't true, of course. I had only just stayed in my room, but the phone kept ringing and I didn't answer it. Was I so depressed that I couldn't function? That's what I believe was happening as I look back upon it now.

Luckily for me, Gene Dusan got involved. He would bring his sons with the team on the road games and they would stay in the room with Lloyd and me. I felt like an older brother to them, the first time I felt like that in two years, and it made a real difference. I began to see that if I could be part of a family, feel as if I belonged somewhere instead of feeling like some nomad out in the desert, then I'd have a reason to perform. Mrs. Dusan also invited me over to the house for dinner and for the opportunity to play with the kids. I needed so desperately to belong to a family that I would have done anything to be a part of their household.

Gene was compassionate and caring. He was humane, but he stayed right on my butt and made sure that I was putting out to the fullest of my potential. He said that he knew that I was so talented that when I played the game in my usual laid-back way people would likely complain that I was either "lazy" or not motivated. "They'll criticize you for relying on your natural talents instead of hustling on the field. You'll have to learn to withstand that type of characterization," he said. He was right, but I never learned it. I always feel upbraided when people say that I am just dogging it.

He told me that the only thing I could continue to do was to make progress. He kept on pushing me, and I kept on pushing forward and gradually broke through during the second third of the season. Gene taught me how to listen as well as how to improve my playing skills. He convinced me to take what he was saying seriously, and in so doing I learned that listening was also an important skill. I ended up hitting a respectable .255 with thirteen home runs in Lynchburg in 1981. It wasn't great, but I contributed to the team and showed the Mets that I was gradually coming along.

But what would I do the following year? we all wondered. Was there any way the Mets, who themselves were under criticism from the press, could try to at least present me in a favorable light when the press descended on my next minor league team? Soon, they and I knew, I would be called up to the show. Showtime! They had to make the transition go more smoothly. They had to find a way to speed up the process. But they and I knew that I still hadn't finished paying my dues. It was in 1981, only my second year out of high school and the pressure was already building. The press was saying that I was a bad investment, the Mets were worrying that my transition to the majors would take too long, and I was worrying about whether I had made the right decision by joining the Mets.

It was all very confusing. And as the rainy California winter soon dried up into a desert spring, I looked with more than nervousness at my upcoming year. I was being moved up, they told me. I'd be going up to double-A ball in Jackson, Mississippi. Jackson, the Deep South; the coming year looked tough indeed.

7

SHOWTIME

Minor league ball is as much carnival as it is baseball. Entire communities come together to party; families bring food; they eat and drink; there's music. Kids can reach out and touch the real-life baseball players. There's a purity to it that surrounds you when you're a player and that often hides the serious purpose beneath the whole structure of a minor league farm team—getting to "the Show." For anyone who hasn't seen a hellzapoppin', high-scoring, A or double-A ball game, it's worth the trip to a local minor league town.

There were "lifers" whose paths you'd cross in A ball who dreamed so passionately about going to the Show they'd wake up in the night with wet sheets. When a bonus player was teleported into their midst who had "Show" written all over him, either they hung around real close, hoping that a little of the magic or good fortune would rub off on them like pollen, or they got real hostile. Pitchers liked to throw at bonus players, as I found out when I picked myself up from the red dust in

Lynchburg, and fans sometimes like to hoot them down. Other fans, like a Starvin' Marvin, welcomed the chance to cross paths with someone who might be going the route of a sports celebrity. It was something to tell your grandchildren about, or even just a bit of familiarity with someone whose photo you might see in a sports section some day. Your own angle on a hero.

All of this was a real mind-expanding experience for me, a side of baseball I'd never seen before. This was "grown-up" baseball, baseball with an edge to it, with a relentless pressure behind it. Guys' jobs were on the line. Their futures were at stake. These weren't just happy-go-lucky teams taking buses from one little town to the next to put on a show for the locals; they were really extended training camps, breeding farms almost. The whole point was not winning, but getting out and getting up. Behind the nine innings of the nightly baseball-circus were the coaching evaluations, the instructional sessions, the endless practice, and the constant traffic of players full of hope going up and the walking wounded being sent down. I was excited about seeing baseball played not as a pastime, but as a business. This was a world I had heard about but never seen firsthand. It was a world full of people whose whole lives were devoted to the business of baseball. It was a world that I was expected to join because, like them, my life was signed over to baseball as well. I had at last begun to live my childhood dream of being a professional baseball player.

Then there's the downside. I'd never been this much away from home before for any reason. The loneliness and isolation of being away from everything familiar threw me way off stride for the first few months in Kingsport and then again in Lynchburg. At the same time, I had to adjust to the pressure of playing pro ball. Each year that pressure increased because you had to learn to play in a more difficult league against stronger players. You inch your way to the majors.

At Lynchburg, I experienced more pressure than I had seen on the Kingsport team in the rookie league the year before. I had begun the season with the hope that I could make a greater contribution than in the previous years, but very quickly I developed the feeling that returning to professional baseball might have been a mistake. Maybe I should have been someplace else, I thought as I crossed paths with players older, more experienced, and better prepared emotionally than I was.

These guys seemed to know who they were. They weren't kids just a year or two out of high school. Most of them had gone to college and learned more about the world than I thought I would ever know at that time. They had learned what I call "real-life" skills and knew how to deal with people. They'd lived in dorms and knew how to discipline themselves. They'd been taught to study and how to apply what they'd learned. They knew how to talk to people and they had a real sense of their own importance. I had none of these skills. I should have been in college, I told myself. I should have spent my time learning how to cope with the ego circus of NCAA basketball and learning methods to cope with the personalities I would come up against. I would have been better prepared for pro sports. There were so many ego trips and head trips that I thought I had slipped into another dimension.

I also experienced firsthand racism from fans. I perceived in no uncertain terms from the attitudes of people around me—the locals, the fans, other black ballplayers—that I was in the South now and that I had to be extra careful. You could hear some of the racist comments from the fans when you were on the field, and my skin would crawl whenever we'd get off the team bus in some town that looked as though the year was still 1950. I understood—actually it was more of a "sensation" than anything else—what racism can do to you.

The racism that I sensed in Virginia was just like a force field of hate. You know it's there; you can see how it changes the light coming through it; you can even feel it like a heaviness all around you. But you can't point to one specific thing and say, "See that? Now do something about it." It's as if there were someone with a smirking grin behind you all the time, but every time you turn around, he's suddenly gone. The racism that I perceived certainly affected me by putting negative thoughts right into my brain. I was already feeling down because I was away from my family, and the comments I was hearing just off to the side or barely within earshot made me feel especially angry and sad at the same time. Why was I here? Why was I putting up with this? These are the kinds of thoughts that can plague a young player's brain during his stint in the minor leagues. It takes a compassionate and understanding manager to recognize these attitudes and deal with them positively.

That's why I was so lucky to have found Gene Dusan. Gene

explained that I would be hearing a lot of personal and ugly comments from fans over the years and that many of them would, in fact, be racist. "You can let them get to you," he said, "or you can understand them for what they are and defeat them by being all the better for it." He told me to keep myself focused on the future.

"There will be a time when you will be a great ballplayer," he said. "You have all the skills that the greatest players have, and you will one day join their ranks. During these years in the minors you must learn to develop a confidence in yourself that will withstand all the negative attitudes you will confront. If you can do that, you can't possibly fail."

It's not just athletic skills you develop in the minors, it's mental skills and character. The more a coach or a manager can instill confidence in an athlete's character, the more that person will be able to accomplish and the sooner he will be able to do it. Gene Dusan did this for me, and the Mets recognized his ability by promoting him along with me to their double-A ball club in Jackson, Mississippi, the following year, 1982.

At first I was more than a little nervous going into the heart of the Deep South where so many bloody civil rights battles had been fought. But I was in for a happy surprise. Jackson is a college town, in some ways like L.A.'s Westwood, and I had a friend at Jackson State. The town seemed like home already. And he showed me places to go, things to do, food to eat, people to see. I felt better at Jackson than I had felt at either Kingsport or Lynchburg. I could even take Gene Dusan and his kids around with me without the disapproving stares of the locals following us everywhere because I felt like a native more than a newcomer.

Gene, too, made things easier from the start by telling me right at the outset of the season in a private meeting away from the rest of the team and the press that he was looking for big things from me that year. He didn't announce it or make any big deal about it. He didn't put any public pressure on me. It was more like one friend telling another friend that he knew how good it was gonna be. He did it in a way that was a form of encouragement and not a challenge to meet a set of expectations. "Nineteen eighty-two's gonna be your year," he told me. "This is where the rookie out of high school that I first met becomes a pro ballplayer. Here's where you learn to use your wings," he predicted. Gene promised to protect me from the press—"a cone of silence," he called it—so that I could deal with the issues of playing ball and not with public relations. "Whatever goes on in the papers is their issue, not your issue," he told me over and over again. "You're not going to let things get to you this year."

All of that made me feel that I'd have the opportunity to develop professionally. I got added support from the Mets when the papers began clamoring for me to be brought up right away during the season. "Why are you coddling Strawberry?" some of the sportswriters had asked management. Rumors began flying through the Jackson ball club that I might skip triple-A and be brought up during my double-A season. "The Show," some of the players were telling me on the bus. "You're going to the Show this year." But the Mets stepped in and squashed those rumors before they did any damage.

Gene told me that the coaches and managers thought that I'd be "destroyed" if I were brought up too early. "But tell you what we might do," one of the Mets' executives said to me. "If you can really make the transition while you're at Jackson, we may move you up to Tidewater to finish out the year. Get you in triple-A faster if it looks like you can hold your own." Fine by me, I thought. "But don't push it too hard," Gene added. "Give yourself the time to develop mentally as well as professionally." I told myself to listen to Gene and to focus completely on playing for Jackson. The better my performance, the more I could tell myself that I was learning what it takes to become a professional ballplayer.

I had a monster of a season at Jackson. I hit more home runs than I'd hit in my two previous years combined, I think, and had a whopping 97 RBIs. I felt in complete control of my game, of my swing, and of what was going on in the field. Maybe the newness of being a Met had worn off, maybe—and I think this is more likely—I was getting used to the minor league pitchers, and probably I had acclimated myself to playing under the pressure to produce in the minors. Whatever it was, I was never more sure of what I could do than I was in the 1982 season down at Jackson. Then, right before I was moved up, I was voted the most valuable player in the whole Texas League. In an interview at that time, Gene Dusan explained to a reporter that "in Jackson, Darryl Strawberry just put it all together."

Another Jackson coach, Bobby Valentine, told a story in an interview that I remembered with great pain and frustration, but which he told me was really an example of what I could do when I was focused. Bobby told a magazine reporter that in Shreveport, Louisiana, in 1982 I had dropped a straightaway fly ball to the outfield that cost the team a run. The next inning I came to the plate with two men on and the fans booed me for my error in the outfield. I had never been booed before and it stung.

"But," he said, "with one swing of the bat, Strawberry silenced a crowd like I'd never heard a crowd silenced in my life. The ball went so high and so far that I was in awe." The whole crowd in the stands just went to its feet and watched the ball travel as if it were going to the stratosphere. "That's how he takes care of the fans," Bobby said.

Bobby worked with me the entire year because, as I found out later, the Mets had wanted him to make sure I got to Tidewater on schedule. I understood that I was in good hands and that the Mets at that time wanted me to make the transition from high-school to Major League ball as quickly but as smoothly and thoroughly as possible. Neither they nor I wanted me to stay in the minors any longer than was necessary. Yet the Mets executives didn't want the pressure of the media to force them to bring up a player who clearly wasn't ready. That kind of premature exposure can demoralize a young player. I was feeling the same way. Sure I'd told the Mets that I didn't want to spend too many years in the minors. I wanted to get to the majors as quickly as I could. But when I was in the minors and saw firsthand what playing under pressure meant, I was grateful for the time the Mets were giving me and the attention I was getting from the coaches. You want to move up, but you don't want to blow your chances. I think most players have mixed emotions about the pressure to move up.

But in 1982, I was feeling good. I was feeling strong, I was feeling ready. The Mets thought I was ready, too, because at the end of that season, on schedule, I went up to the International League to play triple-A ball at Tidewater. I helped the Tides win the playoffs that year. By the end of that season, I was feeling very good about being a member of the Mets. I had a sense that I was in a family in which I was playing an important role. This was a family, I believed, who thought that I was a vital member, and would spend the time to make me feel like I belonged. "Belonging" to the Mets was a very important issue for me during those early years as I began to invest the Mets' family with many of the feelings and hopes I should have invested in my own family. For the Mets, baseball was a business and only a business. I didn't see that very clearly until the very end. Maybe that's why it hurt so much in 1989 and 1990.

Rather than taking off in the winter of 1982, I decided to push the year by playing winter ball down in South America for a team in Caracas, Venezuela. That was a unique experience because it sped up my development, to be sure, and it also led me to see what the world was like outside the United States for the first time in my life. I didn't speak Spanish, but I believed I could make myself understood and I wanted the opportunity to play against aggressive professional athletes who were far more experienced than I was. I wanted to see what the pitching was like and how I'd fare against more established teams.

It turned out an eye-opening experience that almost closed my eyes for good. One day I hit a blast of a home run off a very popular local pitching hero, and the fans didn't take to that too kindly. When I went back into the outfield in the next inning, the fans out there started throwing bricks and stones at me. Hey, bullshit! I could have been killed. The other guys on my team came running out to give me a batting helmet, but I waved them off. I'd have rather stayed in the infield the next inning. I'm glad I'm still here to tell you, it was pretty nasty down there for me. But that incident gave me a firsthand respect for what one of my baseball heroes Dave Parker had to go through when he was on the Pittsbugh Pirates in 1976. Dave had just become the highest-paid player in baseball that year and the hometown fans in Pittsburgh responded by showering him with radio batteries from the stands. Some way to treat a hometown player, right? The man could have been severely injured, if not killed. When I saw those bricks and stones coming down at me, I realized what Dave must have felt when the batteries rained down on him.

I began the 1983 season in Tidewater as a triple-A ballplayer on his way to the majors. I felt confident after my season in South America because I'd been able to hit some of their best pitchers. These were guys who might some day be in the Major Leagues themselves. Davey Johnson was managing down in Tidewater in 1983, and we began our six-year association, which I have to say was never boring.

I had had a great spring at St. Petersburg, Florida, for the Mets, and I know they were considering bringing me right up. But they decided to let me start the season off in Tidewater just to make sure that my performance the year before hadn't been a freak and that I was off and running before they made room for me on the roster. Everybody knew, and I knew, that I would be going up that year. All the newspapers were predicting it, as I eventually came to find out, what the newspapers predicted generally turned out to be the case.

I was nervous at the thought of going up in '83 because everybody was saying to me: "This is it, you're goin' to the Show." "You did too well last year to stay in triple-A." "Write. Let me know what it's like up there." "Don't forget your friends." All that kind of stuff. But I was also excited at getting my chance. I knew what was expected of me. Only a densoid would not have been able to figure out what the Mets and the fans believed I would do. But understanding expectations and meeting expectations are two different things. And I found that out the hard way when I made my first appearance at Shea. Maybe that's why the Mets wanted me to start the season off on the Tides; they wanted me to get used to swinging the bat before they turned the spotlights on.

My first ten or so games at Tidewater were spectacular. Whether I had improved to the point where I could hit anything any triple-A pitcher could throw, or whether the triple-A pitching wasn't as good as it was supposed to be, I don't know. I only know that the fastballs I was seeing weren't nearly as fast as they'd been in the winter league and the curveballs took too much time to move. Maybe that made me too confident, but I was hitting the ball very well and was very happy about it.

At the same time, the Mets got off to a dreadful start. They were getting bombed right off the field like they were mismatched against every team they played. Their pitching staff was struggling because the offense couldn't produce any runs. Whoever managed to get on base—by accident, by a freak hit, or probably by a walk—simply grew a beard and died there at the end of the inning. I saw bits of the New York press's treatment of the 1983 Mets:

IT AIN'T HAPPENING

OH DEAR!

CAN IT GET ANY WORSE?

IT JUST DID!

BRING HIM UP!

WHERRRRRRE'S DARRYL?

I'm down here in Tidewater.

Now I'm up here at LaGuardia. Then I'm at Shea Stadium.
"Now batting for the New York Mets-ets-ets-ets-ets, number eighteen-een-een-een-een, Darryl Strawberry-erry-erry-erry-erry!"
ROAARRRRRRRRR.
My mind tunes in to the press box and I can practically hear the announcers . . .
"*Listen to that crowd, Ralph. They're excited about this young kid making his debut here at Shea tonight.*"
"*As well they should be, Tim. Strawberry comes to the Mets preceded by one of the most formidable reputations I've heard in years.*"
"*What did he do in his last season down at Jackson, Ralph—34 homers? 97 RBIs? Wow. Strawberry can really help this Met team dig out of the cellar.*"
"*That's why he's here, Tim. The papers have been demanding the Mets bring him up, and bring him up they did.*"
"*But look who he's facing out there: Mario Soto.*"
"*Soto's dominating this league, Tim. Part of me goes right out to Strawberry all alone in that batter's box.*"
WWWOOOOSSSHHH!!
What was that? Where'd that ball go? It was here a second ago. Was that a pitch? Did it count? Hey, ump, don't you have to see 'em to call 'em? Just luck, probably. I'll tag the next one.

WWWHHHIIIFFFF!

How did he do that? I didn't know you could do that with a baseball.

"Yer OUT!!!"

When did he throw that? Hey, ump, I wasn't even ready.

"Not an auspicious beginning, Ralph."

"We'll be seeing a lot of this kid, Tim. Something tells me that Mario Soto's gonna be seeing a lot of him, too."

I struck out three times that night and then popped up. At least I hit something so I could remember what it felt like to make contact with a baseball. But what did he have on that ball? I kept asking myself. This guy threw me stuff I'd never seen before in my life. He wasn't faster than pitchers I'd faced in the minors, but he had a million times more control than you'd expect. He knew right where he wanted the ball to cross the strike zone or catch a corner of the plate. He never got behind me, never made any mistakes, never let me figure out where his next pitch would be. By the time I brought my bat around, the ball was long since gone. I looked like a born whiffer, Mario looked like a champ, and the newspaper headlines looked like this:

DARRYL K. STRAWBERRY!

STRAW FANS SEE STRAW FAN

GET A WHIFF OF STRAW

Ultimately, you learn how to hit a Mario Soto. You watch him for a year and listen to the experienced hitters and your batting coaches describe how a Mario Soto will set you up for his change-up or his breaking ball. You'll see how the situations will force certain pitchers to play it safe by not giving you pitches you can pull or hit into the gap. But all of this takes time. And while you learn to hit, you learn what it's like to fan, fish, swipe, and play golf with balls that lead your bat everywhere. You look pretty stupid in the process until you see for the first time exactly how a change-up drops, how a breaking pitch splits away from the direction it was going, and how a knuckleball waves before your eyes until you're seeing double. When you can see it, you can hit it. But it takes precious time.

The fans were cheering me despite my opening-night performance. Most baseball fans, especially hometown fans, give you enough space to find your starting level. It's called a honeymoon. The press usually tells them when to end the honeymoon. Then they let you know what they think. I still had some time on my clock left in New York after that first night. And the Mets in '83 were so terrible, so dreadful, so far below the level of Major League minimal competence that any additions to the lineup would only have helped. I had a cushion.

The Mets were managed in 1983 by George Bamberger when I first came up. George didn't have much to say to me. In fact he didn't have much to say to anybody, other than, "Just go out there and have fun." That was advice I could relate to because I had just achieved my lifelong dream of reaching the Major Leagues. Other people on the Mets, such as Dave Kingman, Tom Seaver, and George Foster, weren't really having too much fun being humiliated on the field by local Cub Scout packs.

I, too, was quickly caught up in the whirlwind of it all as the Mets' season spun into disaster for the fourth year in a row. The newspapers, always ready to lend a helping noose, were already howling about another first. They said—and who was I to argue?—that I was the first black potential baseball star to start his career in New York. I know, I know! Jackie Robinson, Willie Mays, Roy Campanella, Don Newcombe, Monte Irvin, Reggie Jackson, and on and on. But, and these are their words not mine, Robinson, Mays, Campy, Newk, and Irvin all began their careers in the old Negro Leagues. Reggie, of course, had been at Oakland before George Steinbrenner brought him to the Yankees.

Talk about turning up the heat on someone. Here I was, ready and willing, even if not completely able, to face up to the likes of Mario Soto and the starting rotations of all the National League teams we'd be playing, but it wasn't enough just to be a rookie. I was prepared for that; I was glad for that. Believe me, I was thankful that I had achieved my dream of breaking into the majors. But I thought that's all there was to it. You put on your uniform and go out to play baseball. I wasn't prepared for the hype of being the very first black star to begin his career in New York. I didn't understand the honorifics of it all. No one told me how the media game was supposed to be played and what I was supposed to do when I

was told that I was the first young black star in New York.
What did that really *mean*? I actually tried to figure that out.
To me that only meant I could only go *down* from there. No
one, the papers said, had ever before come into New York and
so overwhelmed the city as I had done. But what do I do for an
encore? Was I supposed to walk across the East River next?
Actually that would have been easier than reading every day
in the papers about the miracles I was expected to perform any
minute now. At nights I would lie in bed as sirens blared
beneath my window and planes roared overhead as they circled the city and say, "Mother, get me out of here." I was
absolutely paralyzed with fear!

George Bamberger seemed to be a very quiet, reserved individual. He'd fill out the lineup card and tell you to just go out
there and play. He said to us in the locker room that the team
had to use the assets that we had, and that was all he expected
from us. He didn't say much of anything else and we didn't
have many assets to use. I guess that's why we kept on losing.
He kept saying, "The season's still young and things will take
care of themselves." Things didn't take care of themselves and
the season got to be older with every day and every humiliation heaped upon our shoulders by the sportswriters, who were
sounding more like comedy writers for television sitcoms.

They laughed at us because we were over twenty games out
of first by the end of the season. They laughed because we were
so mired in last place that even when we made twitching
efforts to win behind the pitching of Tom Seaver, they would
have to scrape the cobwebs off our base runners left stranded at
the end of each inning. They also laughed because no matter
who we sent up to the plate, the newly acquired Keith Hernandez, pinch hitter Rusty Staub, or myself, there simply was
no magic at all. We just couldn't hit the ball consistently
enough to score any runs. We were pathetic.

George finally turned in his clipboard and resigned as manager. Maybe the pressure was too much even for him. Rumor
was, and when you're a twenty-one-year-old rookie all you get
is rumor, that years earlier George had had a heart attack and
was on the verge of another one. He resigned for his health.
Worrying about having another heart attack was already too
much for Old Lonesome George. The last thing he needed was
to worry about taking care of twenty-five other guys staggering
around the baseball diamond like walking stiffs controlled by a

flying saucer. On top of that, George had to deal with a press corps that could have put Superman into cardiac arrest.

Frank Howard, who had been one of the more vocal coaches, took over as manager. Frank liked energy. No, he liked to *see* energy. He liked to see his players go up there and swing—swing at anything, even a passing sea gull. Frank was one of those big "powerhouse" hitters of his day, so it made sense that he wanted you to swing. I swung. Who was I to argue with the man? I didn't hit anything, but I swung.

If you were to pay me, I could not define Frank Howard's personality, assuming, for argument's sake, that he actually had a personality. I do remember that he was the kind of man, the kind of big, *big* man you did not want to get too close to if you valued your life. Frank Howard was huge; huge and inarticulate. He made Andre the Giant look like Jaleel "Urkel" White. You just stayed far away from him as he crashed through the clubhouse like the Frankenstein monster, his arms flailing around.

When Frank made a move, you never questioned him about it if you were one of his players. If he said he wanted Rusty to go in there and hit to left field, Rusty went in and tried to hit to left field, even if the situation called for a bunt. If Frank said the steal was on, then you better believe the steal was on until he said the steal was off. It didn't have to make sense. We were in last place, and you did what he told you to do.

Fortunately for me, Frank was never a critic. He said he was there to help his players develop, and believe me, I needed all the development I could get. What Frank did for me, though, was assign hitting coach Jim Frey to stay on my case. As the year rolled on, my case became more and more desperate.

After Mario Soto blew nine pitches by me like Stealth fighters, things went from bad to worse. The magnitude of what professional baseball was began to get to me: the hype of the Major Leagues, the thousands of fans in the stadiums—all of them cheering or booing or whatever—the sense of being surrounded by a huge physical structure whenever you stepped up to the plate, and your name blaring over the loudspeakers. It was more, much more, than I had dreamed of when I allowed myself to dream of being a big-league ballplayer. This was no fantasy; it was the real thing.

The fear at being at the very center of this whirlpool was so great that I began to overcompensate. I reacted to the very pressure I was trying to avoid by saying that I *should* be the man of the hour. The team didn't expect that of me and, indeed, didn't want me to assume that burden. I did it all by myself because something inside me told me I was supposed to jump in and become the leader. Maybe I felt I had to hold the Mets family together somehow. But that was silly. I was only a rookie who'd barely turned twenty-one.

Instead of just keeping myself afloat and learning to hit the ball in the Major Leagues, I wanted instant greatness for myself as well as for the team. I told myself I wanted to do well more than I ever wanted anything in the past. I pushed myself too hard. I only wanted to hit home runs, to make a good impression on the fans, to show the Mets that I warranted the trust and investment they had made in me. No cheap little singles or doubles into the gap for me. As a result, I lost sight of what I was supposed to do on each pitch. I lost sight of the ball and of the pitcher. I was overswinging, trying to blast the ball out of the park instead of just making contact with it to push it through the hole. "We're in last place," I said to myself, "and I'm supposed to be the savior of this team." But I wasn't doing well at anything.

'Round about the middle of June, El Mucho Grande Howard and coach Jim Frey decided to bench me. I know that Frank and Jim felt that I wasn't putting out enough for the team. Jim told me that my problem wasn't attitude or outlook, it was something that trips up a lot of rookies who forget that they have to develop one day at a time. I was struggling, confused, and looking at too many things at the same time. I was worried about being away from home, missing my current girlfriend, seeing new cities for the first time in my life, and facing new pitchers and different types of pitchers. It was all overwhelming. Being in the majors, realizing my dream of a lifetime, actually achieving a serious goal by the time I was only twenty-one just hit me all at the same time in June 1983.

Jim Frey played the role in my life during that period that Gene Dusan had played the year before and the year before that, and Mr. Mosely even earlier. It's a role that I seem to need to have played out for me, Dr. Alan Lans told me years later, because it fills a gap that my father should have filled. However, in 1983, I didn't know any of that. I only knew that I felt myself falling into an uncomfortably familiar pattern and having to rely on the expertise of Jim Frey to get me out of it.

"You've got to be the one to help yourself," Coach Frey told me. "Sure I can help you, but only with the mechanics of hitting. The confidence, the belief in the ability to hit the ball, has to come entirely out of you."

I was truly green. I must have sat there in the clubhouse looking pie-eyed and blank because Frey kept saying that it wasn't so bad. He knew I could do it because I'd done it before. He didn't realize that I was stunned more at the situation I was in than anything else. Here I was, sitting right in the Mets' clubhouse, on the verge of running all the way across country to Los Angeles on my own two feet because I was so overawed by my situation. Orientation, I have now come to understand, is a good thing.

Jim began by stressing the basic techniques of hitting. I thought I knew what they were: how to follow the ball from the pitcher, how to watch a pitcher, how to bring the bat across, and the like. But Jim opened up a whole new world of dealing with Major League pitching. He pointed out that I was my own worst enemy at the plate by wanting to hit home runs so badly that I didn't look at what the pitcher was doing.

"They're not going to give you home run balls," he would say. "You have to *make* them give you your pitch by showing them you can hit their other pitches."

He explained the process of setting up pitchers to me. He told me to keep my own mental records on how pitchers behave in specific situations, what they look for from left-handed hitters, what they're prepared to give me—and all pitchers are prepared to give up something to avoid something worse—and what they need me to do at the plate.

"It's all mental," he would say. "Each of you has to find out what the other can't give up. Then you chip away at him to get him to give it up."

It's funny. You think you know so much when you come up as a rookie, only to find out that you don't know anything at all. A whole new world of baseball opened up for me when Jim began teaching. Part of me wondered why I was even on the Mets at all. If they'd known that I didn't know the first thing about what Frey was teaching me, they would have sent me packing. I actually confided this to Jim once, who just laughed at my naivete.

"Of course they *know* how much *you* don't know," he told me. "Why do you think I'm working with you? It's not for my own instruction. It's to get you to acclimate yourself to Major League pitching as quickly as possible. All rookies go through this," he continued. "Now it's your turn."

I heard Frey's voice over and over in my brain every time I came to the plate. "People want to appreciate you. People want to see you succeed. Think of it as fun. You are here to enjoy the gifts of your talent. Give the sportswriters a chance to appreciate you. Give the fans a reason to cheer. Work on your defense. Study your opposing pitchers. Talk to the other hitters on your team. Find the hitters on the team that bat most like you and ask them what the pitchers do. This is your job, Strawberry. You work here. Treat this like a profession. Don't worry about your salary. Don't apologize for your salary. Don't be intimidated by other players. Most of the players you're afraid of aren't the players they once were. They may know more than you know, but you're a better athlete. Use what you have. You are the best. You are the best. You are the best. You're the king of the mountain. Put that in your head and no one can take that away."

But I still lingered in the slump. I'd get a couple of hits and then be so shocked by the hits I got, I'd forget everything that Jim Frey told me and go back into my slump. Jim never got down on me, though. He never gave up. He'd come to see me in the clubhouse where I'd be moping as if I didn't belong and he'd say, "Why is the best player on the field sitting around here like a sad sack? Get out of here and act like the best player on the field."

I know that sounds a little Mickey Mouse, but when you're a rookie even Mickey Mouse is better than the silence of doubt. Then, right around the All-Star break, it all suddenly clicked in. Instead of trying to hit every pitch and getting down on myself when I couldn't, I began looking at percentage pitches. "I could hit this guy," I would tell myself after watching some video or eyeballing the guy during warmups. "If he gives me this, this, and this. If he gives me that, I won't swing. If I get this, I can take him to left field. If I get that, I can hit to the opposite field. He always starts with this. I can hit this. That's my percentage."

Maybe you don't get your special pitches right off. But if you have the power, you can make those special pitches count. Then the pitchers get afraid of you. They pitch away from you instead of at you. Then you get them making mistakes and getting behind you on the count. Then you can swing at stuff they wouldn't normally throw you because they're afraid to walk you to a base when there's a chance you'll ground out. So they pitch. That's when your percentage goes up.

I got selective. I became aware of what I could and couldn't hit. Then I added to that list what I should and should not swing at. Soon I found myself connecting with the ball more than I was not connecting with the ball. Soon I was getting one hit for every five times at bat. Then I was getting a hit in most of the games I played. I was getting on base. I was being moved into scoring position. I was crossing the plate. I was moving runners around. Then I was hitting home runs, big home runs. I was hitting homers with people on base and my RBIs began to climb. Then I was hitting one out of every four at-bats. At the end of the season, I was at .257, which wasn't bad at all for a rookie. I also hit 26 home runs and had 74 RBIs.

Finally, and this came as a surprise, I was named the Rookie of the Year at the end of the season. I didn't expect to be the Rookie of the Year; in fact, during June and early July, there were nights that I didn't even expect to stay up in the majors. But when I got my head right and started to follow Jim Frey's instructions, I knew that there was a place for me on the Mets. The newspapers said that by the end of July, I was so dominating the league that my selection as Rookie of the Year was natural. It was the effect of the turnaround, they wrote. I started off on wobbly legs and ended up with a respectable .257 average.

I saw it in a different light, and it made me tremble at the power of the New York press to create myth. I knew, when I accepted the award, that had I been playing for Kansas City or Minnesota or even for Pittsburgh, my performance might have been praised, but never awarded. New York sportswriters had made me into an intimidating hitter, a threat to every team we faced. I helped by hitting 26 home runs, of course, but it was more than the actual hits, it was the threat of the hit. That threat was manufactured in the New York papers. I remember reading the papers and saying to myself that I was casting a much bigger shadow over the league than any rookie should have been. It was that the shadow was coming from New York that made it so big and not because it was Darryl Strawberry's shadow. Part of what Willie Mays had said was coming true.

The media can make you much bigger than you are. They can re-create you. They can also tear you down.

Nineteen eighty-three was a time of great adjustment for me personally as well as professionally. Although I found I didn't have to become a different human being in order to play baseball, I did have to mature. I did have to make a distinction between "serious fun" and "deadly seriousness," and I had to understand what it meant to look for the fun part of baseball even while 100,000 eyes were boring into you whenever you stepped up to the plate with runners on base. If you can remember it's all a game, that even the fans are holding their breath, you can remain individually sane.

Nineteen eighty-three was also the year in which I met my wife-to-be, Lisa, at a Lakers game at the Forum. I saw her standing in the crowd and I said to friends, "Wow! Who is she? She kills me. She is gorgeous." I was a Rookie-of-the-Year New York Met and was pretty impressive myself when my friend introduced us. I visited her a couple of times, like a real gentleman, and sent her flowers. Then we began dating. What impressed me most about Lisa was her ability to be happy. She wasn't like me. She didn't have this anger inside of her that she had to work out. She seemed always happy, always smiling.

Had I been more sensitive to what was going on around me, I might have seen the seeds of trouble that were just beginning to germinate while we were dating during 1984. I had already become a local hero in Los Angeles and liked to flirt with women. Women would come up to us even when we were eating out together and begin to flirt with me in front of her. Maybe I should have shut it down right away, but I didn't and it made her mad. I should have seen the writing on the wall, but I was too busy being a Met and a baseball hero. I wanted marriage, too, and I overlooked the obvious danger signs of jealousy and fighting as we drifted into an engagement in 1984.

The Mets team didn't fare as well as I did during the 1983 season, even though there were some solid individual performances. George Foster, for example, had just signed a big deal with the Mets for millions of dollars after having had good years at Cincinnati. The pressure was on him to deliver even more than it was on me, and he wound up with a terrific 90 RBIs and 28 home runs at the end of the season. George had to cope with some jealousy on the part of Mets players who felt that he was getting too much money. There were a few lame jokes, lots of sour grapes, and more than a few bitter comments. George was more of a loner than a socializer anyway, so he didn't miss much by not being invited to the beer blasts. He spent a lot of time with his family, and I respected that. We even got along.

No one ever confronted George to his face about the money or the limo he rolled around in, but I saw from watching how players dealt with him what can happen to big-money players in the clubhouse. It wasn't pretty, but it didn't keep me from going after the salaries that I wanted.

Dave Kingman was a particularly intimidating person on the 1983 Mets. If you thought Frank Howard was big, Dave Kingman was *El Gigante*. He was much bigger than I was, and I felt he could have destroyed me at any time. I used to kid about him because of his name and called him King Kong. It was not something I was going to taunt him with to his face, of course, because he would have snapped me in two like a twig. I'd heard from other guys on the team that Dave liked to play strange jokes on people. There was one time in particular, I heard, when a female reporter came to the locker room for some interviews. Dave had found a dead New York–size rat which he'd put in a box. He wrapped up the box and told the reporter that he wanted to give her a present. It was something, he was supposed to have said to her, that he really wanted her to have. When she opened it in the locker room and saw the dead rat inside, she got quite a surprise—a surprise, I think, that she'll never forget.

Where Kingman always seemed a little unstable, Rusty Staub was just the opposite. He assisted managers George Bamberger and Frank Howard in the instructional duties with the younger players and was particularly helpful to me because he was a left-handed hitter. He would tell me how to pick up a curveball from a pitcher he'd faced many times in the past, which part of the strike zone to look in for the ball, and how to know when the pitcher has made a mistake so you can get the bat head on it and blast it out of there.

I was in awe of Tom Seaver that year, not because his performance was so superior but because he was the only legitimate "legend" on the Mets. Seaver was well past his glory years by the time that Cashen had gotten him back from Cincinnati for the 1983 season, but he still had an aura about him. It was a kind of glow that said, "I've been there and know what it's like at the very top." He had this bearing of tremendous accomplishment about him. He had been one of the Amazin's in the glorious World Series, and nothing he did subsequently could ever tarnish that image. That was a pinnacle I wanted to achieve.

Another personality on the Mets, who arrived the same year I did, was Keith "Mex" Hernandez. Keith had a reputation for loose talk that the press picked up on right away. They designated him the main guy on the team and sought him out for all the juicy quotes they needed to liven up a gray, steamy New York summer morning on the Canarsie local. Keith had a particularly nasty habit of telling the press what he wanted another player to know. It was indirect and almost always hurtful, but Keith knew how to play the media for all they were worth. He seemed to like to show the other guys on the Mets that they had to be nice to him if they wanted him to use his leverage with reporters to get them "good press."

"Watch what I can do," Keith would brag before a game.

After the game, half the New York press corps would track after him into the clubhouse where he would hold court and mouth off about other players.

"Yeah, well, I don't think this guy's doin' well enough," he'd say, as if it were really his place to give an opinion.

But the press lapped it up because they liked conflict, dirty laundry, raw emotion, mano-a-mano stuff, and it always appeared in the paper the next day. Team solidarity? Loyalty? Fuhgettaboutit! Give 'em the dirt and they eat it up. Keith understood how this let him wield a great deal of power on the Mets. When he tried to pull it on me, I told him where he could get off. We had our differences after that.

Nineteen eighty-three was a year under fire for me. I learned how to hit the pitches I was getting and I learned that I could be successful in the majors. I had fulfilled my goal—getting there; fulfilled a second goal—performing well there; and even won the Rookie of the Year award. I could return to Harvard diamond in Crenshaw, look Mr. Mosely in the eye, and say to him, "Look at me. I fulfilled the promise you held out for me." And I could see the pride in his face that one of his neighborhood "kids" had made it to the bigs.

I had a warm glow inside me as 1983 came to a close. And

as I prepared for the 1984 season, I was already excited. Of course I couldn't have realized it at the time, but in 1984, I would meet the best friend I would ever make in my entire life. He was two years younger than I, but headed in my direction.

In 1984, the Doctor would be in.

8

THE DOCTOR IS IN

Nineteen eighty-four was the year the magic slowly began to happen both for the Mets and for me personally—I became engaged to Lisa and we decided to get married the following year. It was also the year the ingredients would come together for the Mets. Frank Cashen's trades and the team's draft choices finally crossed paths in 1984, and the team on paper looked as if it had a chance to crawl out of the cellar. Our pitching staff would jell, our hitting would become consistent, and our defense would begin to play as a team instead of like a bunch of guys playing pickup schoolyard stickball. But I could never have predicted the successes that were awaiting us in 1984 when I packed my bags at the close of the '83 season and left New York for California.

The Mets wound up winning only 68 games and losing 94 in 1983. Frank Cashen didn't have much to say. He did what he always seemed to do when the going got rough. He took off for a quick vacation. Big Frank Howard bit the dust at the end of the 1983 season as well. It was kind of like King Kong falling off the Empire State Building and hitting the pavement with a crash. Coach Jim Frey, for his part, went over to the Cubs, who won the division in 1984. I was glad that Jimmy Frey got himself his own team to manage. I knew from how he helped me that he'd be an asset to any team he worked for. Frey was a player's coach and a player's manager. No matter how difficult a player's situation, he was always able to see it from both the player's point of view and the team's. Then he'd somehow put the two points of view together so that they made sense. When I saw the way the Cubs played in 1984, I realized that Jim Frey's presence on the team was making things happen. He was motivating players. I wish he'd stayed on the Mets.

In October 1983, the Mets named my old manager from Tidewater, Davey Johnson, as the team's manager. Frank Cashen made the announcement during the World Series, in Philadelphia, after Davey had flown up there from Florida. Looking back on it from the vantage point of seven years, I can't figure out how the two of them managed to stay together for so long. Frank was a quiet guy who rarely said anything to anybody, least of all to me for the seven years that I was with the Mets, and only spoke in private. Certain people seemed to have an ear to his thinking, but most people did not.

Davey, on the other hand, was a talkative, "shoot first and ask questions later" guy. He was always putzing around with his stupid computer, even when he was playing under Cashen at Baltimore, and he'd come walking in with these complex stats relating at-bats to the times he was stranded on second base to the number of hangnails he'd pulled off himself in Cincinnati. We'd gotten along for the fifteen minutes that I knew him down in Tidewater, and Frank, of course, had worked with him in that capacity for years. Cashen seemed confident and I was still only an egg so what did I know? It all sounded good to me.

I was pretty much an observer on the Mets before the 1984 season got fully under way. No one, especially Frank Cashen, asked me for my advice on anything. In fact, I was still basically a novice to the business of baseball itself. I was on the receiving end of the rumor mill and had many of the same reactions to news stories about the Mets that anyone else would have had after picking up a newspaper. Even though friends and reporters asked me for my opinion during the 1984 preseason, my only reaction was a kind of "dunno," because I really didn't know. I still liked to follow the game from a fan's perspective and maybe that was one of my early mistakes. I behaved too much like a fan and not enough like a player who "works for" the game at the same time as he plays it.

For example, at the close of 1983 the newly hired Davey Johnson probably thought that he was just going to sail into camp with a Darryl Strawberry, Mex Hernandez, Tom Seaver, and others from the 1983 team, but his plans got a real jolt. Frank Cashen, in one of his blunders, neglected to protect Tom Seaver in the free agency pool. Frank must have thought to himself in the dark of the night, as he sat up plotting in his study, "Who needs some worn-out forty-year-old pitcher? What's he good for anyway—ten games? Twelve games?" That's exactly what the Chicago White Sox thought when they saw his name on the unprotected list, and Roland Hemond of the White Sox scooped him right up. Cashen & Co. were stunned because they never thought another team would have bought into a forty-year-old pitcher. But it was dumb thinking because Seaver had plenty of life left in that arm and a guaranteed twelve-or-so-game winner in your rotation is nothing to sneeze at. "Where in the world can you get a guarantee like that dropped right in your lap?" Hemond said afterward.

I heard about the whole thing while I was in California, and just like any sophomore anywhere, my views were not important. I knew that the Mets had made a mistake because even a high-school ballplayer knows that you don't give up a twelve-game winner unless you can get a fifteen-game winner in return, and on the face of it, the Mets gave one up for nothing. I had a strange reaction to the whole thing. Besides looking at it from a great distance, I kind of told myself that I would have to put out more in order to make up the difference. Looking back, that makes no sense. How could I make up for the loss of a pitcher? But at the time I saw it as a vacuum that I could mysteriously fill by playing extra hard. Two and two don't make four here, but when part of you wants to prove yourself very badly, two and two don't have to make four.

It turned out that the Mets recouped somewhat by picking up Sid Fernandez from the Dodgers. This was one of the better deals Cashen made. When 1984 got cooking, Sid produced wins, the other new Mets contributed, and the team looked a hundred percent improved from the 1980–1983 debacles. Even the critical Frank Cashen was pretty quiet by the time the season was in full swing, although the newspapers kept harping on what the team might have been had Cashen only protected Seaver.

When Frank was taking his pounding from the press, I could see from a distance what it was like to be the target of sportswriters' criticisms. It was like a movie playing on a screen in slow motion. I knew all the parties in the story: Frank Cashen, Tom Seaver, and Davey Johnson. And I knew from other players I'd spoken to that nobody had expected Seaver to get picked up off the unprotected list. But when he was, the papers jumped on Cashen like he'd done it on purpose. I saw the blood fly and I saw how Cashen had to sit still and take his medicine until they were tired of beating up on him and got on to other stuff. I even felt a little sorry for him and believed that if I could make a difference in 1984, maybe the team would win and they'd let up on him. I felt loyalty.

Davey was in a unique position to put together the "new" Mets from their farm teams. Because Davey had been involved with the farm system at all levels and had managed at Tidewater through 1983, he was one of the few people in the whole organization who was in touch with all of the Mets' brightest prospects. Frank Cashen was working out savvy trades to acquire veteran players. Between Davey and Frank an entirely new ball club was emerging. For me it was an exciting time to be a Met because I was at the center of a new ball club that was taking shape right before our eyes. While I played in the minors and the Mets crawled around at the bottom of the division, Cashen was patient about bringing up his new prospects. Now, in 1984, I could see that the years of patience were about to pay off. The chemistry seemed to be right, and I believed that we would begin to make our move in the division. The key to our drive would be the pitching of Dwight Gooden.

The Mets' real big break in 1984 was Davey Johnson's convincing Cashen to let him bring Dwight up to the majors. I hadn't known Doc personally in the minors, but I sure knew *about* him. Everyone in the Mets' organization had heard tales of this incredible pitcher the Mets had plucked straight out of high school in Tampa. Everybody told me that the Dwight Gooden "Cinderella story" was so similar to the Darryl Strawberry "Cinderella story" that Gooden and I were definitely going to be friends. They were right. Doc became my closest friend in the world.

Like me, Dwight had been drafted right out of high school, where he earned a reputation as one of the best high-school pitchers in the country. Sportswriters were making pilgrimages to Florida just to see the Gooden fastball that seemed to go on afterburners as it got to the plate. I'd never seen a fastball like that anywhere. Not even Nolan Ryan's cannon shots seemed to have that extra kick at the end. I still don't know how he does it.

Dwight also had good control over his curveball, which was almost a miracle for a high-school pitcher. When he was still seventeen, Dwight could throw a curve that would nip the edge of the plate at the very last minute and long after you had relaxed. He could throw a curve that would look as if it would brush you back as it came barreling in. And just before you complained to the ump, it would kind of loop in to catch the corner of the strike zone. You weren't even sure where the ball had crossed. Then when the call "Strike" came, you'd just stare in amazement.

Dwight not only was consistent in his control, he knew how to set you up with his curve before blowing the heat right by you at the exact moment when he knew you were forced to swing. With only a three- or four-pitch repertoire, he could strike out over half the batters he faced each inning and get himself out of trouble on the few occasions when there were runners on base. The result was "Doctor K."

Most high-school pitchers never achieve the kind of control Dwight Gooden exhibited. You'll see a smoking fastball, a barely controlled sharp curve, a plucky little sinker once in a while, and maybe even a feisty proto-knuckleball or two. But it's the control that counts. Your curveball ain't worth nothing if you can't keep it over the plate. And the fastball only works if the batter thinks it's going to be a strike. Most high-school pitchers will throw some good stuff, but the majority of their pitches will be so out of control that the pitchers are usually behind in the count. A scout will look for the good stuff, determine how successfully the pitcher can be taught control, and write his report accordingly. In Dwight Gooden's case, not only was his control exceptional, it was downright scary. The scouts went berserk when they saw him because it looked like he'd been pitching pro ball for years.

Doc also thinks when he pitches, unlike many Major League hurlers. That puts him in the same category with Nolan Ryan and Orel Hershiser, two of the most mental pitchers I know. All of these guys think way ahead of the batter. They understand that they have the edge over the batter in one regard. They *know* where the ball is supposed to go. Most pitchers don't realize they have this advantage. Knowing that you have the advantage over the batter means that you can change your mind and work with your catcher to confuse the batter. You can set him up, make him think you're going to give him heat, then throw him the deuce. Doc is also very disciplined and technical when he throws. He's not like the passionate pitchers who try to dominate with sheer force of emotion. These guys break down real quick when things don't go their way, and you can scare the hell out of them easy. Doc doesn't scare.

When Davey Johnson saw Dwight Gooden for the first time, the folktale goes, he was so impressed that he phoned the Mets' personnel office to check on the guy's birth certificate. "This can't be a seventeen-year-old kid," Davey said. "Too much poise, too much confidence, too much control." But the Mets confirmed Dwight's age down in Kingsport, and Davey kept his eye on Doc for the next couple of years. In 1983, after Davey had jumped him up to Tidewater, where he helped the Tides in two International League playoff games, Davey knew that Doc was ready. After Cashen let the White Sox steal Seaver right out from under his nose, Davey knew the time was ripe.

He began working on Cashen as early as that winter. He pushed and pushed. "The kid's ready," he would tell Cashen. "Not another Tim Leary," Cashen reportedly told him, remembering what happened to the pitcher he brought up too early in 1981. "I'm not going through that again for anybody. Gooden never pitched double-A. He needs at least a full year on the Tides."

They compromised even though Davey wanted Doc brought up right away. Dwight pitched his first few games down in triple-A, but Cashen agreed to keep his eye on him too. Gooden's stats weren't mind-boggling—he only struck out nine batters over eighteen innings in five games—but his poise simply blew people away. Before the '84 season started to build up steam, Davey was able to press home his point with Cashen, and Doc was moved up to the Major Leagues. Once on the Mets, Davey treated him with kid gloves. He had this guy on a clock. Work so many innings, rest so many innings; throw so many pitches, lay off for so many starts. It was like Davey wanted to compress a year in Jackson and a year in Tidewater into the space of a few months. He didn't force or push Doc, but used just the right mix of work, exposure, and instruction to bring him along at the speed of light. Whatever I might say about Davey's treatment of me and the dumb mistakes he made after 1986—and I have a lot to say—I can only praise him for his management of Dwight Gooden.

From the moment Doc arrived in the Mets' clubhouse, we became friends. First of all, there were so few black players on the Mets that any new black guy was in an exclusive club automatically. People also compared us because of the similar press we had gotten in high school and in the minors. People were saying that Doc and I were the "new Mets," and that developed a bond between us as well. I also felt kind of protective toward Doc. He was a very young guy when he came up, still a teenager, and even more tentative off the field than I was. We both talked about the pressure to perform that was pushing on us, and we were both anxious about what the coming year had in store. Because I had been a rookie the year before, I could give Doc some advice. That also made me feel protective.

In my family, I was the youngest of the brothers. After me, there were only sisters, and none of them played ball. I often envied my older brothers that they had a younger brother they could bring into the sport. Maybe I saw Doc in the same way that my older brothers saw me. I know that whenever Doc got into trouble on the mound or found himself in a fight on the field, I felt as if I had to protect him.

People said we even looked alike, but that wasn't at all true. Doc and I don't look alike, never have, never will. We're both tall, but that's about it in the resemblance department. Our personalities are very different too, even though people think they're alike because I wound up in Smithers on an alcohol rehab and Doc wound up there to recover from his use of cocaine. I'm sure that we may have reacted alike to the pressure of being in the Major Leagues, and I believe that whatever resulted in Doc's cocaine use and my alcohol abuse started way before we found ourselves in the majors.

The relationship between Doc and me was also forged out of

the roles we had to fill on the Mets. Just before Doc was set to come up, Davey was talking about "Darryl on offense and Doc on defense," like that was the formula for the whole team. I know that in Davey Johnson's mind, that was the equation for the "new Mets." Finally, when Doc did eventually join the club and went immediately under Davey's wing, part of my "unstated" job was to make Doc's transition to the majors as easy as possible. Doc is a very easy person to be friendly with. He doesn't make any demands on a friendship because his professional "attitude" is focused entirely on his pitching. In private, Doc seems easygoing, but he had to face a great deal of pressure very early in his career, too.

Like me, Doc carried the heavy weight of "potential." If I was the black Ted Williams, Doc was the "young Don Newcombe" who would pitch no-hit ball for the Mets. He was the black . . . Tom Seaver? Nolan Ryan? Sandy Koufax? Doc had already shown he could dominate his opponents in the minors. It's one thing to be a player. It's another thing to be so intimidating that just your presence in a lineup forces the opposing team to shift its strategy to conform to you. That's the role of a dominator. You put Dwight on the mound and the other team has to sacrifice some of its options in order to adjust to what a pitcher like Gooden can do to a batting order. I was supposed to be a dominator too. You put me at the plate, and the field has to shift, the pitcher has to adjust, and the opposing team has to adjust offensively as well because of the amount of runs I will put up for the Mets. Therefore, both Doc and I were in training to become "dominators" of the National League, and that helped create our friendship.

Once the 1984 season was under way and it looked like the Mets would be the spoilers of the East, Doc and I would look at each other and kind of giggle like two high-school kids. "Can you believe this?" we'd say. "This is like an express train and we're on it." Sometimes Dwight would say that he wanted to wake up in the mornings and pinch himself because the whole thing seemed like a dream. One day you're a champion high-school pitcher. The next day you're on your way to the rookie league. The next day you're in the majors. That's the way it felt, he told me. I understood exactly what he was saying because even though I spent more time in the minors than he did, I had that unreal feeling too during the first year I came up to the majors. I certainly had it the night I faced Cincinnati.

Doc also knew that he was kind of a "half pitcher" because Davey Johnson had given Frank Cashen a solemn promise that he would not "use him up." Before the season began, Davey got set to use pitchers Walt Terrell and Ron Darling, whom the Mets had picked up when they traded away Lee Mazzilli. But in April and May the Mets' pitching was shaky and the team stumbled badly. By mid-July, Davey had established the starting rotation as Sid Fernandez, Ron Darling, Walt Terrell, and Dwight Gooden with Bruce Berenyi as a spot fifth starter. Except for Berenyi, they were all rookies or second-year pitchers. It was a gutsy move—typically Davey—but these were strong pitchers, and he really didn't have much of a choice. He was also banking on Gary Carter to steady the rookies, who, on paper and in Davey's personal computer, made up maybe the best starting rotation in the National League East. Davey, of course, hadn't figured on the Cubs' picking up super winning pitchers Dennis Eckersley and Rick Sutcliffe, but then who can predict the future? Davey felt we were still strong, and we moved into the summer heat of the 1984 season.

I developed a great deal of respect for Davey Johnson early in the 1984 season. That is why it was all the more painful as our relationship became strained and sometimes bitter in 1986 through 1990. Part of my respect for Davey came from the enormous amount of baseball knowledge and strategy that he seemed to have stored up there in his brain. Whatever he worked up on his computer was plugged directly into his mind. If the situation changed on the field, he didn't have to chew it over the way some managers do. The answer was almost always spit right out because he had so many percentages and averages built right into his thinking. In fact, I was in awe of the way he could take on opposing managers one-on-one in relief-pitching and pinch-hitting duels and almost always come out on top.

In the early years, Davey Johnson was kind. He was good to his players even when they crossed him. I know, for example, that I wasn't the easiest person to work with. I know that when Jesse Orosco and I were in the "scum bunch," drinking beer, spitting nuts, and throwing food in the back of the plane, that Davey probably wanted to storm up to us and tell us to shut up and behave. But he also knew that we were kids letting off steam. Maybe he saw the danger signals ahead, but he hoped that we'd see the same signals and take care of ourselves. I didn't.

As the years wore on, I could see how the pressure changed Davey. As the newspapers came down on him and second-guessed every call, as the terrible trades he'd been pushed into by the front office took their toll on the 1988 and 1989 Mets, and as the team disintegrated under the constant pounding by the media, Davey changed. He was used to operating with complete authority, answering to no one on the field, and running his team with an almost casual abandon. But when each and every lineup change resulted in a kind of "board of inquiry" or court-martial, he became more concerned with keeping to the Mets' "party line." In other words, I had come to know Davey as a country boy who played a country game, but once we were in New York together, I could see how "they" forced him to become "corporate" in his thinking. Corporate people play it safe, stay well within the numbers, and watch the downside. Davey didn't like to play it safe. He liked to stretch the numbers and see how far the percentages would take him. That was the kind of "go for broke" baseball that I enjoyed playing in the early years.

In 1984, all was hope, all was promise, everything was focused on our glorious future. Who would have thought that just a year after being in last place, we would inch our way into first place in the East on July 31, 1984. It was a complete turnabout. The sense of team spirit that grew in 1984 captured all of us. It was here that a lot of the seeds of our magnificent 1986 team and our almost-magnificent 1988 team were planted.

When Davey stuck Ron Darling into the starting pitching rotation alongside Doc, he got himself another focused pitcher to go with Doc. Both of these guys were supported in relief by Jesse Orosco, who, by 1984, had developed the reputation of being able to pitch the Mets out of any dogfight, no matter how ugly it got. Keith Hernandez was exactly the kind of stability the team needed at first. He and I battled in the press for the entire season, but his being at first base and my backing him up in right gave me a feeling of tremendous security, not to mention his consistent .300-plus batting average. Mookie

Wilson was known as a spoiler who could cause trouble for opposing teams in any situation. Mookie was the guy whose hit or walk would start rallies. He was trouble once he was on base. Something about him made opposing teams nervous and got them to make errors. Then there were Rusty Staub and Ray Knight, two of the most consistent threats in the Mets' dugout.

Rusty was never rusty. I would watch this guy walk into a game after not having played for over a week, take a couple of warmup swipes, and unload a base hit to start a late-inning rally. Then I'd see Ray Knight come in right out of the cold, challenge some of the toughest relief pitchers in the league, and punch out a killer double right into the gap. When the starters were faltering, guys like Staub and Knight would make things happen. That's how I knew we were a team touched by destiny.

I was thrilled to be a Met in 1984. Even though I was already in trouble with the press because I was yapping too much about needing to be on a winning team, when we were duking it out with the Cubs for first place around the middle of the summer, I was totally happy. Each day you'd want to get to the park as soon as you could because playing baseball was so much fun. This was exactly what I thought it would be like when I was first drafted. You didn't have to be the world champions, you just had to feel that you could be. And that's exactly how we were as a team. Keith would look at Chicago and say, "They're not any better than we are. So they made a few good trades. So they got Dennis Eckersley. So what? We can take them and don't you tell me that we can't."

Then we started playing games against Chicago, Pittsburgh, Houston, and Philadelphia in which the outcomes weren't decided until the late innings. Davey would say that the late innings were "all Mets" because we had Rusty Staub, Ray Knight, and Jesse Orosco. He was right sometimes, and sometimes he was wrong. But it didn't matter. We *knew*, because we were never really out of contention until the very end, that time was ultimately on our side. Our team was coming together and the pitching and hitting were working. Then there was the thrill that one series, just one streak, just one big game against Chicago might break the back of the Cubs' offense and sit us up there in first for good. The fans saw that too. The K corner started to make its appearance in 1984 and I began to hear the *Darrrrryls* from the outfield stands. What a great feeling to know that you're part of a team that's got the makings of a league champion. But maybe that's where the seeds of discontent also started to sprout.

I certainly had my own problems that year, which I denied because I was able to focus on the team spirit that was obviously developing. But I did go into slump after slump in '84, and the papers kept claiming that I wasn't living up to my potential. Maybe if I'd hit more home runs and hadn't blown so many crucial times at bat, we might have stood a better chance. I was still trying to be "Casey at the bat" more times than I had to, and as a result struck out like Casey more times than I should have. The fans hate when you strike out in crucial situations, especially when they know you have "home run" on the brain, because it makes you look so painfully silly. The press also knew I was trying to hit home runs to impress my family every time the Mets blew into Los Angeles.

It also didn't help that I developed a habit of getting to the field late from time to time and had to be disciplined. In one incident that the press really picked up on, I got to the field for a San Diego game very late and got benched by Davey Johnson. It was humiliating, and I probably shouldn't have let people think that I was sulking around the clubhouse. But sulk, smulk, when Davey sent me in during the ninth inning to pinch-hit I still drove in the tying run to send the game into the tenth, which was when the Mets put the game away. So much for sulking.

People said that I didn't know how to handle myself well in my second year in the majors, but that's a load of baloney. I know that maybe I shouldn't have mouthed off to the press at the first day of spring training. I think I was trying to get a jump on Keith Hernandez, who had a comment about everybody and everything. I've certainly learned my lesson about speaking up and criticizing other players over the years. I said to the press that I wouldn't be afraid to speak up whenever speaking up was needed. "I'll be the one to speak up," I think I told them. That was a direct challenge to Hernandez. Then I said that my heart was broken over what went on last year because there seemed to be so many players that just didn't care about winning. "I've never played on a loser before," I said. "Just on winning teams. When I got to the big leagues, I thought everybody cared about what the team did. Boy, was I surprised that so many guys didn't seem to care." Then I said, without really understanding what I meant, that I wanted to lead the team to victory.

At that time, I didn't know what real leadership was. I thought I *wanted* to be a leader, but I wasn't prepared for the responsibilities that come with the job. I was ambivalent is the nicest way to say it. I didn't know what the hell I was talking about is another way to put it. Leadership is a job. You can't just be a leader one day and say, "Hey, these guys don't want to win," and walk away. Once you call yourself a leader or accept the role of leadership, you do it for the long haul and you stand by the team's performance whether you win the World Series or wind up in the cellar. I wasn't prepared for that in 1984, and I put my foot in my mouth. That resulted in the kind of dissension and discontent that festered on the Mets despite our winning seasons in '85 through '86 and again in '88. I wasn't prepared for it in 1990 either.

From my perspective now, I can see why a lot of veterans might have said, "Who does that kid think he is?" A second-year player, even though he was Rookie of the Year the previous season, really has no right to criticize other players, especially those who had higher batting averages. At the same time, I was surprised that so many of the remarks I made were taken right out of context and quoted in a way that made them seem accusatory rather than what they were—simple observations. Figuratively speaking, I got a bloody nose that day when I saw just how fast your remarks can turn around and hit you right in the face. I learned the hard way that to stay in the locker room all afternoon and give interviews that will only be chopped up and reconstituted when you should be focused on playing the next day is a recipe for disaster.

At first, it's a real kick to see your picture in the paper and read your words. But that feeling fades very quickly and turns into a feeling of terror when you wonder how you're going to be quoted and who the reporters have run to with your mangled quotes for a response. Before you even look around, you're in a public feud with someone, there are hurt feelings, and you want to respond in print or bust the guy in the head for what you've been told he said. And the whole thing was created by sportswriters to sell a few papers. Hey, that's business. That's the hype of celebrity sports. But not for me, thank you. In

1984, I started playing that game the wrong way, and I didn't figure out what I was doing until after I left the Mets.

Although I was criticized for what I said then and for my slumps during the season, the team still made it into first and was a contender for the championship of the National League East until September. Then Keith Hernandez and some of the other players took shots back at me. Keith, in an interview, said that I gave up too easily in tough situations. "When things got rough, he gave in," he was quoted as saying. "In August I didn't think he was giving it a hundred-percent effort, but he was down on himself." While it was certainly gracious of Keith to forgive what he saw as my indifference and the wasting of my natural talent by writing it off to the problems that players have in their second year, and while it was understanding and compassionate of him to sympathize with my second-year blues because he, even he, The Great Hernandez, experienced them himself when he was only a second-year player, I didn't appreciate what he said one bit.

After his interview was printed, Keith came scraping across the clubhouse to me to express the hope that I didn't misconstrue his comments, which were only aimed at making me a better player. They were all taken out of context, Keith explained. And they were a natural reaction to what I had said in spring training that had offended some of the older players. Keith was only there while the other players were speaking up, and the press quoted him instead of them. He hoped I understood, all in good fun, of course, and that I wouldn't take offense. I told him that I was good and pissed. He was pulling the same shit this year that he had pulled the year before. Who made him the manager of the Mets? What right did he have criticizing other players to the press as if he were the public affairs officer or something? Whenever Hernandez was frustrated about his own issues, he would mouth off to the press about players he felt should take up his slack and place them on notice that he was displeased. Maybe if he worried about his own bat instead of other players' performances he wouldn't create such hard feelings. Besides, for all of his chronic complaining, I still got more RBIs than Hernandez in 1984 (97 to 94) and led the team in home runs.

I also got into trouble in 1984 because I had gotten friendly with a bunch of guys on the team who called themselves the "scum bunch." Maybe we were immature, maybe we were just a bunch of jerks, maybe the demons were already sizing us up for their feast, but we used to sit in the back of the bus or the team plane and drink beer, blast our music, and throw food around. We used to have some real "animal house" food fights, too, that, I'm sure, didn't endear us to some of the more conservative players.

The scum bunch was led by relief pitcher Jesse Orosco, who would ultimately play a major role in the Mets' Championship Series in 1986. Jesse picked up 31 saves during the '84 season and always seemed to stay cool under pressure. Maybe Jesse seemed so intense yet calm in crisis situations because he was able to blow off the anxiety and sheer terror that always accompanies a relief pitcher to the mound by acting like a devil-may-care lunatic when he wasn't pitching.

I fell into this group partly because I felt that they had kind of a license to be bad. I know now that it was a mistake because I let the group have too much influence over me. If the scum bunch said throw that hamburger out the window or spit beer on someone, then I'd do it with a vengeance because I wanted to belong. Sure it was fun, but it was also forced. That's not the kind of person I really am, but I was acting out so that I could get the kind of approval first- and second-year players should work hard for on the field and not in the locker room.

Did I get Doc Gooden involved in the scum bunch and mess up an otherwise stellar career? No, not at all. In fact, Doc was never one of the rabble rousers, and that says a lot for our friendship because Doc turned out to be the steadying influence on me during my later years with the Mets. In 1984, Doc was more focused on staying firmly and warmly under Davey's right wing until he was allowed out to pitch next. Then he'd climb right back. Davey wanted nothing to happen to Doc. If I had come up to Doc with a magic lantern and said, "Three wishes, Doc. Let's go to town," Davey would have whipped it right out of my hand and thrown it into the ocean. So the truth is that I didn't get Doc involved in anything, even though some of the newspapers in town said that I was a bad influence on him.

The scum bunch, Jimmy Frey, even Keith Hernandez's criticisms—all affected me more than they should have during my early years on the Mets because I gave each of these "figures" an authority far beyond what they should have had. The scum bunch was a ridiculous group of rowdies and it was blown all out of proportion. Coach Jimmy Frey was a legitimate tutor, but I became so dependent upon him that when he left, I felt abandoned and took the whole first part of 1984 to recover. The Keith Hernandez relationship was the weirdest of all. He gave good advice and was a natural leader, and I looked up to him because of his skill and experience, but I never realized until years later how much I'd put him into a "father" role. That explains why we battled back and forth for so many years and why I always saw his criticism as particularly stinging. I put more stock in it than I should have. Maybe Keith was actually trying to get my goat. Maybe he was just running off at the mouth the way I did. Maybe he really was trying to be professional. I can't tell. But it pained me that I was that open when I should have been more coldly professional. I realize now that I was laying the burden on other people instead of dealing with it myself. Sure I came around after the Keith Hernandez story in the paper when he said that I gave up on myself in crisis situations and that I was lazy when I should have been tough. That's partly what makes me so mad. I'd invested so much in what Keith had to say that even though it was insulting, I still responded. It gives me a cold chill not only to realize that, but to realize what the papers said after I pulled out of my slump.

The newspaper reporters said that I "woke up," came around, and started working again. It burned me that they thought that something Hernandez said had that much effect, as if: "Oh, 'scuse me, Mistah Mex, was I nappin' on my broom, I mean, bat?" Whaddya mean, "woke up"? Did "Overseer" Hernandez have to give the lazy, overfed Strawberry a good kick in the pinstripes—in a typical white-black interaction— to get him back onto the ol' ballfield back home to pick off some pitches for home runs? What an insulting thing to read about yourself. If you're black, when you're in a hitting slump you're just plain lazy. Black players can't have slumps just like they can't have injuries. When you finally pull out of the slump it's because someone—usually someone in a whiter shade of pink or an acceptable variation thereof—has booted you the hell out of the slump. Kicked you off the back porch, so to speak.

"Hey, that Keith Hernandez, he sure made Strawberry sit up

and take notice. Gave him what for, and now look how he's hittin' that baseball."

"Gee, thanks, Mex. I needed that."

But despite the problems that Keith and I had in '84 and would continue to have right through 1989, I still respected him as a baseball player who could consistently hit a solid .300 year after year, play an outstanding first base, and keep a young pitcher from falling apart on the mound despite a crisis situation in a game. Keith solidified the infield for the Mets and helped stabilize our team defensively.

The 1984 season was a heady one for me personally, if not for the rest of the team. I'd never played on a Major League first-place team before, and just being on the Mets for those few days when we were in first a game or so ahead of the Cubs was one of the sweetest, most exhilarating feelings I ever had. I know there were guys who'd been around the league longer than I who got depressed after we slipped back into second, but I didn't. I saw a whole future ahead for me and also for Doc. Maybe I blinded myself to the pressures that were increasing on us. For sure I didn't see that there were tensions already at work that would drive us along our respective paths into the pit of addiction. But for all my rowdiness during the year and my getting myself in trouble with my interviews, I nonetheless allowed myself to become "a Met." I said, in effect, this is my family and this is my new home, and I encouraged Doc Gooden to do the same. So when the bone-crushing pressure of the 1986 Series affected every part of my life and I saw that even the Mets themselves at the height of their glory had turned against me, I was emotionally drained. That was my undoing, my unraveling for my final four years in a Met uniform.

However, as I looked out the window of the 767 as we circled out over the Pacific on our approach to L.A. at the end of the 1984 season, I told myself that I would have no reality until the 1985 season started up again in a few months. It would be like all the nights before all the Christmases rolled into one. I could hardly wait for 1985.

In the third grade.
(COURTESY OF
RUBY STRAWBERRY)

With Michael (center) and Ronnie (left). (COURTESY OF RUBY STRAWBERRY)

Wearing my new uniform as the Mets' top draft pick in 1980. (© GEORGE KALINSKY/MAJOR LEAGUE GRAPHICS)

Receiving the Doubleday Award for outstanding Triple A player in the Mets' organization at Shea Stadium in September, 1982. I was still at Tidewater. (© GEORGE KALINSKY/MAJOR LEAGUE GRAPHICS)

An uncertain rookie, fresh
from the minor leagues.
(© GEORGE KALINSKY/MAJOR
LEAGUE GRAPHICS)

Receiving the Rookie of the
Year Award for 1983.
(© GEORGE KALINSKY/MAJOR
LEAGUE GRAPHICS)

My wife, Lisa. (© GEORGE KALINSKY/MAJOR LEAGUE GRAPHICS)

(Left) Darryl, Sr., and Darryl, Jr. (© GEORGE KALINSKY/MAJOR LEAGUE GRAPHICS)

The first of many great moments in 1986—Mookie, Keith, Gary, Doc, and the rest of the team greet me after I hit a home run on opening day. (© GEORGE KALINSKY/MAJOR LEAGUE GRAPHICS)

In the groove. (© GEORGE KALINSKY/MAJOR LEAGUE GRAPHICS)

A Met, and proud of it, 1986. (© GEORGE KALINSKY/MAJOR LEAGUE GRAPHICS)

I'm somewhere in there, celebrating the final out in game seven against the Red Sox in 1986. (© GEORGE KALINSKY/ MAJOR LEAGUE GRAPHICS)

Mayor Ed Koch and me in the clubhouse after game seven. (© GEORGE KALINSKY/MAJOR LEAGUE GRAPHICS)

(Left) My family—Lisa, Darryl, Jr., and Diamond Nicole in my arms, 1987. (© GEORGE KALINSKY/ MAJOR LEAGUE GRAPHICS)

(Below) At the top, the world champs, but coming down soon. (© GEORGE KALINSKY/MAJOR LEAGUE GRAPHICS)

Facing the Dodgers in the 1988 playoffs. (COURTESY OF MADISON PRO SPORTS)

Surrounded by the press, as usual, during spring training, 1989. (© GEORGE KALINSKY/MAJOR LEAGUE GRAPHICS)

(Below) The last hurrah at Shea. Coming home after a three-run shot in 1989. (© GEORGE KALINSKY/MAJOR LEAGUE GRAPHICS)

Back in L.A. with the Strawberry family. (COURTESY OF RUBY STRAWBERRY)

(Below) Getting ready for 1991 with my new teammate and friend Brett Buttler. (© LOS ANGELES DODGERS, 1991; PHOTO BY JOHN SOO HOO)

Up against Doc Gooden for the first time during spring training in 1991. (© LOS ANGELES DODGERS, 1991; PHOTO BY JOHN SOO HOO)

(Below) Eric Davis is one of my oldest friends. Here I'm hanging out with him before a game at Riverfront. (© LOS ANGELES DODGERS, 1991; PHOTO BY JOHN SOO HOO)

Making a running catch early in the season. (© LOS ANGELES
DODGERS, 1991; PHOTO BY JEFF CARLICK)

(Below) My bat woke up big time around the 1991 All-Star break.
(© VICTOR BALDIZON)

August, 1991, battling for the divisional crown. Dodger fans seemed to appreciate my eight RBI game. (BOTH PHOTOS © LOS ANGELES DODGERS, 1991; PHOTOS BY JOHN SOO HOO)

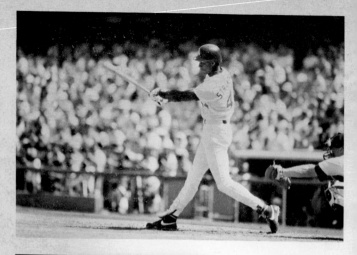

Down to the wire. We were all swinging for the fences and trying to take the extra base, but Atlanta won the West in 1991.
(BOTH PHOTOS
© LOS ANGELES
DODGERS, 1991;
PHOTOS BY JOHN SOO HOO)

9

WIN, LOSE, OR STRAW

I was primed as I read the sports pages over the winter. Frank Cashen was making the moves that would help us go all the way. You could see how he was thinking when he brought three veterans—third basemen Howard Johnson and Ray Knight, and catcher Gary Carter—to the Mets. We got Carter from Montreal in exchange for Hubie Brooks. Now we had a lineup that would include Keith Hernandez, Mookie Wilson, Howard Johnson, Gary Carter, and me. We had been laughable in the early eighties. Now, Frank Cashen, who I had come to look on with a kind of awe because he had so much power to make trades, hire and fire, and move people around, was trying to turn that laughter into respect. I felt like he was supporting me personally by doing that—fool that I was at the time—and I returned that support with full commitment. I was going to be SuperMet: mouth shut, glove open, bat swinging for the bleachers. Even the New York newspapers were saying that with Hernandez, Carter, and

Strawberry in the lineup, the Mets were going to be the team to beat in the East in '85.

I thought at first that adding Carter to the lineup would take some of the offensive pressure off me to turn a Mex Hernandez hit into a run. Keith was a solid hitter who could get on base at least once in every two and a half at-bats. With only me batting after him, the fans expected miracles every time he was on base and I came to the plate. With Carter in the lineup, Hernandez would now be followed by two home-run hitters, or so the thinking went. But when Carter didn't bring him home, either because he only moved him to the next base or didn't hit at all, it put even more pressure on me to get Keith across the plate. I finally found out during training camp that Keith hated to be stranded on base, and when he was, he blamed me, not Gary Carter. Oh dear!

There was so much new hitting power on the 1985 Mets that when the season started the hitters had a kind of camaraderie that hadn't existed the previous year. We each seemed to be able to pick up the slack from the other person. We led off our first few games with artillery blasts of hitting power. Gary Carter was our first hero, getting late-inning and tie-breaking hits that turned around the first five-or-so games. His enthusiasm and raw energy seemed to make things happen from right out of nowhere and infected the entire team with a spirit. It was *fun* to be on the Mets now. Dwight Gooden got off to a strong start, too, when he combined with Jesse Orosco to pull a three-hit squeaker away from the Philadelphia Phillies right down there in Hoagieland before the eyes of thousands of stunned Philly fans. Even the stupid Philly clown stopped dancing to look at the pitching duel taking place on the field.

We were all pulling together just like a family because it seemed like no single player was being held responsible for the Mets' success. As a team, our batting average early on was actually pretty low. But whenever someone went cold, someone else got hot and the team rambled on like a car held together by baling wire. It was a fun time because you never knew what was going to happen the next day. The team was held together by a combination of Mex Hernandez's consistent hitting and Gary Carter's ability to move Mex over or clear the bases with a home run. Gary was backed up by Mookie's hitting as well. When Mookie went into a slump, Davey brought Lenny Dykstra up from Tidewater. Lenny was never known for his power in the minors, but he had a good reputation for being able to get on base. He still seems to have the ability to trick the defense into making mistakes that will turn him into a base runner. I thought he was particularly good at drawing walks or getting pitchers to give him stuff they shouldn't. He's a very dangerous base runner, too, although most pitchers don't realize it.

The first pitcher Lenny faced was—you got it—Mario Soto at Cincinnati. Lenny was known more for his ability to punch a hit where he wanted than for blasting it out of the park. I remember during the game before Lenny's first at-bat when Davey was telling him not to worry about hitting the long ball off Soto. "Tough to do," Davey said. "Just try to make contact." In his next at-bat, Dykstra popped a home run off Mario Soto that broke the game open and won it for us. Who knew he could do that? But that summed up the spirit growing on the Mets in '85. Anybody could be a hero.

A few days later, on May 7, Kid Carter unleashed his bat for a grand slam that broke a tie. We were right up there in contention and Davey Johnson kept picking his head up from his computer screen and saying, "Fellas, the computer says we can do it. All you got to do is go out there, have fun, and make it happen. Don't let anything hold you back."

I was elated and the mood in the clubhouse was the same. There is nothing like the feeling of being part of a scrappy, winning ball club that puts it all together game by game. Sure it's great to be fifteen games ahead of the pack and dominating the entire league. I've been there. Been there twice. But it's something else to come back after an almost miracle year to pull your team back to where they were when the season ended. As the first week of May came to an end, I felt like there had been no break between 1984 and 1985. We'd just kept right on playing and scuffling runs away from the other teams. The spirit on the club had built up, the new players had added to the "family" quality of the Mets, I felt secure and supported by Davey Johnson, and, having married Lisa that February, everything had shaped up.

I felt the wind at our backs by the second week of May, when we belted ourselves into first place for the first time that season. I was strutting around the clubhouse like a rooster—actually more like Mick Jagger—joking with Doc about how we were in first to stay while Keith was telling us that there were still four and a half months to go. "You guys conserve your strength," he kept saying. "You'll need it for the stretch."

Then in a game against the Phillies on May 11 in which Sid Fernandez was pitching a shutout—I'll never forget that play —Juan Samuel, now my teammate, hit a blooper to very shallow right. I saw the angle on it, I timed how it was dropping, and I really thought I had a play on it. But the harder I dug to get to it, the more it seemed to drop, as if the wind, but there was no wind, had taken it and was plunging it down. But I was whipped up by the gutsy spirit of the Mets and thought, as I stretched, "I can get this. It's not out of reach." But as I dove for it, I jammed my right thumb back into my hand and felt the pain shoot up through my whole arm like an electric shock. I rolled over on the ground, grabbed my thumb, and held on to it as if someone was going to take it away from me. I couldn't believe the pain. It was throbbing and pumping up and down my arm and wouldn't stop. I kept cursing, "No, no, it can't end here." I thought my world had come to an end as I finally stopped rolling and tried to get to my feet. The next thing I realized the trainers were lifting me up. They hauled me out of the game before I even remembered my own name. They X-rayed the hell out of my hand, arm, brain, everything they could X-ray, and found out that I had torn the ligaments on my thumb. And oh man, did it ever hurt. It hurt my heart, too, because I knew just from the way the base of my thumb felt, as they kept packing it with ice and telling me everything was going to be okay, it was going to take a long, long time to get back to normal. Davey Johnson told the press the next day that it was his "darkest hour." I can still feel the pain to this very day.

When Davey Johnson and I looked back on that summer, he told me that the whole season turned around for him at that point. "It wasn't just your injury," he said. "It was the kind of event that stops you in your tracks." He told me he could see the team, which had been on a roll, begin to stumble. At the time I was heartsick because I knew we had the Eastern Division right in our hands. It was ours; we knew it and the rest of the teams in the East knew it, too. But when they took me off the field, the other teams licked their chops.

Had we been any other team than the '85 Mets, maybe we would have fallen out of it. But although we were not about to run away with it, we pulled together and promised to hang tough until our lineup was healthy again. I felt the support of the entire clubhouse well up around me. There wasn't the kind of groaning that "Darryl let us down" then. They were genuinely concerned, even Keith Hernandez. He told me that you have to learn when the risk of injury is so great that you have to let the ball drop. But nobody said I was grandstanding, and I really believed that I would have made the catch had it not been for the crazy backward spin on the ball that took it down and away from me.

Fortunately for us, the Chicago Cubs began to stagger at the same time, mainly due to injuries, and we stayed neck and neck with them through the spring and into the summer. By then, however, Vince Coleman and his St. Louis Cardinals, as well as the Montreal Expos, had begun to make their move and we looked around to find that our hand-to-hand combat with the Cubs had turned into a four-team free-for-all. Good. I was glad to be back in the lineup even though my thumb was killing me. I still couldn't get the grip on the bat that I needed and therefore couldn't get any power into my swing. In fact, though I returned to the lineup on June 28, I didn't really "come back" until somewhere in early July.

Things had gotten really tense in the National League East because we had refused to fade away or disappear. St. Louis had actually knocked Chicago all the way down to fourth in a crucial series, and that left us sitting in third about three games out. At that point, we began an all-out series against Atlanta that Davey said would really test our mettle as contenders. "This is where the rubber meets the road," he would say. "This is where I get to see if I have a team of late-inning sluggers or a bunch of rookies who still need to learn what the game is about."

The big test came on July 4, 1985, when we faced Atlanta in a grueling nineteen-inning game in the Atlanta tropical heat. We got on the buses to leave our hotel for the ballpark at about five in the evening and didn't get back until sometime after five the next morning, when the sun was already coming up. The game was delayed by rain before the start and again right in the middle, but it didn't release the tension we all were feeling. We were frustrated because we knew we had a better team than the Braves, but we just couldn't put them away. Gary Carter got five hits that night. Keith Hernandez hit for the cycle. I contributed too. But the Braves just kept coming back on us again and again. Each time it looked like we could close it down in the top of the inning, they came back in the bottom to tie the score. Finally we had them up 16-13 with Ron Darling pitching in relief, the first time he had pitched in relief since he was in college. But while we sat there in the dugout, vacant-eyed and hollow, Ron pitched through the final inning and we piled on the buses to go back to our hotel. I was asleep before the bus even pulled out of the stadium.

Later that month we met the Braves again at home and I pounded a grand slam off them in my first at-bat and then hit a three-run homer in my third at-bat. We won that game 16-4 behind Doc Gooden. The next day we beat the Braves 15-10. We were truly back on a roll when August came, and the spirit was bubbling out of us again.

Davey was so proud of the way we came back from our "June swoon" that he said we had "championship" written all over us. He exhorted us in the dugout. "You guys will eventually go all the way," he would tell us. "You're havin' fun. You'll put it together this year or next." He was right, but we thought it would be 1985.

On August 5, Davey was hugging the hell out of me after I hit three home runs against the Cubs in Chicago and we took over first place. First place for the second time that season and for the second time in as many years. It was a good feeling. I was two years in the majors and now on a winning, first-place ball club. Davey Johnson told me and told the press that if it had not been for injuries to me—I was out of commission for almost two months—and to Mookie Wilson we would have gotten to first place much faster and stayed there for the whole season. But it was still a thrill for me because I knew that 1984 was no fluke and the first part of 1985 was no fluke. We were a first-division ball club, if not always a first-place ball club, and nothing anyone could say about us would ever change the record. I was playing on a club of winners where I knew I belonged, and I wanted to take them all the way.

After we returned from the two-day players' walkout in early August, we picked our winning streak right up and blasted through the next week or so knocking off everybody who came into the ballpark. We swept the Cubs and took three out of four from the Phillies. But edging into September, the Cardinals had express-trained right through the National League

East and were ahead of us in the standings by two games. The championship was still ours for the taking. We had six games to play against the Cards and a series coming up in Los Angeles, in which Doc Gooden would do battle with Fernando Valenzuela.

We were a young and confident club in September 1985, led by a manager who was not afraid to defy conventional wisdom. Davey also looked out for his players. That kind of bare-knuckles management works, of course, as long as the team wins and stays in contention. But when you're an "almost" for three years after you won all the marbles, the fellas upstairs start to get nervous. Then when you start to fail and the team gets shaky under you, they call your number. That was the way it was with Davey. But in 1985, we still had a glorious future waiting for us.

We ate our way through the Western Division clubs in early September like Drano through a clog, beating San Francisco and sweeping San Diego in short order. Gary Carter was magnificent, belting home runs as if that was all he could hit. No matter what they threw him, inside or outside, slow curves or change-ups, Carter seemed to know exactly what was in the pitchers' minds. In our last two games against the Padres, Kid hit five home runs while the San Diego fans just sat there in the stands with their jaws hanging open. Were these the same Mets of 1983, who were the dustmats of the entire National League? Hey, no way! These were the championship Mets, home run kings of the National League. Stay out of our way if you don't want to get rolled over. Or so we thought.

On September 6, the day we were to begin a crucial end-of-the-season series against the Dodgers, Keith Hernandez had to be in Pittsburgh to testify in a cocaine trial. In very dramatic testimony, Keith confessed publicly to having regularly used cocaine when he was on the St. Louis Cardinals. He was in recovery now, he said, and had stopped using the drug. After his testimony, Keith flew back to Los Angeles for that night's game, arriving in time to enter the game in the fifth inning.

It was a warm evening—the Santa Ana was just starting to rustle up from the desert—and we were facing Fernando Valenzuela. I was home, playing before hometown fans and friends. I desperately wanted to succeed. Dodger Stadium was jammed, and long lines of cars were still snaking into the parking lots from Highway 101. People were hoping to get a ticket to see the hottest Mets series of the summer. Talk about wanting to strap on your rocket pack and fly down to the stadium. Everybody I had ever even vaguely known called me to wish me luck, even against the home team. I was feeling mighty good.

Oh yeah, about the game.

Valenzuela and Doctor K duke it out for nine long innings, scattering hits here and there, but pitching scoreless ball. No true baseball fanatic in the stands is disappointed that these guys pitched themselves out of jams time and again. Can you dig this? Nine innings and it's still 0-0. I don't even feel tired, I'm so nervous.

"Hey, Ma, look down here. It's me, Darryl."

Are they looking?

After the ninth inning, Davey sees that Doc is tiring and pulls him out for a pinch hitter, but the move does not produce any runs. Tension, tension, tension, tension. The Dodgers threaten the Mets in the eleventh and twelfth innings, but cannot push any runs across. More tension. Then, in the top of the thirteenth, with two out, we have two runners on base against Dodger reliever Tom Niedenfuer.

Now the cameras play on me, Darryl Strawberry, rising from the on-deck circle. Static electricity fills the air. Again, I can practically hear the announcers in the press box . . .

"I've never seen a Dodger Stadium crowd like this, Ralph. The fans here tonight have just gone crazy over this pitchers' duel."

"And here comes Darryl Strawberry at the nucleus of this Met batting order and the hometown fans are screaming."

"He's a local hero, Ralph, no matter what uniform he's wearing."

"This kid's only twenty-three years old and he's already become a dynamic presence in this National League, Tim."

"But can he hit Niedenfuer? That's the big question here in this thirteenth inning of an absolutely scoreless ball game with two Mets on base."

Niedenfuer is trying to pitch me outside and low—breakaway balls that will leave me off balance. He doesn't want to give me any time to get under a pitch and really tag it. I can see the outfield shifting ever so slightly to the right. The signal is on and my chest is filling with confidence. They're compensating for me. Here, in Dodger Stadium, barely a few miles from where I grew up and played baseball, my hometown team is shifting to compensate for what they think I'm going to do to their top pitcher. I'm not about to disappoint them. Although it's still the top of the inning, and the Dodgers will have a final at-bat no matter what I do, it's *showtime*.

Niedenfuer's next pitch is almost identical to his first: low and away. But this time, as I lift my right foot I plant it slightly to the left and golf my bat under the ball as it breaks toward the outside. I bop it as hard as I can near the top of the bat and the sonofabitch flies off into left field in a long line drive that doesn't give anyone any time to recover. It's a hit. No doubt about it! By the time both runners on base have scored and the ball has come flying back to the cutoff man, I'm standing on second as if I were on a cloud. Right in front of my family, friends, and half of the world of people that I know and love in Los Angeles, I've put the Dodgers in their place. I've hit the Mets to victory.

Now it's up to Jesse Orosco, leader of the scum bunch, to pitch his heart out in the bottom of the thirteenth. The Dodgers load up the bases and things are lookin' mighty grim. But Jesse hangs in there. My friend Jesse! He stays with each batter pitch after pitch, his brows furrowed. He's pitching on instinct alone down to the final batter and . . .

Yes Jesse, yes!

As they say in Century City, it was UN . . . believable.

By October 1, there were only two baseball teams in the entire world: the Mets and the Cards. And it was the Mets, just three games out of first, who pulled into St. Louis for a National League East series that would draw more interest than the World Series itself.

When Keith had returned to Shea Stadium for the first time after his confession at the cocaine trial, our hometown fans gave him a standing ovation. But now in St. Louis, where he had played so well for ten years, the fans booed him unmercifully, until the drama of the game itself stopped them cold.

Oh my, how Ron Darling pitched that first night. He and John Tudor battled for nine nerve-wracking innings of absolutely scoreless baseball. Then Darling was replaced by Jesse "the Fireman" Orosco in the tenth, who continued to pitch scoreless ball. To open the eleventh inning, the Cards replaced

Tudor with Ken Dayley, who struck Keith out first and then sent Kid Carter whiffing back to the dugout. I stepped into the batter's box next. I was swollen with power and fury, ready for baseball. "Dayley, you're meat!" I screamed to myself. Then the jerk tried to smoke me. Smoke me!

KA-BOOM!

The ball wouldn't stop flying. On and on it went, deep into right center field. Up and up it soared, high over the bleachers. The entire stadium went to its feet as the ball bounced high on the scoreboard and disappeared somewhere in the superstructure of the stadium. Yes! Yes! Fireworks. Cheers. Victory! The whole world comes alive with a home run. I love hitting home runs.

We were two games out of first.

Imagine that! After roiling about in the cellar two years ago, to climb into second place the following year, to be playing out a three-game series for the division championship the year after that. We were walking proud as Mets and I felt finally like I'd proved myself at home. The whole team was walking around with chips on their shoulders now. This was it, we said to ourselves as we took the bus to the hotel; this was where we'd nail down our Eastern Division title and pin the Cards' ears back to the wall. We formed up a wall around Mex Hernandez, too. Nobody boos a Met with that level of personal insult and gets away with it. Nobody!

On the very next night, Doc Gooden took the mound for the Mets. He had an off night—only struck out ten batters—but our own offense struck early and hard and left the Cards gasping for breath, 5-2.

We were one game out of first.

The next night we almost did it. Almost, almost. First Mookie singled to open up the game. After Wally Backman grounded out, Keith Hernandez singled Mookie home. Then Gary Carter and I both singled. Good grief, this was it. The bases were totally loaded and there was only one out. We were a hair's breadth away from first place. But then Danny Cox got tough and forced George Foster to ground to Terry Pendleton at third who scooped it up and threw Keith out at the plate. Mex didn't like that at all. Now there were tears in our eyes as Gary Carter, myself, and George Foster stood on third, second, and first bases, peeing in our pants over a 1-0 lead in the first with two outs, when grand slam hitter Howard Johnson stepped to the plate. HoJo had belted Danny Cox out of the park for a grand slam three weeks earlier in Shea. So we knew this was gonna be it! This was the home run. Good night, Danny. Have a nice winter. This was the game winnerrrr, rrrrrright heeerre. Crack! Gary streaked for home and I headed for third. The ball bounded down the third base line and I raced it as fast as I could. Dig, Darryl, dig. Bobble it, Pendleton. Drop the stupid ball, Pendleton. Go near that bag and I'll run right over you.

NOOOOOO!

"Yer *out*!"

By the seventh inning the game had settled into a managers' duel of relief pitchers while the Cards settled into a 4-2 lead. We clawed another run out of the Cards in the eighth. Then, in the ninth, Keith got to first base on a neat two-out single over shortstop and we had a chance to tie the game when Gary Carter came to the plate. Our hearts started pounding again. Just get a hit, Gary, any hit. Get on base, Gary, and I'll get you home. Whitey Herzog brought Jeff Lahti in to pitch to Carter. Gary tried as hard as he could, but Lahti got him to hit a fly ball to right that, with two outs, ended the game for us right then and there.

Hoowie da hoowie, yeah!

We were sorrowful as we returned to New York. Weepy as we knocked off Montreal while the Cards beat the Cubs. Then the next day the Cards beat the Cubs again while we were losing to the Expos. Our season was over.

On October 6, we played the bottom of our roster against the Expos just to keep the fans happy while the starters sat in the dugout. Frank, even Frank Cashen, must have been moved by the kind of year we had. Maybe the fans wouldn't see the starters on the field tonight, but Frank had another idea. Give the fans a show. Give the fans, those wonderful Mets fans, on the last night of an amazin' season, something to take home. In a burst of inspiration, Frank had the big Shea scoreboard flash highlight films of our year, a magic year, but a year in which we didn't go to the playoffs. We knew that in that moment, Frank Cashen loved his Mets, and we loved him, too. Shea was suddenly alive with feeling. This was the way baseball was supposed to be. Glory, but I was glad to be a Met that night.

We stood up in the dugout watching the scoreboard while

the fans were cheering for us. I couldn't believe it. We were almost there, almost into the playoffs, but the fans were still cheering their New York Mets. I started to cry. Then a few of the guys acknowledged the cheering fans when they ran out on the field and started waving to the stands. The fans went crazy. More of us went out and began tipping our hats to our wonderful, wonderful New York Mets fans. The whole of Shea Stadium was alive with love. It was warm, it was happy, it was like one giant 40,000-person family all wishing the season would continue but thanking each other for what they had.

Wally Backman, out of nowhere and just because he loved the fans as much as they loved him, spontaneously threw his Mets cap right to a fan in the stands. The whole Shea Stadium crowd came alive. People were screaming, "I love the Mets," and then Keith threw his hat into the stands and then we all threw our hats into the stands. There was even more cheering. There were tears. The team was crying on that October night in New York City. We thought the whole place would explode in love. The fans love us. We loved our Mets fans, loved them with all our hearts.

Next year, New York. Next year!

10

"ONCE UPON A TIME ON THE METS"

It's early morning in early March down in St. Petersburg, Florida. The year is 1986, and everyone has great expectations. The pressure is already building. So is the hype. We've all assembled for the coming baseball season like "the posse" out of a Sergio Leone Western. There's Mex, standing tall in the tropical sun, publicly confessed and publicly rehabilitated, already holding court with the reporters on the practice diamond, talking about the fortunes of a club that, he says, has "world champs" written all over it. He casts a long shadow over first base. "Doc's year," he says laconically, throwing a baseball into the webbing of his glove for emphasis. "Yyyyyup. Doc and Straw, that's about the way it is. Kid!"

Gary Carter is running laps around the bases, still working out the knee that underwent surgery the year before and taking deep, manly breaths to test whether he feels any pain from all those ribs he broke last year. Gary Carter is the perpetually wounded Met who always gets up from the dirt when you think there's nothing left of him. He always gets up. There's a rumor circulating around the clubhouse that when he got that busted rib in a third-inning collision at the plate, he'd grown a new rib by the eighth inning. And even when the game's going down the tube, when you look at Gary you think you're winning. It's his expression. He's always winning. It's uncanny. I won't know what his secret is until 1991. Carter's our secret weapon in 1986, only we don't know it yet.

Wally Backman is taking his practice cuts in the batting cage, concentrating heavily on each stroke he takes. I can sense a deep anger brewing inside Backman these days, something sullen and dark in his personality. Did he show too much personality last year when he tossed his baseball cap into the stands? Did he give too much of himself away? Backman doesn't like me, I can tell. There's an edge to him whenever we have anything to do with each other. Does he think I talk too much? Earn too much? We're heading for a clash down the line; I can see it coming.

The pitchers are loosening up their arms for the long campaign. Keith Hernandez thinks we have the best starting rotation in the National League, he tells the reporters. There's Sid Fernandez. People thought at first El Sid had washed up on our shores a washed-up pitcher, good for only seven or so games a year. "Arm's shot," some of the newspaper reports had said about him. But Davey Johnson and Frank Cashen thought differently, believed in Sid Fernandez, and he became a dominating pitcher for the Mets who surprised the opposing batters each and every time he popped up in the rotation like a gremlin.

Doc is like the "quiet man" in the old John Wayne movie. Most people see only his intense, dominating personality on the field, but never see his personal side. We've gotten to be close friends since he came up from the Tides in '84, but there was still an aspect of Gooden that even I didn't see. It wasn't until after he went to Smithers for drug rehabilitation that I understood just how much the pressure got to him as well. Maybe it was just because Doc seemed perpetually young, but you always got the impression that underneath his armor, he was seething. It was as tough to be Dwight Gooden as it was to be Darryl Strawberry, and on a team with very few black players, it was tougher still. There was just too much personality you had to keep hidden.

Nineteen eighty-six would have to be Dwight Gooden's year to soar. He'd spent two seasons under Davey Johnson's personal protection, and last year he showed that mostly every time he hopped out of the nest, he could dominate Major League hitters. Now he had to keep flying. The pressure would be on Doctor K to produce again, at least 17 to 20 wins this season out of his spot in the rotation. Talk about pressure, this great pitcher now had to prove that last year wasn't a fluke.

When Bobby Ojeda was on the mound last year, he always looked like he was just one pitch away from disaster. He never was, though. Maybe it was the look of panic that seemed burned into his expression, maybe it was that his pitches were just this side of sane, but whatever it was it frustrated the hell out of opposing batters. You walk up to the plate, you see this guy on the mound who looks like he's about to burst into tears if you just take a practice swing, and you think, "I can hit this guy." Then he throws you a pitch that you go after and it's in the shortstop's glove. Next at-bat, you say, "Well, maybe I shouldn't try to pull the pitch so hard," and the next thing you know you've bounced it over to second and you're out of there. That's the way it goes when Bobby O's having a good day. And you never know why.

Like Bobby Ojeda, Jesse Orosco always seems on the edge of tears, but Jesse has a reason to be. He's rarely called to the mound because someone like El Sid, Doc, or Ron wants to share the wealth or the glory. "Hey, c'mon in, Jesse. These guys couldn't hit a volleyball with a tennis racket. Pitch a few perfect innings and then we'll toss back a few brewskies and party the night away." Nope, when Jesse came out it was to face a caveman with a club, no outs, bases loaded, and the Mets with a one-run lead in game three of a crucial series. And that's exactly how his face always looked, even when he staggered up to the mirror in the morning to shave. "Yo, Jesse, chill it out. The game ain't even started yet and you only goin' to the shower." "I know, Straw, but I'm just gittin' ready for tonight."

Ron Darling also looks like he's always in trouble, but that's just because he thinks too much. His computer's in his head and he's got each batter's pitching program figured out for each at-bat. Hit him once, though, and you can knock him right out of kilter. I've seen this guy get belted so bad he didn't know where he was. When he was on, it was like he was a psychic. When he was off, they'd have to orbit a navigational satellite over the plate so's he could find it.

Howard Johnson and Ray Knight are like a one-two, left-right combination at third. They're more like a pair of halfbacks than baseball players, because Davey can shift them around according to who's pitching and what he thinks he sees on the field. Howard Johnson is Mr. Consistency all year long. He's usually good for a hit a game, and his hits usually come in crucial situations. But Ray Knight makes things happen out of nowhere. He's afternoon thunder and lightning on a summer day. You put him in and suddenly he starts a rally. Then Gary Carter gets his hit, then Keith, then comes my home run. By the end of the World Series, Ray will have had one of the greatest years of his career, joining me in hitting a Series-winning home run in the final game and earning the World Series MVP honors.

Moooooookie Wilson is the fans' delight and the only player I know who can "will" himself to first base. When he's on fire, he seems to make perfect strikes suddenly veer away or drop to the plate. Never get behind him on a count, or you're gonna walk him. And once he's on first, he's gonna get himself to second. Nobody steals second with as much drama as Mookie. One minute he's on first. Don't blink! You missed it. Now he's dusting off his uniform after his slide into second. More than anyone in the clubhouse, Moo-kie was the amazin' Mets, because Mookie himself was amazing.

And then there was Lenny Dykstra, the second coming of Pete Rose. On the playing field, the resemblance between Rose and Dykstra is unnerving. Both of them hustle around like they're on personal missions to win the game. Both are aggressive head-first base runners who have no compunction about knocking a fielder standing in the baseline into the middle of next week. Were somebody to have asked me about the Mets' bench back in '86, I'd've told 'em, "Don't mess with Lenny." Opposing managers never put much stock in Lenny's bat, until they saw him at the plate. Dykstra can get a hit out of a paper plane flipping over the plate from the stands. Lenny could get us hits when they were pitching baseballs the size of Ping-Pong balls, and he could turn a Ray Knight single into a three-run rally. Nineteen eighty-six was going to be his year of greatness.

It's 1986 and the Mets are the dream team. It's going to be our year and we know it in our gut. Davey Johnson knows it in his computer. "Stay healthy," he says. "Stay healthy and the National League is ours. Numbers don't lie." And that more than anything defined Davey's style of management.

Davey Johnson believed you had to make things happen. He believed that individual talent would always make the difference. He believed that if you weren't putting out your best effort you'd bring the whole team down. But he also believed in the power of numbers, the law of averages. If Davey says the numbers work, bet on it, the numbers work!

But you also have to make them work *for* you, he'd say to us over and over again. You don't work for them. This was not the year to be laid-back. Being laid-back is what always gets you in trouble. This year Davey is more than optimistic, he's downright prescient. This year, he orders, "We won't just win the division, we'll dominate it." That was it. We'd be more than winners, we'd be the *dominators*.

In the dugout, Davey's like a walking calculator. He knows all the stats and can tell you when somebody is due for a hit after so many games, whether a Ray Knight can get a hit more easily off a Bob Knepper than a HoJo can, or when, I'm so sorry to say, to pull the double switch. He doesn't talk much in the dugout. He just kind of stares. Davey Johnson and Tommy Lasorda, for example, are so different from one another you'd think they came from different planets. Tommy talks it up; Tommy seethes; Tommy glares; Tommy comes after you when he wants something; and Tommy gets out of the dugout and leads the hometown fans in ninth-inning cheers that rattle opposing pitchers into making game-losing mistakes. Davey, on the other hand, puts his grand plan into motion and lets it take care of itself. He doesn't play Billyball, but he's a gutsy manager who's not afraid to take chances. But Davey is adamant about one thing: it's his team and he wants to run it his way.

Many managers like to play a corporate style of baseball. They keep an eye on the attendance figures: who draws the most fans, who creates the biggest market. So what if the team wins or loses? If it makes money, we all share the wealth. "Christmas bonus time, boys. Turkey for everybody. Line up and get it while it's hot." Listen to the front office, cover your ass at all times, make sure that you run things by the boys in publicity, compliment the gals in accounting—"Helluva nice dress. Lose any more weight and you and me gonna do a little tango"—and make sure your players smile for the camera, lay off the firewater, and stay out of jail.

Davey wasn't corporate. He'd have his numbers, he'd work up his plan, then he'd put it into motion and expect you to do your part. If you didn't, then he'd bench you and let you know what he expected you to do next time. If he needed some extra oomph out of you, like he did out of me from time to time, he'd call you into his office, close the door, and have a heart-to-heart. "Darryl," he'd say. "I don't need you to do any more than your end. You see these numbers you've been putting up during the past series? Now you've fallen down a little bit. We all need you to get back to those stats. If you can do that, the rest will follow naturally. Any problems you want to talk about? Anything I can help you with? Don't wait for me to ask you if you have a problem." These were Davey's good years, and even though we had very public fights from time to time, I could relate to his style and his attitude.

After Davey told us the numbers were in our favor, he turned his attention toward the St. Louis Cardinals. The division wasn't theirs to win last year, he told us; it had been ours to lose. Look at the newspapers. What did *USA Today* say: CARDS WIN? No way. METS LOSE! Was St. Louis pissed? Hooowie, were they ever. Whitey Herzog began the 1986 season by singing the blues in the night because all the papers were talking about the Mets instead of the Cards. "Who do they think they are?" Whitey was rumored to have asked a reporter. "If you listen to the way they talk, they think they won the division for the past two years in a row."

We were propelled by arrogance and cockiness. Ron, Keith, Gary, Lenny, and I were all spoiling to fight anybody who crossed our path. Gary wasn't afraid of taking anyone on physically. Ron Darling had no misgivings about brushing back pitchers who threw at our batters. And Keith Hernandez would give as good as he got. Lenny became the feisty base runner who'd look for the collisions to take fielders out of position. I tried to be the most intimidating person on the team. Anybody who laid down the challenge to me or to Doc got himself laid out fast. I wasn't afraid to push someone if I thought it might intimidate the person, make him think twice about trying to intimidate us, or make him blow his cool. We were looking for the edge—"Davey's percentage," we called it —in everything we did. Give Davey the numbers, the story around the clubhouse went, and he'd bring us to the championship.

We had a sense of destiny in 1986, a belief that it would all come together for us in a great, historic display of baseball power. Davey said it was in the numbers. We felt it was in our hearts. We had been separate players in 1984. We had come together as a team in 1985, and the fans had showed us they cared about what we almost accomplished. Now we had matured in 1986 and we were going to bring it home for all New York to see. Look out, National League East, it's the Amazin's. Weee'rrrrrre back!

Davey set the tone just as the season started. He held up the schedule and pointed to a four-game series in St. Louis's Busch Stadium in late April. "You win it all right here," he said. "Numbers are numbers and we make them work for us right here. We break the Cardinals at home, we own them for the rest of the year. Other teams will know that we're taking back what should have been ours last year." When he explained that we already had the psychological edge over St. Louis—he always stressed "psychological edge" as the push that the numbers needed—we understood exactly what he meant. He wanted us to go right at the Cardinals from the moment the season started and establish our dominance. He warned that they would throw the best they had at us just because we thought we should have won last year. He reminded us that the Cards' manager, Whitey Herzog, had already told the papers that the Mets were the team to beat in the East. That's what he meant by the psychological edge.

We came from behind to pull games out in late innings so many times in 1986 that the press began calling it the Mets' lightning that struck late in the game. That became our psychological edge, and the teams we played became accustomed to rolling over in the seventh inning because they expected we'd come from behind. There were games during the year where you could almost see the other team not playing hard during the early innings because they were saving themselves for the later ones, believing that whatever they did early would have little effect. That became our edge. The teams that made mistakes early lost the game by the fourth inning and made our late-inning lightning simply a continuation of what we were already doing. Other teams made mistakes in the late innings because they believed that we were going to score runs.

We went out hard and clean and took the games right out of the Cards' hands. In the first game, we were tied after nine innings. Almost a replay of the first game of our series with them at the end of '85. But we'd scored two runs off their ace reliever, Todd Worrell, in the ninth and got another in the tenth to walk away with the win. Doc brought us back into Busch the next day and held them scoreless and frustrated while we stomped them for nine runs. Wally Backman came up with an impossible play in the field in game number three that choked off all their hopes for a win: we beat them 4-3. And in game number four, while they were still reeling from the beating, Bobby Ojeda stepped up on the mound and kept them popping out and grounding out for nine innings while our hitters banged John Tudor for five runs. We beat the man who'd beaten us the year before on his home turf and then blew out of town with a four-and-a-half game lead.

We were the first-place team, and every other club in the league was after us with a vengeance. Pitchers threw at us, runners banged into us, fans booed at us. But we didn't take it. We fought back. A pitcher would throw too close to my head and I had the bat down and was halfway to the mound before four guys would jump me. I wouldn't throw any punches though. I wouldn't give the ump a chance to throw me out of the game. I'd stand up to umps, too, just to let them know that I was aggressive. That kind of attitude translates very quickly into things breaking your way on the field. If an ump knows that you're going to voice your opinion, he may think twice before making a hasty call. Sometimes you can even get the calls to go your way if the ump is "conditioned" to go in the direction you're pushing him.

Whenever I thought someone was throwing at Doc, I was out of the dugout before anyone could stop me. I knew my size intimidated some of the other players. I knew that my aggressiveness was also a threat on the field. Hey, if I got in a good punch before the ump pulled me off, the other guy was gonna feel it. And because we weren't willing to sit back and take a licking, we were involved in more bench-clearing brawls than any other team in the league that season. That made the out-of-town fans especially mad at us and looking to ambush us. You can imagine walking into a bar in Philly after kicking the Phillies right out of the Vet.

People think that baseball is only played on the field.

They're wrong. Baseball is a head game as well as a body game. You have to pump the energy, the cockiness, the aggressiveness. You have to pump up so much testosterone that if someone even looks at you funny, you're punching his lights out. You have to tell yourself that there are no consequences, only winning and plowing under the bodies of anybody in your way.

A team on the march to the championship that develops this attitude is no longer a team—it's more like a gang. You hang together, you chill together, you go to war together. You play kick-ass baseball until you're the only ones still standing on the field—and you expect to have your asses kicked as well. But once you're into that mind-set, once you've told yourself that no matter how much pain you get, you're not changing the program, the machismo builds and builds until you're no longer human, you're like a Terminator. That syndrome split my three-year-old marriage up for the first time during the 1986 season and, I'm sure, put other marriages in the trash bin long before mine came rolling along.

Sure we took our share of lickings along the way. But we put the Band-Aids on, sobered up, and showed up to play the next day, when the fans booed us because some local newscaster reported that we tore up a local bar. You have to do that, too —march into somebody else's city and raise a ruckus at a bar on his turf. Let him know you have no respect for his territory. Piss on him if you have to, but stomp away having swept the series. We tried that in Houston, at a place called Cooter's Sports Bar, on July 18 during a four-game series in Houston that the Astros took three games to one.

We won the first game of the series, on July 17, but lost the next game 3-0. That night, we all went to Cooter's to celebrate the birth of Timmy Teufel's first kid. Darryl, Jr., had been born the month before, so I was in the mood to celebrate too. Now when you consider the tension of the series and the reputation of a heavy jock, down-home, good-ol'-boys watering hole like Cooter's you might say that we should have picked a more quiet and dignified place to hoist our glasses in a toast to the newest Teufel. But no, that's not the way it was going to be.

We had our reputation of being fighters that we'd earned the hard way on the field. Houston has its own fighting reputation. After all, isn't that where George Foreman comes from? So here we are in Cooter's after being shut out, drinking and toasting and toasting and drinking and drinking and drinking and drinking. The music's loud; the sawdust tickles our throats and makes them drier; we're in first place; I look around me at the faces of the other people in the bar, as our little group— Timmy, Ron Darling, Bobby Ojeda, and Rick Aguilera—gets louder and rowdier. I may be tough, I think, as I check out the slack-jawed mugs on these country boys, but I'm not a masochist. These guys are looking to size us up for a whupping. I say, "Sorry, fellas, I gotta go. Got a big game tomorrow. Maybe y'all should be thinking about packing in tonight, too. It's been real. We must do this again sometime. See ya."

That's all she wrote, and I hit the hay. I heard from someone later that at five in the morning, there was a phone call that said Timmy and the other Mets had been arrested and were going to jail unless someone bailed them out. The newspapers picked up the rest of the story from there.

It was last call, so the story goes, when the new father, proud of his offspring and wishing for more drinks to welcome the youngster into the world, had asked the bartender to play more music while he downed the rest of his brew. But the barkeep was not a man to be messed with, especially when it came to violating the beverage control laws of the great Lone Star State. No, sir, the man said; it's closing time and when you gotta go, you gotta go. So, the story continues, Timmy Teufel, with his brew still in his hand, followed the crowd across the sawdust toward the door, where he was stopped by two of Houston's finest, serving in an off-duty capacity as bouncers. It's the law, they say; you can't leave a bar with a drink in your hand. The law's the law, right? But old Timmy was also not a man to be messed with, especially after Houston's best pitcher had humiliated us on the very day of the birth of a young Teufel. The point where the bouncers tried to explain to Timmy that he could not take his drink into the parking lot is, coincidentally, where the story breaks into two distinct versions: New York style and Texas style.

Texas style: "I'm sorry, sir, but the Texas beverage control law absolutely prohibits patrons exiting an establishment serving liquor from taking their liquor with them. Liquor must be consumed within the establishment. Liquor to take with you can only be purchased from state-licensed package stores."

New York style: "Hey dickhaid cocksukah, y'all carr' that glayuss outta dat bahhh an' Ah bust yawuh haid lahk a can-

nalope den Ahma shove dat deah glass raht up yawuh y'all
know what so's y'all cain't set fawuh muuuunth. Heah?"

What's the truth? Who's crazy? In both versions, the rest of
the story plays out along very predictable lines.

In the Texas version, Timmy reportedly refused to return his
drink and was impolite when told that he had no choice. The
bouncers reportedly identified themselves as off-duty police officers, subdued Timmy and the other members of his party who
tried to intercede, and arrested the whole pack of them. The
Texas version claims that they had assaulted the police officers.

In the New York version, the bouncers were so abusive to
Timmy and the rest of the party that although Timmy wanted
to comply with the law, he believed he was being aggressed
upon. When the bouncers, according to this version, jumped
on Timmy without giving him a chance to comply with the
law, his teammates had no choice but to intercede to protect
him. The bouncers, the New York version of the story claims,
never identified themselves as police. It was only when they
were being bested by the Mets-in-a-jam, who thought that it
was just a bar fight and nothing else, that they identified themselves as off-duty police, made the arrest, and called for
backup.

Although I wasn't there, I heard that the bouncers, who
were really cops, jumped Timmy, and the guys with him
jumped in to help. Timmy and company claimed the bouncers
never identified themselves as police officers, that the bartender called the police, and that when the cars arrived to
break up the fight, the bouncers pulled their badges and filed a
complaint against Timmy for assaulting police officers *and* for
attempting to take liquor in a glass out of a bar. Timmy
claimed that the bouncers never showed any badges—so how
could he have known they were cops? As for leaving the bar
with a glass of booze, Timmy claimed that he was going to
bring it back—"Honest, I was, Your Honor"—but that the
bouncers who never identified themselves as police didn't give
him a chance. Teufel and Darling were charged with aggra-
vated assault of a police officer. Ojeda and Aguilera were
charged with hindering Teufel's arrest. The papers had a field
day. End of story.

For the rest of the season after that, we were even more
arrogant, we were cocksure, we'd held our ground against a
hometown bar's bouncers. We kept our attitudes up by brag-

ging and drinking—except Gary Carter; we kept our spirits up by being rowdy; we had the scum bunch to keep us laughing and Jesse Orosco to keep us in control of the games we were in danger of losing. We kept our tempers whetted to a razor sharpness, took no prisoners, and gave no quarter. And as this attitude became my "family" attitude, I got sucked deeper and deeper into the maelstrom of drinking, partying, and hell-raising.

I gave my personal demons a feast in that summer of 1986. I became estranged from my wife, estranged from my friends, and so totally fixated on the game, the game, the game, that the rest of the world faded away. When that happens to you— as it has to if you're going to take it all the way—you're supposed to understand that you'll repair the damage at the end of the season. But I didn't understand that. I'd found a "championship season" type of life that I could relate to, a kind of lifestyle that made myth into reality and made superhuman feats into daily accomplishments. When you're on that kind of high without the weight of real life to bring you down, you tend to fall down. Hard! But I didn't know I was already falling until after the World Series.

But on the field I was a Met, one of the killers of the National League. No matter what they did to us, we were never out of first place for the rest of the year, and we marched into the National League Championship Series against the Houston Astros with more than a 20-game lead. It meant a return to Houston and the memories of Cooter's and the charges still hanging over Timmy and the others who had jumped in to help him.

Houston pitcher Mike Scott, whom Cashen had traded away years earlier and who had it in for us because he thought he'd gotten a raw deal in New York, had mastered the art of throwing what was generally agreed to be the most unhittable pitch in baseball: the split-fingered fastball. Most fastballs come smoking toward the plate on a fixed path. They can be high, low, inside, or outside, but if you can follow the ball from the pitcher's hand, you can determine where the ball will be. The split-finger comes barreling in just like a normal fastball, but as it reaches the plate all resemblance between it and any other pitch becomes purely coincidental. The split-finger can drop like a stone, take off like a rocket, or veer away from the plate as if it has an iron core and somebody in the stands has a huge magnet. What's the result? You swing at an invisible ball. "What are you swinging at, Straw? A golf ball?"—because the ball has dropped to the plate and you've tried to follow it. You get my point: the split-fingered fastball makes batters look stupid, and batters don't like to look stupid.

Mike Scott had led us around like dogs through a hoop during the regular season. We were afraid of him. In fact, given our whole ballsy season, Mike Scott remained the one soft spot in our platinum-coated attitude. The soft spot was just big enough to throw a baseball through and have it split away just after it spins through the hole.

Mike Scott was also Frank Cashen's personal nemesis. Now that he was in Houston, he was the reminder of what might have been if only Cashen had given him more time to develop. But, you might say, baseball is also a game of bad decisions made too quickly that are slowly regretted in the hours right before a big game. Baseball is also a game where everybody and his uncle have perfect hindsight and track your decisions like a hound dog snuffling down a trail. There's just no escape from it.

Mike Scott loomed over the mound to haunt us and remind us of our 1982 debacles. He had beaten us badly too many times for us not to worry. "We gotta hit this guy," we'd complain to Davey Johnson. But Davey didn't answer. "I can't follow this guy's ball," Keith Hernandez, the most consistent and accomplished hitter on the team, would say. "We gotta have a program," I said to Davey. And he replied from behind the oracle of his computer. "It's simply this, fellas; the numbers don't lie," he said. "How many times can Scott pitch during the series in a regular rotation? He pitches the first game, he pitches the fourth game, he pitches the seventh game."

"But if he pitches the seventh game, they win," Dykstra or somebody else who whined like him piped up from the rear of the clubhouse.

"That's my whole point, fellas," Davey said, rising from behind his computer to make his whole point. "There ain't no seventh game!"

"Nooo seventh game," we said in unison, finally understanding the brilliance of this man's mind.

"That's the ticket, fellas," he said. "No seventh game. You win games two, three, five, and six. Simple as that."

But wait, there was Nolan Ryan, already an institution all by himself in baseball, who was the other powerhouse in the Astros' rotation. Then there was the "Junkman," Bob Knepper, who threw pitches that were so cheap, rummies on the Bowery would have walked by them without taking a poke. Scott, Ryan, and Knepper—these pitchers completely dominated the National League West by shutting down the division's most powerful batters. There were even some New York Yankees fans yakkety-yakking on the southbound D train about wanting Houston to win the National League pennant just for the opportunity to see Mike Scott duke it out with Roger Clemens for twelve or so scoreless innings. The pitcher still standing on the mound at the end of twelve wins.

So you can see, the National League Championship Series was highly charged physically, very emotional, and pumped up with all sorts of bravado and craziness. But the games themselves were incredible athletic contests. I had never ever been in a tougher series of games.

Our strategy was as simple as any strategy can be: the nights when Scott wasn't pitching were *must* wins. One loss to any pitcher besides Scott meant that we'd probably face him in game seven and lose the championship. Davey's law: "The numbers don't lie."

Game one in Houston was almost too predictable. Split-Finger Mike kept us looking, fanning, and dribbling little grounders along the third base line. We could barely get a man on base, and when we did, he died there from boredom. But we roared back against Houston the next night and two nights later in game three in New York. Then we faced Mike Scott again in game four, and Frank Cashen tried to sideswipe him with a bit of the old lawyer's finesse.

Frank had been watching Scott carefully through the year, he claimed, and again very carefully during game one. He said he was convinced that Scott was roughing up the surface of the ball with a piece of emery or a file or something to give himself more surface to grip and use to control the ball's spin. Finally, before the start of game four in New York, Frank raised his "scuffing" charge against Scott and the Astros with Chub Feeney, president of the National League. Cashen was serious about this because you can't scuff up a baseball in the Major Leagues, just like you can't throw a spitball. After Mike Scott had beaten us singlehandedly in the first game of the playoffs, Frank Cashen, ever the liggle iggle, told the batboys to gather up every discarded ball from Scott in game four when we were scheduled to face him again.

"Get every one you can find, boys, stash 'em in pails, and run 'em upstairs," he ordered. "We'll nail dem sonovaguns. You'll see." Sure, we were hoping Cashen could knock Scott out of game seven. Maybe he could even get a disqualification for game one or four and replay the whole shebang.

Buckets of these discarded balls were delivered to Chub Feeney, who gave them the once-over and ruled, after a special hearing he convened right after game four: "Dey ain't got nuttin' on 'em. Play ball!" And so ended l'affaire-du-scuff episode of our championship series with Houston.

Was Frank grabbing at straws? Maybe so. I'll never know, but Scott had developed such an awesome pitch that it seemed to defy the laws of physics. We'd watched him during the year and said, "This simply cannot be." Balls don't do what Mike Scott's making 'em do. "Sum'pin' stinks, Frank," Davey said. "It ain't kosher," we agreed. People who play baseball every day know that nothing defies the laws of physics but that it has a reason. Frank's reason: Scott was putting extra surface on the ball to get the spins he wanted. "Say it ain't so, Joe." But the league president ruled otherwise.

So we had played Scott in game four and folded up like a tent. But our strategy had worked so far and it was Scott two and the Mets two going into game five against the other Houston ace, Nolan Ryan. Win game five and it's three-two. Win game six and it's "Hello, Beantown."

Meanwhile our lives were falling apart all over the place. Guys who normally didn't drink were nipping at the sauce. My wife, Lisa, had come down to Houston to "work out" difficulties, but I couldn't give her the time of day. I was too busy doing everything I could during games two and three to keep my sanity so that I could contribute in games five and six. This was it. We lose here we lose for the year. All the juices, all the aggression, all the pure animal hate that we'd worked up to get us to this point suddenly bubbled right to the surface. Ask me a question and I'll snap back at you. Push me and I'll take your head clean off. No more talking. I was as juiced up on tension and raw combat-ready testosterone as any human being could be. Bring 'em on. I want my Maypo. This was *High Noon* and I was going to lay the bodies out and sort the bones later. No prisoners! No tomorrows! If we lost but one game, we'd have to face Mike Scott in game seven. Each game was a must. And now—after a Monday off, but still in New York—we had to face Nolan Ryan.

Outta my way, Lisa. I'll talk to you later. I mean it. Don't push me. There ain't too much of me left to get pushed.

Ryan was a tough SOB who had the right stuff in his pitching arm to shut down a ball club's offense. We, of course, had Doc Gooden, who had been so effective for us all season long. In the early innings of game five, Nolan kept striking us out and Doc pitched himself out of some tight spots. Our defense was spectacular. Our acting, specifically Mex's acting, was even more spectacular.

After getting out of a first-inning jam, Doc was in real trouble in the second inning. Kevin Bass led off with a single and Jose Cruz followed with another single, moving Bass to third. Doc then struck out Alan Ashby, looking for the first out. Next, speedy Craig Reynolds grounded the ball sharply to second baseman Wally Backman. Wally flipped to shortstop Rafael Santana at second to nail Cruz for out number two. As Bass streaked for home, Santana fired the ball to Mex, who was into his stretch at first. Reynolds came flying down the line and across the first base bag as Mex went into a split, gloved the ball, and then, in a moment of absolutely brilliant inspiration, screamed "Out!" at Reynolds and first base ump Fred Brocklander. Before Keith's voice had died away, Brocklander jerked his thumb at the stands and screamed "Out" as well. Matt Galante, who was coaching at first for Houston, simply exploded all over Brocklander. I've never heard such screaming. Reporters said later that from the press box they could see what all America had seen in that moment (and what was confirmed by the slow motion replay) which was that Reynolds was safe at first and that Bass should have scored. Much later, Keith admitted to having "suggested" the out call to Brocklander rather than having him come to his own decision. Mex Hernandez should have been given the Oscar that year for best performance by a first baseman in a leading role in a playoff series.

Later on, in the fifth inning, I made my contribution by nailing Ryan for a blast that tied the game at 1-1. The game stayed tied and went into extra innings. Ryan was pulled for a pinch hitter in the top of the tenth, and was replaced on the mound by Charlie Kerfeld in the bottom of the inning. Jesse

Orosco came in for Gooden in the eleventh. In the twelfth inning, Dykstra led off by grounding out. Backman then walked and advanced to second on a wild pitch to the next batter, Keith Hernandez. So Kerfeld intentionally walked Hernandez to get to Gary Carter, who had been slumping badly throughout the playoffs. Was that an insult to the Kid? You better believe it. Gary had been a standout all year and now had been publicly humiliated by the Astros, who had purposely let the Mex get to first. Gary was also stung by Charlie Kerfeld's having waved the ball in his face in game three, after Gary had grounded back to the mound when Charlie was on in relief. Was Kerfeld still rubbing Gary's face in it by walking Mex? We'll never know, but Gary is not a man to be insulted. He has ways of making you regret it.

Charlie threw three balls in succession, making the count 3-0. Then Gary laid off and watched Kerfeld throw two perfect strikes, for a count of 3-2. You could feel the entire stadium rocking from the cheering fans. People were hoarse from screaming, and on that damp, chilly October night in New York, they were awash in nervous perspiration. Win the game here, and we have a chance of avoiding Mike Scott. Lose it here and we could lose the entire season.

Now Charlie and Gary get into a war of nerves at the plate, Charlie trying to hit the corners with his next two pitches and Gary fouling them off. I want to send my spirit out there to infuse Gary Carter with courage, but he doesn't need any. He has more than enough for the whole team. My heart is pounding as Charlie winds up for pitch number eight. He's gotta strike this guy out or get him to bounce it to short for a possible double play. But Gary brings his bat around like a sledgehammer and smashes the pitch right over Charlie's head and up the middle for a base hit that sends Wally Backman sliding into home and winning game five for the Mets.

What I was pumping up so I could kill on the ballfield was making me kill what was left of my marriage. Lisa wouldn't let up at all. Every night we were having violent arguments. My adrenaline was flowing; I was putting my fists through walls; I was so crazy with passion and trying to maintain my edge that I wasn't thinking clearly about anything—least of all, domestic issues. I was in some of the toughest most intense kick-ass baseball I had ever played in my whole life and I was fighting with my wife over who the hell knows what. "Hey, girl, put it on hold!" I'd scream at her. "My head's in another place." But the fighting continued.

Try to put yourself in this situation. You've got to go out there and perform in a hyper-pressure, aggressive, macho, physical, shoot-first-and-ask-questions-later kind of situation. You have no time to think about anything else but beating up the other guy or he'll beat you up. We're facing Mike Scott and Nolan Ryan, who take no prisoners. If I zone out for even a second to think about the issues Lisa's raising or to worry about whether I have a marriage or not, I'm letting myself down and all the guys who rely on me, not to mention the zillions of New York fans watching the game.

They don't want to hear that Darryl Strawberry's busy being sensitive to his domestic issues. They don't want to be told, "Sorry, the reason that pitch went by me is that I was concerned about addressing personal problems." They want me to hit the freakin' ball so far nobody ever sees the thing again. They want me to charge into a catcher blocking the plate and take the guy's head clean off. They want blood. And they want it served up in living color during prime time so they can go to work the next day and kick their competitor's ass right across Broadway. You don't think every ballplayer in every sport doesn't realize that? They're called bragging rights, and they pay me $20 million these days just to make sure that when you plunk down your money for an L.A. Dodgers hat, you buy the top-of-the-line bragging rights along with it. And if you don't think it pumps you up to the point of violence, then you're just not a competitor.

I am a competitor. Nobody gets in my way when I want something. I wanted the National League championship so bad I would have killed for it. I was young, this was my first playoff series, and no wife, nobody, was going to mess up my mind when I had to face Split-Finger Mike Scott or Junkman Bob Knepper at the plate. I'd make the Junkman eat his junk if I could.

There was no backing off and no backing down as Lisa and I kept on fighting. I could feel the violence rising inside me like the howling of so many demons. I was out of control. I was being paid to be out of control and physical. I'm sorry for what I did, but I did it at a time when everybody around me wanted violence and a display of raw power. I tried to tell her to stop. I almost begged her just to wait for another week or so. Go back to California. Go to New York. Go stay with your mother, for heaven's sake. Just don't mess me up while I'm trying to play this game. But she wouldn't stop.

I know there's no excuse for hitting your wife, just like there's no excuse for being an alcoholic. But the truth is that I'm an alcoholic and I hit Lisa so hard I sent her flying backward and broke her nose. I'm sick to my stomach over what I did and how I hurt her, and I blame myself.

It was another one of the incidents that marked what was going on with me as my life gradually deteriorated, at a time when I should have been on the greatest roll and highest high of my existence. Maybe I never felt comfortable with the celebrity status that was accorded me in New York and on the road. Maybe I felt that I could have had any young woman from coast to coast to party with and to feed my ego. Maybe I felt that because I was big, tough, and on a first-place team, I could do exactly as I pleased. Maybe all of that is true, but the closer we came to actually winning the division and entering into the playoffs, the more the pressure of having to perform on a championship team got to me. It overheated my brakes and I had no way to stop myself. I bet it would have helped for someone to have sat me down and said, "Listen, this is what's going to happen to you as it gets heady in the playoffs. You're going to feel like Superman, but you're not. You're still human, so play ball and then put your Superman costume in a suitcase at night." But no one did, and I was an accident waiting to happen. It got worse throughout the playoffs and into the World Series, so that by the end of the season, I was burned out while the rest of the team enjoyed our victory.

I put it all behind me, my marriage as well, when I got to the Astrodome for game six and all the marbles.

The Mets had gotten a well-deserved reputation for not folding up when games entered the twilight zone of thirteen, fourteen, and fifteen innings. But never, I believe, had a playoff game gone to sixteen innings, with the managers of both teams throwing everybody they could into the battle. This sixth game of the 1986 National League playoffs would be fought in the long, long shadow of Mike Scott, who had shut us down in games one and four and who, we feared, had what it took to shut us down in game seven. Therefore, whatever we did, we had to avoid game seven and Mike Scott at all costs. "It all boils down to game six now, fellas," Davey says. "Lose it and we face Mike Scott. Win it and we send the Astros home for the winter. What's it gonna be, fellas?" We're ready for the bloodbath in Houston.

Bob Knepper was the third big gun on the Houston Astros pitching staff. The left-hander was known for his off-speed, deceptive breaking balls that got batters to swing at nothing. Power hitters found themselves hitting pop flies to shallow center or easy grounders to short and second. I had blasted him earlier in the series, but it was still frustrating to try to swing hard on the guy. His job was to hold us at bay so Mike Scott could face us the next night. We weren't afraid of Mike coming into game six as a reliever if Knepper got in trouble, because even if Scott could pull game six out, he'd be worth nothing in game seven, and Houston manager Hal Lanier knew that.

In the top of the first inning, Knepper retired three Mets in a row, but Bobby Ojeda allowed three runs to cross the plate in the bottom of the inning. However, as commentators would say years later, Bobby recovered early enough in the inning to shut down an Astros' rally that should have resulted in even more runs. It was going to be up to the hitters, Davey said in the dugout as we came in for the top of the second. We were already behind, and Houston showed no signs of sleeping at the bat.

I led off the second, but couldn't do anything except bounce out. Neither could Gary Carter or Ray Knight make anything happen, as we went down one-two-three. Fortunately, in the bottom of the second, Bobby O put the Astros down one-two-three also.

The third inning promised fireworks when Rafael Santana and Mookie got on base, but Knepper pitched himself out of the jam with no damage and Bobby Ojeda shut the Astros down again. That brought us to the fourth inning of a game that had settled into a pitchers' duel. I knew, Gary knew, Keith knew, and all the New Yorkers watching the game knew that if this game was going to be turned around, it would be by the Mets' power and not by the Mets' pitching. Bobby had to keep the lid on, and our batters would have to win the game.

The duel continued into the bottom of the fifth inning. Davey was uncharacteristically nervous. He leaned on the dugout steps and chewed at the inside of his mouth. When I dared tear my eyes away from the game, I could see Davey begin to pace. With two out and Bill Doran on second, Billy Hatcher hit a slow roller to Ray Knight at third. Knight, with no play on Hatcher at first, turned and threw to shortstop Rafael Santana, who had come over to cover third. Doran beat the throw to the base but then came off the bag, and Santana tagged him out. Brilliant play! Even Davey clapped. Davey was pumped and began to work the magic of his numbers. His numbers brain was the best in the league. And we were still confident, even though the Astros still led by three.

Davey pulled Bobby O for pinch hitter Lee Mazzilli in our sixth, but Lee didn't make anything happen and we went down one-two-three. Rick Aguilera replaced Ojeda on the mound and had to pitch himself out of a jam in the Astros' sixth, and we were still trailing 3-0 in the top of the seventh, still facing Knepper, who kept dinking us into Palookaville, again sending us down one-two-three. In our eighth, he forced Rafael Santana to hit into a double play to end what might have been a run-scoring inning. Fortunately, Aguilera held off the Astros through the eighth, too.

Davey opened our ninth by sending Lenny Dykstra to pinch-hit, and he powered a base hit into center field that Billy Hatcher overplayed and allowed to get by him for a triple. You could feel the team come alive. Davey had saved Lenny for just the right time. Now the power was coming to the plate. Now the Astros would feel the might of our bats. Next up was Mookie, who went with Knepper's third pitch, on an 0-2 count, and rifled it into right field for a base hit that scored the speedy Dykstra.

There were still no outs and we were down by only two runs, with Wilson on first. Knepper was thinking double play and got Kevin Mitchell to hit a ground ball to third. But the ball was hit so slowly that they had no play on Mookie at second and had to settle for throwing Kevin out at first. Now we had another run in scoring position, only one out, and Mex Hernandez stepping into the batter's box. Keith was as cool as any batter I'd ever seen under such circumstances. He didn't go after the garbage that Knepper had been feeding us for eight innings. He forced Knepper, in a war of nerves, to pitch right to him, and belted a double to right center that brought Mookie home, made the score 3-2, and put the tying run in scoring position.

Now it was up to Gary and me, and we knew it. Gary had

been the hero the day before and still had what it took. Astros'
manager Hal Lanier pulled Knepper for Dave Smith to pitch
to Gary and me. Dave Smith had been sitting in the bullpen
until just this inning and he was still not fully warmed up.
Gary knew this and played a war of nerves with the pitcher
until he got ball four and trotted off to first. "Hey, Gary, anyway you can," I called out from the on-deck circle. The whole
dugout had come alive.

"Yes, Darryl, yes!"

"Go, Straw!"

I stepped into the batter's box and for a second flashed Dave
Smith my "screw you" glare. But, like Gary, I held my bat back
while Smith pitched me four balls to load the bases with one
out.

"Good eye, Straw," I heard Davey call.

Ray Knight was up next and golfed a long, high sacrifice fly,
bringing in Keith from third with the tying run. That was it for
us in the ninth, but Roger McDowell came in and held the
Astros scoreless in the bottom of the inning and we headed for
extra innings. This was our territory. It was where we became
killers.

We played scoreless ball for four innings: we created no real
threats against Astros pitchers Dave Smith in the tenth or
Larry Andersen in the eleventh, twelfth, and thirteenth; while
the Astros couldn't damage McDowell, who pitched five innings, through the fifteenth. In the fourteenth, the Astros sent
in Aurelio Lopez to face Gary Carter, me, Ray Knight, and
Wally Backman. Gary pounded a sharp single into right. I
walked because Lopez was afraid to pitch to me. Ray Knight
tried a sacrifice bunt that resulted in Carter's being thrown out
at third while I advanced to second and Knight got to first.
Then Wally Backman stepped up to the plate. When Wally
singled into right field, I saw my chance to score the go-ahead
run. Kevin Bass tried to get me at home, but his throw was late
and too high, as Backman advanced to second and Knight to
third on the play. Now the score was 4-3. HoJo then popped
out to the catcher, Dykstra was intentionally walked, and
Mookie struck out. So the inning was over and the Astros
were one run down. Jesse Orosco came in to pitch the bottom
of the fourteenth, and the pressure was on him to end it once
and for all.

"All yours, Jesse," Keith bellowed from first.

"Your game, Jesse," HoJo called out.

Jesse was grim, but Jesse was also game. With one out, he went toe to toe with Billy Hatcher, but with the count full he couldn't get the fastball by him, and the center fielder slammed a home run off the left-field foul pole.

"Still you, Jesse!"

"Don't ease up, Jesse."

Very few pitchers in baseball would have hung in there after a shot like that. But Jesse was one of those pitchers. He stayed jaw to jaw with the power of the Astros' order and got Denny Walling on a grounder to first and Glenn Davis on an infield fly to Wally Backman. The game went into and out of the fifteenth inning with a dogged sigh as both Lopez and Orosco retired the sides without any scoring. If it went any longer, the managers feared, there'd be no one left to play a seventh game. We could hardly stand up any longer.

"The numbers still don't lie, fellas," Davey told us in the dugout right before our half of the sixteenth. "We may be in extra innings, but they're your extra innings. We've pulled out almost every extra-inning game we've played this year." Then Davey just got crazy. He wanted this—perhaps more than we did. "It's got to happen *now*!" And he shouted right into my face. "Now, Darryl, you hear? Numbers, Darryl."

I led off the top of the inning loaded for bear. I told myself I was due for a home run as I stood at the plate. I could see that Lopez was as tired as any of us. He wasn't going to trip me up. Then I saw Billy Hatcher moving around in the outfield like he couldn't figure out what to do next. Hey, Billy, don't bother to move around so much unless you can climb into the stands, I thought, because that's where this ball is going. But Hatcher still kept moving back.

Aurelio threw me a pitch that I expected would be a fastball. What else can you get from Senor Smoke? But the son of a gun tricked me. As I swung like a monster for the right field stands, the ball came in like a corkscrew and I only caught it with the top of my bat and squibbed it high in the air. As it drifted into very shallow center, I realized that Hatcher wouldn't be able to make the play no matter how hard he dug.

As I rounded first, I saw that the stupid ball had taken an extra-high bounce off the artificial turf and had popped up between Hatcher in shallow center and Doran, who had drifted back from second. I turned on the speed, dug for second, and reached the bag standing up. Whatever I had—a single and an error or a double—I didn't care. I was in scoring position all by myself. Ray Knight was stepping out of the on-deck circle. He was also due.

Ray saw how tired Aurelio was, and when Lopez just laid the ball across the plate, Ray pounded a base hit to deep right and I came home easily, breaking the tie, while Ray rambled over to second on the throw. The score was 5-4 with a runner in scoring position and no outs in the top of the sixteenth and Lanier pulls Lopez out for *Jeff Calhoun*? This guy hasn't pitched in a dog's age. My oh my, I said to myself in the dugout, there's panic among the Texans in Houston.

Calhoun tried to pitch to Wally Backman, but walked him, in the process throwing a wild pitch that moved Knight to third. Then, facing Jesse Orosco, Calhoun threw an amazingly wild pitch that allowed Ray Knight to come stumbling home with the speed of an uphill freight train and moved Wally Backman over to second. It was 6-4 and things were getting interesting. Jesse squared around and bunted Calhoun's next pitch, sacrificing Wally over to third. One out and Lenny Dykstra was stepping up to the plate. Lenny didn't even wait to be polite. He took the first pitch he could get a piece of and put it into right field for a base hit that drove Wally home and drove the lead to 7-4. Any hopes we had of a really major rally, however, were dimmed when Calhoun settled down long enough to get Mookie to hit a double-play grounder that closed down the inning. It was up to Jesse, up to Jesse, up to Jesse.

With one out in the sixteenth, Lanier sent in the veteran Davey Lopes to face Jesse. Lanier didn't have to tell his batter, "Get on base any way you can." Lopes had been around the league long enough to know that. No heroics, and it doesn't even have to be pretty. So Lopes waited. And waited. And waited. And by the time he had finished waiting, he had drawn a walk off Jesse and was on his way to first. Next up was Bill Doran, who pounded a single to center, sending Lopes to second. Hey, wait a minute, this thing wasn't over yet.

Billy Hatcher, the man who had homered in the eleventh to tie it, was up next and got a base hit off Jesse, who at least kept him from hitting it into the stands. But Lopes had crossed the plate and the score was 7-5 with only one out and men on first and second. Our hopes were starting to fade. Jesse *had* to put out the fire. Our infield came to the rescue on the next play. Denny Walling's grounder was eventually flipped over to Rafael Santana at second to nip Billy Hatcher for the second out, while Doran moved to third. They still had the tying runs on base and the potential winning run in Glenn Davis, who was coming up to the plate.

The Astrodome was alive with screaming fans. Jesse could barely stand up on the mound, and our whole team knew that Glenn Davis could put the game away. He was that strong. Keith Hernandez came over from first to settle Jesse down. What did he say into the pitcher's ear? Only Keith and Jesse know for sure, but the word on the street is: "Throw so much as one fastball and I'll kill you."

Jesse didn't throw the fastball, but Glenn Davis dropped a bloop hit in front of Dykstra that drove in Doran and cut our lead to one run, with two down and men on first and second. There was another conference on the mound as Kevin Bass stepped up to the plate. This game had gone on for so long and had been up and down so many times, no one even knew where he was. All except for Jesse.

From where I stood out in right field, the conference on the mound was like a football huddle. There were so many arms around so many backs for that brief moment that I wanted to run in to put in my two cents. But I stayed put and can only relate what they told me later in the locker room. "Slider," someone said. "Slider," Keith echoed. "Slider"—Gary Carter nodded. But Kid Carter added this: "I want you to look at me like you're trying to get the sign. I want you to shake it off. I want you to nod. I want everybody to think we're having a dialogue out there. But whatever I give you and whatever you take. You throw me the slider."

The slider—the cheapest, dinkiest, dumpiest pitch in all of baseball.

That's what Gary wanted and that's what Jesse threw. Three of them were balls. Two of them were strikes. "Momma, I can't take this anymore," I said to myself, ready to leap over the wall if I had to in order to go home and go to bed.

Then he threw the sixth pitch and Kevin Bass swung with

all his might. I heard the sound of the ball hitting Gary Carter's glove. Kevin had missed Jesse's sixth slider.

We had won the National League pennant—not with a thunderous crash, not even with a bang, but with a sudden whoosh of air. And the air was so, so sweet.

11

GOODNIGHT, BEANTOWN

The thrill of knocking off the Astros had us acting like a bunch of teenagers. We were laughing, half drunk from the champagne and whatever else was flowing, bumping into walls and into each other from exhaustion, hugging, kissing, backslapping, high-fiving, low-fiving, giddy from the release of tension, and stone cold toward the rest of the world. After a while, we collapsed on the locker-room benches and most of us just passed out. There was nothing left of us as they scooped us out of the ballpark.

We pulled into New York to nothing less than a hero's welcome, and, of course, we were delirious with joy. And I mean delirious. We were so wiped out that most of us thought the season was already over and we'd won it all. You don't cap a six-game series with a sixteen-inning nightmare and then pick right up to play the World Series, especially when the press is already claiming that nothing could be harder than the series you just won.

"Of course the New York Mets are the odds-on favorites to

beat the Sox," the reporters said. "Look at what they did to the Astros. The Mets are invincible." Invincible? We couldn't even stand up on our own two feet when we staggered into Shea. I tell ya, there was nothing left of us, absolutely nothing. The Astros series had left us physically and emotionally depleted. We needed some time to recover, to let our wells of energy recharge. But there was no time.

We were also unfulfilled and bitter in the wake of our victory. Why shouldn't we be? After winning a series like the one we'd just been through, the season felt over. But now we had to play Boston as if it were really serious. Yuk! Who wants to play Boston? Don't they have their own league or something? I guess that's the point of a World Series. But why? That's the question we were asking. Why? Anybody could see that we were already the best team in the majors. But no, we had to play the Bosox. Who were these guys, anyway?

"You fellas rest up," Davey said.

That was an understatement. I could have fallen facedown beside home plate and stayed there for the rest of the year. "Hey, Doc. Wake me up when it starts to snow. Zzzzzzzzzzzz." Rip Van Strawberry. But we only had two days, *two days*, to prepare for World Series game one at Shea.

As crazy as it all was, and as heady as our victory was, the emotional cost of getting there was especially high for me. During the heat of competition, you put aside all other worries in your life. I was also drinking to blot out the physical pain of having to go out there every night and work muscles that were past the point of strain. Like the rest of the guys, I just pushed through it until the pain wasn't there anymore. I don't know "firsthand" who else might have been abusing which substances, but months later Doc went to Smithers to recover from cocaine addiction. If he was using cocaine during that series, I wouldn't have been surprised in the least because the pressure was so intense, it made everybody do crazy things.

The scum bunch was scummier than usual, especially because Jesse Orosco was so much at the center of our victory. This guy had pitched in relief in four of the six games, in the tensest situations imaginable. On television, it looks easy, but it's not. If Jesse lost the edge to one batter, he had to gain it on the next. No human being is really capable of sustaining an emotional drive like that without giving way a bit along the seams. We sewed those seams back together by partying with each other and getting badder and madder at the world.

When my wife, Lisa, stepped into that world, she was blown out. I didn't want to fight with her, or with anybody else for that matter, but it wasn't me doing the fighting. It was the "udder guy," you know, the one who makes the magic happen. Real human beings are vulnerable. They should be able to admit mistakes, open up, let the pain help them understand. Baseball players in a life-and-death struggle for the league championship are not vulnerable—they can't be, or else they lose. They become fixated on "the play." Nothing else matters, especially relationships. They deny their pain and mask it any way they can. You pump yourself up to confront your enemies until confrontation itself becomes the issue. You have only one piece of programming: ON CONFRONTATION-ATTACK.

So there I am in my hotel room in Houston mentally pumping up, pumping up, pumping up. It's like I'm a nuclear reactor on the inside with the control rods pulled all the way out. I have to go back out on that field the next day and show no mercy. So there's no mercy in me. Physically, I'm barely strong enough to hold a glass of rum; that's how drained I am. Each game is a physical beating, so your mental energy has to overcome the bone weariness you feel and the actual pain from your muscles and bones. Mentally, you're not even lucid enough to carry on a simple conversation, let alone have an argument. Lisa wants to confront me about our problems, my problems. That's why she's in Houston, she says.

"Confront?"

"Did you say, 'confront'?"

"You confronting me?"

I'm distant, drinking, and downright ugly-mean. Now she wants a confrontation.

I'm out of control.

KA-BOOM!

Memories were flooding back now, images of that night. What had I done? There was no thinking, no weighing consequences, not even a drop of human kindness. *Nada!* Only an instant flash, an autonomic nervous system reaction and Lisa was getting up from the floor, cupping both hands around her nose as tears ran down her cheeks and through her fingers, frantically rummaging around for ice, cursing me and everything about me, and jamming whatever she owned into whatever bag she could find. And then I was alone. And then we won game six. And then I thought I might have the time to think about being alone. But I didn't.

At least we didn't have to fly right to Boston.

The memories of that night in Houston were playing out against the backs of my eyes whenever I closed them to rest. The memories gave me no rest. There was something so frightening about what I had done, as if I'd tapped into a current of family insanity or something, that it wouldn't let me alone. It was like a dream that you keep remembering when you wake up, not because of what happened in the dream but because of how the dream made you feel; old, old feelings that come up from somewhere deep inside of you that suggest things about you that you don't want to know. What were these feelings that wouldn't let me loose? I was really afraid that they had very little to do with Lisa at all.

I began feeling like I was two people. "Detached"—that was the word Alan Lans would use years later. I was the guy who started the rally and scored the go-ahead run in game six against Houston, just a couple of nights before. Now I was supposed to dominate the Series, but I was so shaky I couldn't even figure out which end of the bat to hold. "You better get outta this, Straw," I said to myself. "Run into the wall a few times until you're good and bloody, but don't walk around like this. You're a sitting duck." Nothing I did worked and I couldn't talk to anyone about it because I didn't want to scare anybody else. I had to lick this on my own, I thought. Maybe just a few drinks.

As bad as the players felt going into another series after only a couple of days to recover, Davey Johnson had to feel worse. We were numb when we weren't aching or just plain dog-tired, but he must have been feeling a sense of foreboding about what was coming our way. Like any good manager, Davey had his numbers worked up way in advance. But like an even better field general, Davey knew that his plans were falling apart. Now he had to reassemble a winning team that had already chalked up the big win for the season.

"This ain't over," he told us in an informal clubhouse meeting.

"But we're the favorites," we said. "The numbers don't lie."

"You don't work for the numbers," he reminded us. "Got to make them work for you."

Deep down inside, we all knew that we still had to go out there and win. We had to find whatever it took to bring us to the Series and turn it against the Boston Red Sox, who were like bulls pawing the ground, waiting for the gate to open so they could charge into us. But where was it?

By now Lisa had probably moved in with her mother, I told myself. I'd actually lost track of the time. We were in Houston, then I was in New York, then she was in California, soon we'd be in Boston. Too many cities! Too many lives to keep track of! And I was very much alone.

We were not only still in this, but all of Boston was coming into town like an invading army. In California, which is so big and so far away from everything, major cities aren't just a "drive" away except for Vegas. But Boston and D.C. are only a few hours away from New York by car. Philly is a commute. And in the Northeast they have trains, real trains, like they used to have in the West. Hey, jump on the Metroliner you're in New York in two hours. Half of Boston suddenly took over most of the bars in New York. I thought *I* drank. We'd walk into a bar in Queens the night before one of the games and we'd see these girls from Boston chugging entire pitchers in something like a single gulp. How do they breathe? Through their ears? I turned to Teufel and said, "Hey, if they got girls who drink like that, these guys can beat us."

"Don't worry, Straw," he said. "It's Boston."

I didn't know what he meant until game six, but at that point I was out of the game and wouldn't get back in until game seven.

I had to snap myself out of this feeling of walking through a desert. When I saw the other guys on the team, I could tell that they were a little out of it themselves. Gary Carter wasn't. He was up and rearing to go. They would have to hold him down with straps.

"Ya ready, D? Ya ready, D?" he'd say, his fists all balled up like he was goin' downtown to punch out some drunk in a waterfront dive.

"Oh yeah, yeah. Ready, ready." What was I supposed to tell him, that I was going to lay myself right down and die in the outfield? That's what I eventually did, but I was trying to avoid it before the Series began.

Brrrring! Brrrring!

"You got to get up for this, Straw," someone whose voice I

barely recognized from the old neighborhood in Crenshaw said into my ear. Maybe he was a cousin. Maybe he was a friend. Maybe I was so hung over I didn't care. Maybe it was a friend from New York. What crawled in and died underneath my tongue?

"What time is it?" I asked.

"Too late," the voice said. "Be too late fuh you 'less you git yaw head on."

Click!

I didn't need that bull at this hour of the . . . afternoon. Damn! Davey was gonna have my neck if I messed up any more, but there was nothing, nothing I could do to shake myself out of this. Nothing was working for me except the hope that when I went back to Los Angeles after this was all over I'd have some sort of a life again. It had been too much sacrifice. I had gotten my dream, but I had never realized what it would cost to get it.

Ron Darling opened for us in the first game and seemed settled and in control for the first four innings, striking out the power of the Boston order and settling easily into a duel with Bruce Hurst. Our batters went up and down so fast, it was like they were targets in a shooting gallery. Mookie struck out, Lenny struck out, Keith flied out, and the inning was over. It was like punching a time clock in the dugout. Gary Carter bounced out to start off our second inning and then someone tapped me on the shoulder to tell me that I had been struck out. I looked around and I was at the plate. How did I get there? I didn't even see the pitches. I didn't even see the game. Low, ugly boos were starting in the stands.

Hurst wasn't that good a pitcher, you know. I mean maybe he did beat us in two games, but we beat him the seventh. He just wasn't as good as a Scott, Ryan, or Knepper. We weren't even in the games those first two nights, and that was the problem.

I was walking through the game. I was called out on strikes in the second inning, walked in the fourth inning, was called out on strikes again in the sixth inning, and walked again in the ninth inning. Oh, I caught some fly balls.

Somebody scored in that game—let me see, Jim Rice. That's it. Rice scored on Timmy Teufel's error when he let a ground ball get through his legs. We were in such a coma in the dugout that we didn't even know we'd lost. Actually we didn't know the game had started. Davey tried to whip us up and we kept on saying, "But it's Boston." And Davey kept on talking about a "bad moon on the rise," but we didn't know what the hell he was talking about.

Ron was very gentlemanly about Teufel's error. "Hey," he kept on telling everybody who would listen, "Teufel didn't lose the game. We didn't score any runs. Hurst won the game."

"Right, Ron. Whatever you say. Where you guys wanna go after the game? You comin', Doc?"

"No, man, I got some business."

"Whatever."

And that was how we staggered into game two.

Ah, game two. Doc was going to draw us even. Doc was going to shut the Red Sox down while Keith, Gary, Lenny, and I knocked Roger Clemens out of the box. The New York fans had the K signs out even before they played the national anthem. It would have been nice if my brain had showed up for game two, but I couldn't get my mind off Lisa. Had she left the house? Was she at her mother's house in Altadena already? What would I say to her when I got back home? What about little Darryl?

"Yerrrouttt!"

Huh? Three strikes already? Jeez, man, but that was fast. Clemens ain't so puny. Hey, Davey, what's the score?

"Whaddayoo care? You ain't even in the game."

Sorry I asked. Don't worry, Doc. We'll pound 'em outta here in the next inning.

"You better hit, Darryl!"

Say what? Who said that?

Now it's Clemens coming up to bat for Boston in the top of the third with Spike Owen on first base—Gooden walked him on a 3-2 pitch—none out. He sets. There's Doc's pitch. It's a bunt down the first base line. Owen is on his way to second, Keith Hernandez scoops it up, spins, throws—it's into the dirt right at Santana's feet and Owen is safe at second with Clemens safe at first. I score that an error on the throw for Hernandez. That's his first error in a long time, but what a time to have one.

Hey, Keith, man. What's up?

Waaaaaaake up, Hernandez!

In the game, I struck out in the second inning, flied out in the fourth to Dwight Evans on the warning track (I thought that one was gone, but it dropped on me), struck out again in the fifth, and grounded out to Owen in the seventh. We lost game two 9-3. Wade Boggs, Bill Buckner, and Marty Barrett hit Doc hard, and Rick Aguilera didn't do much better. Nor did El Sid. It was a disaster. Everything we'd accomplished all season was unraveling right before our eyes. Even the Astros were calling the clubhouse to find out what was wrong. "I'll pitch," someone told me Mike Scott had volunteered while he watched game two on TV. "Give me a set of pinstripes. Bygones are bygones." I heard that Nolan Ryan was complaining that we were playing so badly we were making Houston look bad.

And what happened to Darryl?
Where is he?
Darryl sick?

"I wanna talk to Lisa."
"You just wait till the Series is over and you talk all you want."
"How's . . . ?"
"Boy's fine. Watchin' you on TV. You come back when you're ready.'
Click!

"I want you guys to rest," Davey told us after game two. "I want you guys to stay in your rooms and don't go out." He was serious and mad. He hadn't even scheduled a practice on the day before game three. "Some of you have played in Fenway before in exhibition games and you know darn well that this is a crazy park. No big green monster. No walking through on the numbers. We're gonna win this game by hitting Boyd's ass right off the mound. We can hit this guy; he's very vulnerable to the kind of batters we have. Go after him early. Take whatever you can get. Don't let him get set up. Hit him and he falls apart. Now rest."
He didn't have to tell us twice. We just dropped in place and stayed there for twenty-four hours. We didn't think about Boston or Oil Can Boyd. All we thought about was solid sleep.

Davey took a dump-truckful of criticism for giving us the day off.

"Dem slobs?" the papers wrote. "Whadiddeydo ferrah dayoff?"

But Davey Johnson stuck to his guns, even though, according to rumors, the boys in the Mets' front office were getting itchy under the collar about our performance. "They don't need practice," he announced to the press. "These guys are bone tired. With a day's rest, they'll clean up."

And so, on the evening of the third game, Oil Can Boyd looked into the eyes of the Mets batters. Two pitches into the first inning, Lenny Dykstra belted a home run into the right field stands. Here it comes.

Before Mr. Boyd could even think about getting it together, he'd given up a single to Wally Backman, another single to Keith Hernandez, and a hard double to Gary Carter that drove in Backman and moved Keith to third. We were ahead 2–0 with none out, and Oil Can was staggering around the mound like he had just gone a round with Tyson. Oil Can didn't even know where he was. Whatever had gotten to Boyd's pitching was infecting the entire Boston team.

My turn. Watch this, guys. See that green wall over there. Just watch this.

WHIFFFFFF!

I barely even looked up at Ray Knight, who passed me coming out of the on-deck circle. Maybe he said something like, "Nice cut, Darryl," but I didn't even hear him. I stood looking at the dugout floor, my back to the field. I could feel Davey Johnson's eyes burning into me.

There was one out now, mine, when Ray Knight tipped a slow grounder down the third base line and time seemed to stand still again. It was gonna break Boston's way and end our little rally, or so it seemed. Wade Boggs scooped up the ball and threw to catcher Rich Gedman to make the play on Hernandez, who had broken for home. At the same time, Gary Carter was on his way to third. Gedman chased Keith back toward third and then threw back to Boggs, but Keith slid headfirst safely back to the bag. Boggs then threw to shortstop Spike Owen to nab Carter on his way back to second. Carter stopped and was in a rundown. Suddenly Keith Hernandez faked a break for the plate, Owen turned to throw home, Keith returned to third, and in that moment Gary made it back to second. Davey Johnson was jubilant, jumping up and down at the teamwork between Keith and Gary. "See that, see that," he kept on screaming in the dugout. "You gotta believe!"

Ray Knight, of course, was safely on first and the bases were loaded on what the scorecards said was a fielder's choice. But the Boston fans were staring in complete shock at what was unfolding on the Red Sox infield. Could this really be happening?

Inside the dugout, Davey was wild. If the guy could have kissed himself in public and gotten away with it, he would have. "I knew it," he kept saying to anyone who would listen —coaches, players, fans, umps, anyone. "Sonofabitch, I knew it! All these guys needed was a little sack time."

I wish I were a part of this team. I hope I get a hit.

Up to the plate steps our designated hitter—after all, this is an American League park—Danny Heep, who lines the first pitch right over second base for a clean single. Keith and Gary score, and Ray advances to second. Mookie then strikes out and Rafael Santana bounces one to Wade Boggs, who makes the play on Heep at second to end the inning. So we're up by four runs and I'm cheering as we go out there to shut the Red Sox down. The Sox scored a run in the third, but Bobby Ojeda did the rest of the job for us, with help from McDowell, who came on in the eighth. We scored three more runs late in the game and we went back to Fenway the next night only one game down.

"You gotta focus on the game tonight, Straw, and not on your problems," Davey said to me privately before the start of the third game. "Whatever it is, it's got to go on the shelf until this Series is over."

What else could I do but nod? I was trying. I was trying so hard my brain was hurting. I even told myself I wouldn't drink, wouldn't go out on the town so's I could keep my head clear. I was near the end of my rope. I knew Davey was near the end of his rope, too. If I walked through another game, my ass would be outta there and there was nothing I could do about it. Damn, I hated how women could mess up your concentration. If she had only waited till after the playoffs, we coulda worked all this out. Instead, she pulled the trigger and then split. I couldn't blame her, though, only myself. And that was the problem. Had to put it away. Had to put it away. Had to put it away.

Game four, second inning, no score.

CRACK!

Shoot! The ball only squirted off my bat. Bad pitch. By the time I'd taken three steps toward first, Marty Barrett had already fielded the ball on two bounces—right into his glove—and flipped it to Bill Buckner at first for the first out. I was in the same rut I'd been in the night before, making nothing happen. I heard the crack of Ray Knight's bat behind me and saw our dugout get up and cheer Ray's base hit. Any minute now the public address announcer was going to tell how I'd beaten up my wife in Houston and how she had moved out of the house and wouldn't talk to me on the phone. Would that have made things easier or harder?

I turned around to see Danny Heep ground into a double play that ended the inning. As the Mets piled out of the dugout, I could feel what the guys were thinking, but not saying—"Good work, Straw." "Nice going, Straw." And worse, "Thanks, Straw."

I was beginning to dread going up to bat again. We shut Boston down in the second and third, and in the dugout for our half of the fourth, Davey again was staring at me so hard, I could feel the pressure from behind his eyeballs. As he walked by me, he whispered, "Try *not* hitting a home run. Just connect and don't worry. You're due. The numbers are with you."

Too bad the force wasn't with me, I thought, as Backman opened the inning with a rifle-shot single over pitcher Al Nipper's head. Nipper threw a strike to the next batter, Keith Hernandez, and then Davey put the hit-and-run sign on for the next pitch. Somebody in the Boston dugout must have read his mind because Nipper's next pitch was a pitchout, but . . . *Whoa!*

Mex threw his bat at the pitch and actually hit a grounder to the shortstop. Keith was thrown out, but Backman made it to second and we had a runner in scoring position with Gary Carter in the batter's box. Gary didn't wait for Nipper to start setting him up. He belted the first pitch right over the big green monster in left, bouncing it off the screen and leaving the Boston fans gasping for air, while the thousands of Mets fans who had driven up to Fenway were screaming. Then the Boston fans recovered and tried to shout them down. This Series was beginning to feel like a South American soccer game.

We were up 2-0.

"Do it for *you*, Darryl," Davey said to me. "Pressure's off. We're already ahead."

He was wrong, but the psychology was appreciated. There is sometimes more pressure to join a winning team than to create a winning team. I was already writing this Series off because I couldn't whip up the emotion. Then I saw Nipper's pitch curve away at just the right speed for . . . *Crack!*

The fans leapt to their feet as the ball soared into left and bounced off the green monster, and I was standing on second with a double. The Boston fans were quiet as Ray Knight stepped to the plate. He and Nipper dueled till the count was full. I led off second: "Yoo-hoo, Geddddd-man. Here I am." Then Ray lined the next pitch right over Nipper's head for a base hit and I took off like a rocket. I didn't look at anything except third base coach Buddy Harrelson as he waved me home. And I didn't stop running until I was at our dugout steps and high-fiving everybody I could find. I was run number three, and we were finally getting it together again, right here at Fenway.

Davey came over to me again in the sixth, just after Gary Carter hit a little double down the right field foul line that confused the hell out of everybody. "Move the runner, Darryl," he said. "We don't need the homer. We're already ahead. No outs, just get Carter to third."

Maybe this will work, I thought, as I swung at a tempting little just-too-high curveball, scooping it out of Rich Gedman's mitt and yanking it hard and deep to right. I'd hit the thing harder than I thought. Dwight Evans almost fell over backward on his way to the fence. That woulda been a kick, getting two or three bases on an error. But Evans recovered himself and made the catch against the wall. Gary tagged up and made third easily. Though we didn't manage to score Carter, I'd done my job, and I could see Davey kind of half winking at me from the dugout. "That's using your head, Straw," I said to myself. Now if only I could block the pain in my soul over what was happening with Lisa, I might have a good Series yet. If she would only talk to me, then I could stop punishing myself.

When they brought in Steve Crawford to relieve Al Nipper in the top of the seventh, Davey said that Boston believed they could still pull the game out. If they could shake Darling for a few runs and shut us down, the numbers gave them an even chance. Then he looked around the dugout at all of us who were due and gave us the glaring eyeball that said, "Hit the ball." With two outs, Mookie Wilson was still on first after having singled, and Davey clearly was not happy. Lenny Dykstra was up and he took Crawford's first pitch low for a ball while Mookie stole second. Crawford's next two pitches were strikes, and Davey was holding his breath. Then on Crawford's next delivery, Dykstra swung with all his little might and pounded an inside curve deep into right, where I had sent Dwight Evans the previous inning. Evans got the edge of his glove on the ball, deflected it up as he stumbled, and actually lifted the ball over the right field wall for a home run. It was happening to Boston again, as the numbers came right up and stood beside Davey in our dugout.

Now the score was 5-0 and our batters were finally getting their range. Keith led off the eighth with a deep fly to right that Evans—a busy man that night—caught just before it went bye-bye. Then Gary Carter let Crawford get two strikes on him before taking on the green monster again with a home run into the screen in left—6-0. Got to get in on this, I said. Get aggressive. Got to make runs happen. I drove a single past second baseman Marty Barrett, who was playing too close to first. Maybe I could steal off Rich Gedman, too.

We were six runs up, so when Ray struck out and Gedman seemed to pause, I broke for second: "Got to make things happen." But Barrett got to the bag just in time to take the throw and slap on the tag. Hurt, too, and Davey didn't like what he saw. I could see it in his face. But he didn't say anything, and the game ended at 6-2 Mets.

Now the World Series was tied at two games each and had settled into a duel of managers. The Boston sportswriters accused Sox manager John McNamara of throwing the fourth game away by starting Al Nipper, who had an ERA of over 5 for the season.

What's the point? they asked. *The guy gives up too many runs. Where's Clemens? Where's Hurst? Give Boyd another chance.*

We got it knocked, ya dummies, McNamara replied. *Lookit— Hurst, Clemens, Boyd all get to pitch on at least four days' rest while Gooden and Darling only get three days. Davey Johnson's in trouble and he knows it. This is our yeeah, boys.*

Davey tried to settle us down before game five, but we could see that there were so many possibilities playing out in his brain that he looked like he might go on overload. He knew we weren't playing up to speed. He knew that Boston just wasn't as good as we were and that we shouldn't be 2-2. It just wasn't right. Better than 3-1 theirs, he said, but 3-1 ours was more what it should be! The key was Hurst. We should be able to beat Hurst.

But in game five, while Davey thought about the laws of probability, Bruce Hurst scattered ten hits through nine innings, allowing us only one run in the eighth and another in the ninth. Meanwhile, the Red Sox jumped all over Doc, who had to be relieved in the fifth. Boston won the game 4-2. Sure I got a hit. Sure there were nine other hits. But we weren't playing as a team, Davey said in the dugout. He was pissed. Hurst had managed to break us up as a team, so all we got were two runs for our work. And now, down 3-2, we had to face Roger Clemens in game six. Even if we beat him, Davey said, a smart manager would start Hurst again in game seven. Why not? He had beaten us twice, and this time there was no magic sixth game that would keep him away from us.

"No, fellas," he said. "This time you got to win six *and* seven. And you get Hurst in game seven. I gotta shake you guys up."

Davey's confidence in his numbers was getting a little shaky. This situation wasn't in his computer. There were a few of us, including Keith, who thought that maybe Davey saw the numbers going the other way. Clemens and Hurst—both of them had dominated us before. It did not look good. At least we had a day off to drag ourselves back to Shea. At least I could try the house again.

"It's like I told you," I heard that voice in the receiver again. "Like I *been* tellin' you. Like I'm gonna keep on tellin' you every time you call from New York. You ain't gonna get nothin' fixed over the phone while you in New York playin' ball and she out here watchin' you onna TV. You kids just gonna start fighting again and somebody's gonna hurt somebody and you got a little boy to watch out for. You wanna talk to Lisa. You get done with your game and get yaw *butt* home! Darryl, you got to grow *up*!"

No help at that end! I still feel rotten. What's new in Queens?

"The outcome of this Series depends on your fortitude, your endurance, your perseverance, and your stout hearts," Cashen said. We didn't know what he meant, but that's what he said.

"And we still can do it," Davey rejoined. Davey, poor Davey, whose numbers, he himself feared, had finally taken a powder. But Fortune, ah, that was a different story. Fortune, who had been dismissed by Davey Johnson as fickle in favor of his probability equations, finally decided to spend her time with the boys from New York City.

Game six: The Day the World Stood Still. History! Drama! Art! It needs an epic rap to re-create it, not just a few lines of sportswriter's prose. You have to perform it, not just describe it.

You would have thought this was a rerun of *Rocky* from the way the New York papers described the face-off between Bobby Ojeda and Roger Clemens in game six. "This is not a one-on-one thing," Bobby kept saying. "It's a team effort." He said that he had no grudge against Boston and had nothing to prove against Roger Clemens. Clemens is one of the finest pitchers in baseball today, Bobby said. Ah, Bobby, Bobby, Bobby, very political. Just the kind of stuff that the papers like to feed on. It's not a grudge match, oh no. So what if the Sox traded you away, kicked your butt out of Boston in favor of Clemens and Hurst? Kicked you so hard that you didn't land until you made two orbits around the earth and came crashing through the Mets clubhouse roof. Now, Bobby, you have your chance. In uptown New York dance clubs—waaaaay uptown— by the fountain in Washington Square Park, along the streets in SoHo, even up and down La Brea Avenue in my hometown, little brothers with their boom boom boxes everywhere will be rappin' your sound:

Bobby Ojeda in the top of the first,
Throwing his pitches with a furious thirst.
Sez: "I'm not Lendl and Clemens ain't Mac,
The Mets will take the momentum back."
Davey felt his numbers pounding in his brain,
Roaring through the tunnel like the Sev-en train.

Game six. In the top of the first, leadoff hitter Wade Boggs singled off Ray Knight's glove. Bobby got rid of the next two batters, but then Evans lined a long double into left that scored Boggs: 1-0 Boston.

We looked like losers against Clemens in our half of the first as both Lenny Dykstra and Wally Backman were called out on strikes and Keith Hernandez flied out, all so fast you'd think we were tired of having to bat. The Sox got another run in the top of the second inning, and I almost made a terrible error, but recovered just in time to catch Billy Buckner's fly ball to right. I was still thinking about Lisa, and I knew that Davey was watching every misstep, every hesitation, every swing and miss. Soon, unless I struck some fear into the Boston pitchers, he would do something. I began to be afraid and frustrated, not good feelings to have in a World Series.

They walked me in the second inning, the stupid SOBs, and I stole second. See that, Davey? Heads-up baseball. See that? But Davey wasn't looking. He was bummed because Gary had flied out before I got up, and Ray Knight and Mookie Wilson both struck out afterward. Not good, fellas.

Bobby O throws deuces, curving down and in.
Whiffs Jim Rice and Gedman with his deadly spin.
Bobby buzzing beeballs never seen but heard,
Blowing by the Bosox in the top of the third.
Davey felt his numbers pounding in his brain,
Roaring through the tunnel like the Sev-en train.

"Why don't you guys just blow taps?" somebody called out in the dugout with two out in the bottom of the third. "Liven this place up."

"Go, Lenny!"

Bam!

Owen twists out of position at shortstop in order to play the odd bounce.

"Dig it out, Lenny!"

Yerrout!

That was the Mets' third inning.

"Go, Gary!" (With two outs in our fourth.)

Bliiiip. (Ground ball to Clemens.)

"Dig it out, Gary!"

Yerrout!

Davey Johnson was screwing up his face into a frown and twisting the end of his mustache. Then in the fifth inning:

Darryl draws a walk while waiting for his pitch,
Then he steals second like a son of a bitch.
Knight, Moo, *Moo-kie* single right over first.
Darryl streaks home like a lightning burst.
Evans out in right field bobbles like a nerd,
Looking for the ball, he lets Knight take third.
Heep's double-play ball cuts Knight loose,
Ray truckin' home and it's all tied at deuce.
Now Davey sees the numbers playing on his brain,
Roaring through his psyche like the Sev-en train.

"Play your numbers." Davey had to make moves to keep McNamara guessing. In the seventh, he pulled Bobby O for Roger McDowell, who walked Marty Barrett. Barrett eventually scored after an error and a double-play attempt, and that put Boston up by one. In our half of the seventh, we did nothing. In the eighth inning, McDowell got into trouble again. With two outs and the bases loaded, Davey pulled Roger for Jesse Orosco, who put out the fire by getting Bill Buckner to fly out to Lenny Dykstra in center.

Then, in the eighth, Fortune crossed the field. First, in the top of the inning, Clemens developed a blister on his pitching hand, and McNamara removed him for a pinch hitter. So, in the bottom of the inning, Calvin Schiraldi was on the mound. Davey sent Lee Mazzilli up to bat for Jesse Orosco. Lee bounced a hard single into right on Schiraldi's first pitch. I could see Davey looking approvingly at Lee's aggressive cut. I could guess what was going through his mind as he cast a meaningful glance in my direction, but I'd already stolen a base to put myself in scoring position, so I wasn't worrying. That Crenshaw H-U-S-T-L-E was back in my base running, and everybody saw it. At least I hope they did.

Lenny Dykstra, trying to sacrifice Lee Mazzilli to second, bunted right back to the mound. But Schiraldi threw late to second, and Lee and Lenny were both safe. First and second with no outs. Wally Backman moved up both runners with a sacrifice bunt, so McNamara had Keith Hernandez walked intentionally to load the bases. Then, on a 3-0 count, Gary Carter hit a line drive to deep left field that was caught but allowed Lee Mazzilli to score and Lenny Dykstra to take third. One in, two out, game tied 3-3. Davey Johnson gave me the hairy eyeball as I walked to the batter's box from the on-deck circle:

Fans are shouting DARRR-UL, all of Shea's a din.
Schiraldi looks around the bases, pitches down and in.
Fans are shouting DARRR-UL, I gotta hit the ball.
Lisa's out in Altadena, she won't take my call.
Davey's in the dugout, giving me the glare.
I close my eyes and take a swing, but all I hit is air.
Now I hear them booing. Why did she leave town?
I hit a fly snagged deep in center, and close the rally down.
"Lee, take right. Straw, take a rest. You chased a sucker pitch!
I need guys now who'll hit the ball, not wallow in a ditch."
Now I see how numbers flash in Davey's brain,
Roaring through my eardrums like the Sev-en train.

I'd like to describe the rest of the game for you, but I didn't see it. I can describe what the ground looks like in the Mets' dugout at Shea because I got to know it pretty well during those two innings when the whole world was watching the most improbable ending ever to a World Series game. The fans who watched that game on television got wonderful close-up shots of me—some say sulking, others say pouting, others say crying—slumped in the dugout.

I heard from Keith Hernandez, who actually tried to console me in advance of game seven, that Rick Aguilera blanked the Bosox in their ninth, and Calvin Schiraldi did the same to "us" in the bottom of the inning. By the tenth, I was still pretty miserable because it seemed the whole world had turned against me at what should have been one of my proudest moments. I'll never drink again, I promised myself. I'll beg her to come back, I promised myself. I'll do anything!

When Dave Henderson hit a home run deep into the left field stands to lead off Boston's tenth, you could hear the rustling of fans moving toward the exits. I was thinking about going for the exit myself. The whole year, I told myself, was about to end in the tenth inning of game six after I'd been pulled because my brain was somewhere else. With two out, Wade Boggs doubled to left and Marty Barrett singled to center, scoring Boggs. It was 5-3 Boston before Rick Aguilera could put the fire out. But it seemed it was already too late.

Well, maybe not. Leading off the bottom of the tenth, Wally Backman hit a fly ball that drove Jim Rice back a few feet before he caught it in left. Then Mex hit a long drive that looked like it had possibilities for a couple of seconds, until Henderson got under it right near the warning track in center field and brought it in.

Keith just ran by me in the dugout and continued through to Davey's office in the clubhouse. He thought he'd watch the rest of the game on television, he told me afterward. He needed quiet. He needed to be alone. He felt sad, mad, and frustrated and wanted privacy. Wanted a brewskie. Who could blame him? The Boston Red Sox were already whooping it up on the field, jumping up and down like a bunch of stupid schoolboys. They were just asking for a licking, but would probably walk away with their first Series championship in a long, long time. Keith had a right to be pissed. Any New Yorker watching that game had a right to be pissed at that moment.

Davey was probably pissed too as he watched Gary Carter foul one off, take two balls from Schiraldi, and then belt a single into left. Keith watched, too, not daring to move. I looked up, still sulking, but aware that something might be happening. Davey sent in Kevin Mitchell to bat for Rick Aguilera. Hey, this was for the marbles, right? Davey wasn't missing any chances.

Kevin had one strike on him when he drove the next pitch over second for another single. We had the tying runs on base. Davey began to pace. Even he knew that the game might just be heading into strange waters. Ray Knight waited until he had two strikes on him to bloop a single into center that scored Gary Carter and advanced Mitchell all the way to third. Now the tying run was on third and the winning run was on first. McNamara had had enough. He replaced Schiraldi with Bob Stanley. Too late! The fans began calling for the impossible as their favorite player came to the plate.

The fans are screaming, "MOO-KIE, gotta make it
    rain.
MOO-KIE, MOO-KIE, MOO-KIE, even up the game.
Hex 'em, jinx 'em, MOO-KIE, scare us up a run.
Get Kevin Mitchell home from third before the
    inning's done."
Mookie gives the evil eye as Stanley rears and
    throws.
The ball then takes a wicked dip—off Gedman's
    glove it goes.
Mitchell comes home standing up—run number five
    for us.
Game's all tied, Knight's on second, and Davey's
    numbers bust.
"MOO-KIE, MOO-KIE, MOO-KIE," it sounds more
    like a prayer.
He hits the ball toward Buckner's glove, but wait: *the
    ball's not there!*
Suddenly the numbers explode in Davey's brain,
Lighting up the scoreboard like a Sev-en train.

We won game six partly because of Davey's faith in his
numbers and partly because the Boston Red Sox were just
thinking about their champagne too much. Keith Hernandez
saw the whole play and the unraveling of the Boston infield
from Davey's office in the clubhouse. He told me later that he
decided not to go back out on the field. He said he was glad he
stayed in Davey's office to watch the game because it gave him
a different perspective. It allowed him to enjoy it, beer in
hand. He saw on Davey's big TV how Billy Buckner finally
realized that the ball had rolled between his legs, as Ray
Knight came in to score the winning run. It was the Mets, 6-5,
and we were all tied up at three games apiece. I looked up from
the dugout floor as the field exploded and people were rushing
around everywhere as if a fire had broken out, and I uttered a
promise to anyone in hearing distance: "I'll play my heart out
tomorrow night. And I'll go back to California and another
shot at doing things right. I *believe* in the magic. I saw it
work!"

On the next day, a storm rolled up the Atlantic Coast, the
dark gray skies opened up, and there was a drenching, damp,
beautiful Northeast rain that beat down on apartment win-

dows and house roofs, that slowed the traffic in New York City to a crawl, and that rained out game seven, allowing me to stay in bed for as long as I wanted. It was a rest that both teams needed, especially us, because it felt like we'd been running a marathon since April. We'd played so many extra-inning games that we were hurting in places where we didn't know we had places.

I let the magic of the night before wash over me. You'd have to be made of stone not to feel that magic. Sure I felt that I'd messed up. I felt I'd been cheated of glory. I felt humiliated. I said to myself that bitter wounds were opened up that night that would still remain long after the World Series. Part of me, the part that wanted the world to go my way always, no matter what, was as mad as could be at Davey for putting me on my ass on the bench the night before. I gnashed my teeth and said I'd never forgive him for humiliating me. But then there was this family thing. At the very moment I'd been told to sit myself down in front of millions of fans around the world, I couldn't deny the part of me that *wanted* to see the Mets win because I had made them into my surrogate family. So I said to myself I would give it all another try.

I had slipped so badly during the year that my life had fallen completely apart. And yet as I rolled around in the bed that rainy morning in October on that day off, I could not make the Series go away. Rum would take the world away at nights, but the world would come back in the mornings like the tide coming in. I knew that I was screwing up in the Series, walking up to the plate like I had shit for brains and swinging at anything that looked remotely like a baseball, but the team was still alive. I was bitter, but I also sensed that there was another reality at work that I couldn't define or describe. The end of game six still seemed like it came out of a Looney Tunes cartoon instead of the sports pages. What was happening to me? To us?

I wouldn't "get it" until five years later—I certainly didn't see it that morning—but even in 1986, in the pit of my drunkenness, bitterness, and self-pity, there was a force at work in my life that was moving me to an acceptance and an understanding of who I was and what I had to do. It was still a long way off, but what happened in game six made an impression in me that stayed even during the dark years of 1987 through 1990 when at times I felt no better than a dog chained to a backyard fence. At those times, when I looked back on the afterglow of it, the magic of game six in the 1986 World Series told me that there was still hope in the world.

Maybe John McNamara still felt he had a little luck left as he looked up at the gray New York rain from inside his hotel room. Now Bruce Hurst would get the extra day's rest he needed to pitch the final game in his third appearance in the World Series. How many other pitchers have won three times in a World Series? I don't know if McNamara had the figures in his head, but Davey did.

"It's a rare occurrence," he told us. "It's rare enough that I don't put any stock in the numbers. He's working against the law of averages, only he don't know it. And I'll tell you a secret of life, fellas. If a man thinks that he's working with the numbers when he's really working against the numbers, then you got him."

"Does that mean we win?" we asked Davey.

"It means you don't have to be afraid of Bruce Hurst or anybody. Bruce Hurst is vulnerable, and you guys are the folks who will show him just how vulnerable. The numbers rarely lie. But when they do, it's for a good reason."

But Davey wasn't Mr. Mellow in the bottom of the second inning of game seven. Darling took leadoff batter Evans to a 3-2 count and then Evans took him over the left field wall for a home run. And I wasn't happy at all when the next batter, Gedman, hit a stupid fly to right that I wound up knocking over the right field wall for another homer. That didn't endear me to the hometown fans. But then again, I wasn't in a fog anymore and was determined to help win this thing for the Mets once and for all. I was sick and tired of this Boston bullshit as I stood there in right field waiting for the next batter to send one of Ron Darling's basketballs into the atmosphere. I was especially pissed at Davey, but then Lee Mazzilli had gotten that hit two nights ago while I mooned around like a high-school kid. Well, not tonight, guys. Tonight I kick some Boston ass all the way back up Route 128. But the Sox still weren't finished in the second inning: Wade Boggs singled to score Marty Barrett, and the Sox ended the inning up 3-0. We had to make trouble.

Our own second inning was painful. It was frustrating for me because even though I had a good swing, I flied out to left. Still, I knew I was back in the groove. It would happen for me tonight, I told myself. I was going to get a home run tonight. I would tell Davey the same thing just in case he had designs on my position in right field. Meanwhile, after Ray Knight singled, Gary Carter and Kevin Mitchell both grounded out, and Knight was left stranded on first.

I was even more confident after my next at-bat, in the fifth, when I jerked a deep fly to right field that drove Evans back so far, I thought he too might just knock the ball over the wall. But he backed up against the wall and made the catch. Everybody at Shea knew it was just a matter of time, and now I knew that Davey knew it too. We just had to keep Boston from pulling too far ahead before we started our own rally, because our own rally was definitely coming. We knew we were going to win game seven because nobody could win game six the way we did and still go out losers.

After Boston went down one-two-three in the top of the sixth, Davey decided to turn the hitting machine on. He had replaced Darling with Sid Fernandez in the fourth, and now he pulled El Sid out for a pinch hitter, Lee Mazzilli. It was the right choice, because Lee drilled a single through the gap between second and third, and Mookie Wilson followed with a single right over Wade Boggs's head. All the guys in our dugout were on their feet. Hey, it was the seventh game and Davey knew that we could win it all. This was what we had waited through '84 and '85 to experience, and Davey was telling us not to let down the fans who had supported us last year. This was to be our tribute to them.

To my eyes, Hurst seemed to be tiring quickly and losing his control. He walked Timmy Teufel to load the bases, and Keith Hernandez, seething mad and full of power, walked up from the on-deck circle. Keith showed Hurst no respect whatsoever. He sent his second pitch deep into left center for a long single that scored both Mazzilli and Mookie. Timmy went to third and Davey sent Wally Backman in to pinch-run for him. Gary Carter's blooper to right scored Wally, but Keith was tagged out at second, Evans to Owen. Then I belted a line drive toward Jim Rice in left that I thought would drop in for a hit, but he made a diving catch. The inning was over, but we had three runs and a tie ball game.

Now I was satisfied by the way the game was turning around. I forced myself to put the bitterness I was feeling on hold. Like my problems with Lisa, I would deal with it later. I even thought that maybe it would float away on a sea of Remy Martin and get lost over the horizon. Come back to me in a bottle after the season. I had planned some heavy drinking later.

I was trying to act like a part of the team again, to help pull out this game and become a member of a world championship team. I was trying, at least for now. It was a positive act. Davey wasn't hostile to me, because he knew that I was trying even though I wasn't getting hits. "Settle down," he kept telling me. "You're due. Just believe in that and don't push the bad pitches." He told me over and over again to keep my head clear, and that made a world of difference.

Davey was working with me. He knew I was dealing with problems, but he was helping me postpone them until *after* the game by showing he understood. Just the knowledge that Davey understood I was in trouble was support enough. I could handle my problems, knowing I had just a little bit of emotional support. It's a bad, bad feeling when you're out on a limb all by yourself and can't turn to anyone for help. You don't actually have to get help. You just need to know that there's someone there who knows you're hurting. Davey did, right during the game, and that's what helped me get out of the hole I was in. He made me feel part of the family instead of just a troubled kid who'd been told to stand in the corner.

In the seventh inning, Roger McDowell relieved El Sid and retired the Red Sox one-two-three. In the bottom of the inning, McNamara sent Calvin Schiraldi in for Hurst, who'd been pulled for a pinch hitter. Our leadoff batter was Ray Knight, who'd been hitting like a machine during this Series. Schiraldi wasn't ready for Ray's incredible intensity. Knight fouled off the first pitch and then took two balls. Now he knew he had the edge. He hit Schiraldi's next pitch over the left center field wall to put us into the lead by a run. Dykstra, pinch-hitting for Kevin Mitchell, then hit a single. He advanced to second on a wild pitch to Santana by a very tired and nervous Schiraldi. Everybody could see he wasn't long for the game. Davey Johnson could see it too, and was back to his confident—"the numbers are on our side"—self. He even urged me to go for a home run, though he also told me we didn't really need it. A little reverse psychology, Davey?

Rafael Santana kept our rally going with another single, which scored Dykstra. McDowell then moved Santana over to second on a sacrifice bunt. McNamara had had enough and pulled Schiraldi for Joe Sambito, who walked Mookie intentionally and Wally unintentionally, to load the bases. The Sox were looking for a double play to close the inning, but Keith Hernandez found his range and took a Sambito pitch deep to left center for a sacrifice fly that scored Santana. McNamara pulled Sambito for Bob Stanley, and the Bosox looked like they were in a panic. Stanley got Carter on a grounder to retire the side, but we'd picked up three runs and led 6-3. At last we looked like the first-place team that had beaten the Astros, the team that the oddsmakers had picked to win the Series. At last we were playing like winners.

In the top of the eighth, Boston mounted a rally against McDowell, throwing a dramatic scare into the Mets fans at Shea and watching on television. Billy Buckner and Jim Rice led off with singles, and Dwight Evans doubled, scoring both runners. Whoops! No one out, tying run in scoring position. Time for the fireman. Time for a little scum bunch action. Davey Johnson brought in Jesse Orosco and gave him his final instructions just by the look in his eye. No need for a computer printout, Jesse. You throw whatever you have to throw, and you don't have to make it look pretty. You get us outta this inning and maybe Straw will give you something more to work with in the ninth. Whaddaya say about that, Darryl?

Do it, Jesse. The scum bunch sticks together.

Jesse got Rich Gedman to line out to Wally Backman at second. He struck out Dave Henderson. And he got Don Baylor, pinch-hitting for Spike Owen, to rap an easy bouncer to Rafael Santana at short. The side was out. Thank you, Jesse. You kept your word; now I'll keep mine.

John McNamara ain't lookin' so good. Maybe he sees I'm putting the evil eye on Bob Stanley, so he brings in Al "my new pal" Nipper to face me. I *own* Al Nipper. He's mine! I let the Nip Man throw two strikes by me—"ain't my style, Al"— waggled my old bat for his next pitch, and then welcomed him back to Shea with a home run blast from the past that went way over the right center field wall. As I rounded second in a slow, *slooowww* trot while waving to the screams of the 55,000 Mets fans, I saw Davey looked ready to jump up and down. Now we were ahead by two, 7-5. We both knew that I was going to be facing some serious problems in the off season, but as I came home from third, I felt that nothing could take this away from me. Despite the Nip Man's deep glare of hatred in my direction, we were going to win, and I was a part of that victory.

Al Nipper had barely recovered from the earthquake that had just rocked Shea when Ray Knight stepped up. He singled right up the middle. Lenny Dykstra then got too anxious on a lousy pitch and bounced out short to first. One out, but Ray had advanced to second.

Now McNamara decides to get fancy. He has Rafael Santana intentionally walked, to get to Jesse Orosco and set up a force play at third. Maybe Jesse will hit into a double play and close out the inning for you guys, whaddaya think? Hey, be careful, Al. This is a National League park—no DH—and our pitchers sometimes hit the ball.

Now whadda *you* wanna do, Jesse? Nipper throws him a ball and then a strike. You see what I see there, Jesse? You can hit this guy. Boston's already given up on winning. You can smell it. Get yourself some room for the ninth, Jesse. Get it with your bat. Nipper delivers his next pitch and old Jesse slices a bouncer right up the middle for a base hit that scores Ray Knight for another insurance run. Now we lead 8-5 and Santana is on third.

McNamara decides he's had enough of Nipper, who takes the long walk to the showers. Now it's Steve Crawford facing Mookie Wilson with Santana on third and Jesse on first. Steve ain't Mr. Calm and Collected himself. He bounces the ball right off Mookie, who says, "I ain't mad, I just got a base," and trots down the first-base line, loading up the bases. From a sure victory in the bottom of the tenth, two nights ago, Boston is now staring at a sure loss. The Boston dugout was not a pretty sight.

Wally Backman is up and he wants in on the action. He raps a sharp bouncer to second, but Marty Barrett grabs it and fires to the plate to get Santana for out number two. The bases are still loaded for Keith Hernandez. Mex tries the same deal, bouncing the ball to second. This time, Barrett fields the ball and steps on second to close out the inning.

Now it's the top of the ninth and it's all on the shoulders of Jesse Orosco. Jesse bears down on Boston's Ed Romero with a look of controlled fury. He delivers a snake of a pitch that Romero chases and pops to Keith Hernandez, who makes the play in foul territory. Insult to injury on that one. Then Jesse's

cheapest slider tricks Wade Boggs into bouncing a high chop-
per to Wally Backman at second, who throws to Keith at first
for the second out.

It's breath-holding time. Davey has by now figured luck into
his equations for strategizing his ball games. Now the part of
me that was trying to be mature was sitting on my shoulder
and saying in my ear: "Straw, you hit your home run. You
rejoined this team. You're one out away from winning your first
World Series. You succeeded! Live your success and go home
and work out your problems." Those were the feelings clashing
in my mind and spirit as Marty Barrett stepped up to the plate.

How many Red Sox fans were jawing about the "Boston
curse" at that very moment, complaining about the Mets'
magic and the luck of Davey Johnson? How many fans spinning on bar stools in Sunnyside, Queens, or watching TV in
their living rooms in the huge housing projects along Lenox
Avenue, or sitting in taverns from Old Lyme to Poughkeepsie
to Sag Harbor to Bay Head Junction to Lawrenceville, were
not even daring to take a beer-drinker's whiz for fear of missing
the last out of the Series? How many people were watching the
look in your eyes, Jesse, as you went into your final windup?

WHIFFFFF!

Strike three!

Keith Hernandez and Wally Backman rushed to the mound
first. Then Gary Carter and Ray Knight. They were hugging
and kissing that sonofagun like the hero he was. Old Davey
lumbered out of the dugout as Mookie, Lenny, and I ran in
from the outfield to join the huddle. If the fans could have
come down from the stands, they would have. Frank Cashen's
favorite scoreboard exploded in fireworks as hundreds of reporters rushed to the Mets' clubhouse for their exclusives. We
were laughing and crying at the same time. Davey peeked out
from the huddle and gave me the winking eye. The part of me
that wanted to love him for his genius, courage, and comfort
smiled back. The part of me that always hated to be told "no"
held back. This was my greatest moment, and yet something
invisible was still holding me back as the rest of the world of
New York sports fans wept tears of absolute joy.

It had taken four full seasons for the Mets to build themselves into a world championship ball club. We almost made it
to the top in '84. Almost again in '85. And now in '86 we had
gone all the way. We had shown that we were made of better

stuff than most of the other teams in the National League. This was also the kind of year that any young baseball player looks forward to, the kind of year that defines you as a professional, the kind of year that also shows you your weak spots.

There would be ticker-tape parades and salutes. We would be honored by the mayor and other dignitaries. But deep down inside me, deep where not even I could feel them moving, my personal demons were already unraveling what should have been one of my greatest moments of personal triumph. I was feeling strangely empty, dangerously hungry, needy, and unfulfilled. I could already feel the pain that was waiting for me in California. I knew that my triumph would soon dissolve into loneliness and anger. I knew that this celebration would only be a small envelope in time, and I tried to hold on to it even as I felt it slipping away with the slow-motion whooping and wailing of my teammates on the Mets. They were my summertime family, but the winter was closing in.

I didn't like it, but I couldn't stop it. Evil was at work, throwing long shadows across my triumph, like the coming of night.

12

AS THE STRAW STIRS

February 1987, and I was flat on my back in my bed looking up at the ceiling fan in the damp, tropical, early spring Florida heat, trying to put the last three months together in my mind. It had been a straight slide down from the high of the playoffs and World Series in October. Since then, my life had fallen apart, and I was trying desperately to put the pieces together before the start of the new season.

I still had hard feelings toward Davey Johnson from last year. The whole world had turned against me since the end of October, I thought to myself. Davey was just another one of the enemies. You better believe I confronted Davey about that double switch in game six of the Series, when he took me out of the game. I told him right off that he'd made a mistake and I didn't appreciate looking like a fool. But he said that sometimes you don't agree with what your manager does and that's just too bad. He made the decision and I had to accept it.

Maybe someday I'd understand it, he said. But at the time it was a done deal, and fighting about it wasn't going to undo it.

On the flight home to California after the Series, I'd known that the troubles with Lisa weren't going to end. We got back together again during Christmas in our New York condo where we tried to piece our marriage back together. But there were too many demons, too many bad feelings. Lisa didn't want to be in New York; she wanted us to live in California. I wanted to live in New York. I was a champion. We got into another violent fight. There are different versions of that fight, but in divorce papers she filed later in Los Angeles in January 1987, Lisa charged that I hit her with a brass picture frame that I threw at her. I told her then and told her later that that was an accident, but at the time she was in no mood to believe me. Lisa didn't stay around to fight with me any longer. We needed to be separate for a while and she moved back to California to stay at her mother's house in Altadena. I wasn't happy about that and followed her to California to try to talk to her. I didn't know where we were going as a couple—our lives were coming apart so quickly—but I didn't want to make the same mistakes with her and little Darryl, Jr., that my father had made with my mother and us. Once we were on the way down, though, no thoughts of my father and mother or of the fights down in Crenshaw were enough to break our fall.

I was drinking very heavily in the winter before spring training camp opened. I was an alcoholic, but wouldn't realize or admit it until January three years later. My drinking with the boys in the scum bunch was only a beer drinker's party. But eventually, I needed to drink just to keep myself from seeing that the game of baseball I was trying to play and the pressures from the press and the fans I was trying to satisfy were impossible to reconcile. I continued to drink just to blot out the pain of having to face the impossibility of life. And as I started to fail, as each day gave me more and more opportunities to fail, and as each day I felt more and more alone in my misery, alcohol became more important. I drank at parties, I drank at clubs, I drank on the bus, I drank on planes, I drank alone.

During the middle part of January, I began going over to Lisa's mother's house early in the morning and howling like a tomcat for her to let me in so we could talk. "Lisa! Lisa!" I was in a lot of pain and I wanted my family back.

She charged, in the divorce papers she filed, that I was causing a disturbance and waking up the entire household. I denied that. I tried to break through the barrier she had put up around herself and my son. I didn't want to leave him without a father the way my father had left me. I was feeling angry—because I was trapped in the middle of two generations, without a father and kept from my son. I was losing control of myself fast, and the Mets' camp was only weeks away from opening. The Mets would become my family again when the season started, but I had hard feelings toward Davey from last October to work out. Why couldn't I just be mature? I needed some kind of a family around me if I hoped for any success at all.

I made one last attempt to talk to Lisa right after the Super Bowl in Los Angeles. It would be my last weekend before I had to go down to Florida, and I wouldn't be able to get away from the team until we had a break during the regular season. Whatever domestic problems you have during the season, you put them right on the shelf until after the season. That's why so many problems in baseball families remain unresolved for years, until the couples just drift apart. You're home one night, on the road for the next ten days, then home again.

In a professional team sport like baseball, basketball, football, and maybe even hockey, it's like you're married to your teammates and they become your family during the year. The performance of each member reflects on the entire group. You become tied to them in many ways as you compete with them for attention and money while supporting them for the team. You rely on them to support you. You rely on their loyalty. When it's pulled away from time to time during the season, you better be flexible enough and strong enough to understand why and fix it. I didn't. Too many marital relationships can't stand up to that kind of team pressure pulling you in different directions. My relationship with Lisa couldn't.

Lisa charged in her complaint that on Super Bowl Sunday I came over to her mother's house, where she and Darryl, Jr., were staying, and beat her. She said that I was drunk and violent and that I took her purse and stole money, jewelry, and credit cards out of it. The court granted Lisa an order barring me from contact with her, from going to her mother's house in Altadena, and from taking any of our joint assets. I also couldn't see my son, Darryl, Jr. I was not a happy camper in February when spring training camp opened.

To me, there's nothing so emotionally wrenching as a divorce. There's nothing that so obviously points up your failure as a human being. And there's nothing that reinforces your negative view of yourself as reenacting your parent's worst flaws in the presence of your own child. A voice starts up in your brain that says, "Life is hopeless." To be in a physical confrontation with my wife in which I acted out the role my father played in my life knocked me out more than words can describe. I think that began the final two-year slide for me that ended up in my having to go to the police station the night I threatened Lisa with a gun.

By the time I went to Port St. Lucie, I felt like a walking disaster. I wanted to pity myself because I had had a father I could only see from a distance at the park on weekends, and now my own son would have a father that he'd only see on television when the Los Angeles station broadcast the Mets' games locally. "Daddy's blowin' into town. Let's catch him at Dodger Stadium." It was making me sick to my stomach to think about it. I was trapped in a script I couldn't rewrite. But in a larger picture, it seemed like the whole world all of us on the Mets had created in 1986 had fallen right down around our ears after the celebrations of victory and the holidays. We had barely had time to rest and repair ourselves when the new season began.

I wasn't the only person going through hell as I lay there on my bed in the Florida heat. In January, the long-standing charges against Ron Darling and Tim Teufel in Houston were finally resolved, when they pleaded no contest to a misdemeanor charge of resisting arrest. Then Doc Gooden was charged in Tampa with possession of cocaine and a whole new situation flared up on the Mets. Dr. Alan Lans was flown to Florida in advance of our opening up camp down there to talk to Dwight and begin whatever had to be set into motion for Doc to go through rehabilitation.

There were some in the press who said that I was being blamed for Doc's problems because I was a heavy drinker and had influenced Gooden. He had fallen into the evil clutches of the scum bunch, they said. But it wasn't true. In fact, I didn't even know that Doc had a drug problem for sure until the news broke. There were rumors, of course, that Doc was in trouble. There were times when some of the players would be getting ready to go out after a game or go to dinner and Doc would have to go back to his hotel room to get something. He would tell us he'd meet us at the restaurant, but then he'd sometimes not show up at all. This wasn't what you'd call "aberrant" behavior or anything, but it was inconsistent and led to rumors that maybe Doc might be having problems with drugs. But no one knew anything for sure.

Athletes on professional sports teams are among the highest paid performers in the world. There's a certain craziness about putting on a uniform and going out to get physically beaten up by other people just like you, verbally abused by fans for whom you are performing, and criticized by a bunch of wimps in the press who couldn't do ten percent of what you do and have no idea what it takes to go back out there on the field day after day. If we didn't like it, we wouldn't do it, of course, but that isn't to say that it still isn't a little crazy.

In the middle of this oddball situation, the players, most of whom are actually millionaires in their twenties and thirties, have to be combinations of pure, emotional kids, business-minded adults, and politicians when it comes to the press. They have to go from risking injury by throwing themselves into an outfield wall just to stop a ball from going over a fence to handling very personal questions about the most intimate aspects of their lives. "When *did* you stop beating your wife, Darryl?" "How long were you porking that skirt over in Detroit?" "So how much will you have to cough up in this settlement?" "Do you have any *other* illegitimate children?" You have to answer questions like this right after you've had to pump up like a Green Beret just to gain a single game on another team. You walk into the locker room, find that all the problems you had before the game haven't magically gone away, and someone shoves a mike in your face. What would you do?

Therefore, and this is a major therefore, you have to pretend that the other athletes you play with are all adults who can handle their own problems even when you *know* they can't. It's denial, sure, but the kind of denial you have to practice in the artificial atmosphere of pro sports. You give each man his privacy and a great deal of personal space because you know that his space will be constantly invaded by outsiders throughout the year. Everyone you play with will be watched by the public on more levels than politicians or movie stars because they will be judged on the most basic levels of masculinity and physical performance. So if a player is having a problem with drugs, alcohol, or a relationship, as Doc and I were, you tend not to make it a topic of conversation or throw it in the guy's face. You stay far away from that guy's personal life unless he brings it right to your locker in the clubhouse and forces you to deal with it. That's how it was with Doc and me.

In that same January, Doc was also trying to work things out with his former fiancée, Carlene Pearson, whom he had broken up with the previous November after the World Series. At about the same time, Doc's parents told the press that eight months earlier, Dwight had fathered a child by another woman. Doc and Carlene agreed to meet in New York, but when she came to pick him up at La Guardia Airport in Queens, a routine X-ray search of her purse showed that she was carrying a .38 handgun. The newspapers said that she was charged with possession of a stolen handgun. Poor Doc must have been rocked to his knees.

The Darryl and Doc show was ready for another performance in 1987, except that Doc was being packed off to Smithers for rehab. Seeing Doc disappear behind the walls of Smithers like he'd been swallowed up was a scary thing because I knew I was on the same track, even if I wasn't admitting it to myself at the time. I told myself that booze was different from blow, but in my heart I knew that I was sliding down the same chute. The shadows of night were getting close, and despite the heat down in Florida, I was feeling the chill.

By March, things in my life had gone from bad to worse. The press had gotten hold of Lisa's complaint—it was, after all, a public document. It's bad enough to have to fight out your domestic problems using lawyers, but to fight them out in public is another matter. And things weren't coming together on the Mets either. The team seemed to be coasting on its victories from the previous season and not putting together a winning team for the coming season. I was as guilty of that as the next guy because I was letting the emotions of what I was going through spill over into my dealings with other people. That might be expected, but it's also expected that you'll control it.

Now I can understand that I was out of control because I didn't have a clue about dealing with my problems. When I felt the burden of what was happening on the team or with my career or with Lisa weighing down upon me, I'd either go out drinking or open a bottle of rum and drink it at home. Drinking had become my way of dealing, my way of forgetting what I had to face. The people at Smithers would eventually say that I was "medicating" myself with alcohol. But now I know that it was the demons, the unearthly spirits, that had taken control of me and were living on my fury. Once I exorcised them, I was able to see it all.

In one of our early exhibition games, we faced the Boston Red Sox in a replay, as the press always says, of the World Series. Replay my ass. When you play those types of exhibitions the only thing you want to do is to walk away without somebody breaking your legs or spiking your balls off. Nobody really cares, anyway, because you have a whole season in front of you, and this game doesn't even count. But it counted for Al Nipper, who was not a forgiving guy that spring. Okay, so I put it in his face when I pounded that homer in game seven and then took—what was it?—five or so minutes to walk around the bases while the fans went crazy. It was my first Series, my first Series game-winner, and my last home run of 1986. So maybe I wasn't cool about it. But then I'm not always Mr. Cool.

That was definitely no reason for Nipper to put a fastball right in the middle of my back during the exhibition game. Hurt! Hurt like hell. I threw the bat down and went stomping toward the mound to pound the brains out of his head, but a bunch of guys from the team and plate umpire Dave Pallone jumped all over me. Then both benches got up and squared off for a fight, but they separated us before anybody could throw a punch. But I was mad. I knew when I was being thrown at, and Nipper wasn't just trying to brush me back. He'd thrown to hurt. That was how the 1987 baseball began; with fighting, pain, hurt, and frustration. And that was how the entire year played out.

After our championship season, we had no more axes to grind. We felt there was nothing left to prove: we were the champs. That's why it's tough for a team to repeat. The myth of "all we gotta do is try" is gone. When you start the season by trying to take away somebody else's title, you believe that all you have to do is beat the other guy to win. But you don't "know" what it takes to beat him until you've won.

Then you learn that there's much more to it than simply winning by the rules. While you're basking in the glow of that World Series flag, getting mellow, you see that it took all sorts of things that "shouldn't" have happened to get you to the top. You "know" what it took to win and you realize that it was impossible to have pulled it off from the start. Once you test the truth—that you are vulnerable and impossibilities aren't supposed to happen—you are aware of gravity. You've seen the edge of the cliff, and you know that people who walk over it are supposed to fall off. Somehow you become softer. The memories of the pain are still too raw. You lose your edge. And everybody else is gunning for you and will pull many of the same tricks you pulled on them the year before. So you'd better be prepared to fight them just to stay alive. It makes you frustrated and it makes you angry. You begin to doubt. You begin to turn on yourself. We were protecting what we already had instead of going after what somebody else had, and that made us vulnerable.

By contrast, just the year before, we were aggressive, nasty SOBs looking for a fight, because we were carrying a grudge from 1985 when we thought we should have won it. That grudge, born during the three-game series in St. Louis, drove us through the entire 1986 regular season, even after we had beaten St. Louis in April and permanently taken over first place in the East. When games hung in the balance, we weren't afraid to increase the tension by getting into a brawl or telling other players off. Other teams began gunning for us. We turned ourselves into "top guns" physically as well as mentally, and had to pay the price fighters pay. We got beaten up as many times as we did the beating, but it created a psychological edge for us by making us seem intimidating. We were too worn out to repeat that in 1987.

In one of my favorite *Dallas* episodes, the year after J.R. was shot, Bobby Ewing complains to his father, Jock, that no one will give him the power to run Ewing Oil the way he sees fit. J.R., though still recovering from his wounds, is still in control. "Nobody gives you power," Jock tells Bobby. "Power is something you *take* from someone else. It's not worth anything unless you take it away from the person who has it. Then it's yours." Much the same can be said for winning a baseball championship. Most players feel they have to take the championship away from another team. They go after what somebody else has. In 1986, we went after the division championship that had been taken from us the year before by the Cardinals. After we won, we had fourteen more games to play to win the World Series. In 1986, everybody thought the National League pennant belonged to Houston because they had Nolan Ryan and Mike Scott and because they had beaten us so convincingly during the season. Therefore, we took it away from them. In the World Series, the victory was ours until Boston took it away from us by winning the first two games. We didn't have to look at what the Las Vegas oddsmakers were saying to realize that we had already given it up. Now we had to take it back. We did. And we kept on taking it back right through game six, when fate itself intervened on Mookie Wilson's and our behalf, and then in game seven, when we overcame a 3-0 deficit.

In 1987, there was nothing for us to take. We had it already. We were still not a mature enough team to sit back and beat away all comers. That was what the powerful New York Yankees did from the 1920s through the early 1960s, when they won at least five pennants in each decade. A team has to grow to that level of year-after-year performance. The Mets were far away from that. We didn't know how far until 1987 ended and we had to fight our way back in 1988.

Like most of the other players on the Mets, I had lost my edge. Like many other players, I was trying to put my life back together from out of hundreds of jigsaw puzzle pieces scattered around my room. And I had no set of instructions, no picture of the finished puzzle to guide me.

Then there were the baseball issues. I wanted to succeed, but I was still working out my feelings about Davey's having benched me last year. And to make matters worse, I'd look around the practice field at St. Petersburg and see guys just walking through the drill. Then Davey would look at me as if I was the only player on the Mets who was required to contribute anything. These guys didn't have their hearts in it at all, so I had to carry the team. I wanted to be on a team, not be the team; there's a difference. These guys felt like they were the world champions and the team to beat. Let the other teams work hard. The Mets had already won it. Now I was feeling that I was being made to carry the burden of the entire club and that I would get punished if I slacked off. Once that feeling starts to eat at you, you begin to throw your own quirks into the pot.

So I showed up late. I overslept. Sorry, Davey. But the guy fined me five-hundred-bucks. Here I am shelling out thirty-plus thousand a month to support my wife in her mother's house while I'm not even allowed to talk to her and Davey zaps me with a five-hundred-dollar fine. Hey, that was food money. I got mad and told him that I wasn't going to practice anymore if I was going to be singled out for such abuse. "Fine," Davey said. "Go home if you want to, but it's going to cost you another thousand."

Whaaat? I'm outta here.

"Darryl's not wet behind the ears. He's an established veteran who should know what's expected of him," I read in *The Sporting News*. Guess who said that? C'mon, guess. You know. Who's the guy who'll mouth off to anyone who puts a microphone in his face? It's Keith Hernandez. Who else?

Guys on the Mets were walking around like zombies that month. Gary Carter looked like he'd already taken a furlough for the year and Keith Hernandez was awash in his own problems. Davey's fining me for being late? There were guys whose bodies were standing on the field but whose brains where a million miles away. Late to batting practice? These guys weren't even there. "Hello, Lenny, anybody home?" But Davey focused all of the problems of spring training on me and my attitude. Sure, sure, everybody knew I was drinking more than my share, and they were pissed about it. But sometimes I think it was more than the booze, because of the way I was singled out. Let the other guys goof off as long as Darryl gets his hits. Darryl Strawberry will take care of us all, *and* he takes the blame when things go bad. It's bad enough panting around the Mets' clubhouse because you want them to let you into their family. After having to solve the whole team's problems during the day, you get to lapse into a Remy Martin–induced stupor at night. And that was mostly how I spent the 1987 season when I wasn't having to answer questions from Lisa's lawyers.

I was the fall guy because it was my fault that the team was in such trouble. Look at what some of the other players had happen to them: Timmy and the boys get into a fight down in Houston and there's no big to-do from the club; Doc goes to Smithers and I get the blame; Keith confesses to using cocaine in St. Louis and he gets a standing ovation. But here I was in the middle of an ugly and painful divorce and the club treats me differently from everybody else. Why? Why was I the only guy in the clubhouse who had to go out and play under the worst circumstances, when there were guys sleeping on the locker room benches. I killed myself to help the club that year and only got abuse. Maybe I had the look of an alcoholic about me. Maybe I didn't have the maturity to walk into Davey Johnson's office, tell him off for the umpteenth time about benching me in game six, and demand that he and I work out our problems once and for all. I simply let myself walk through the clubhouse with the awful sensation that I wasn't as good as the next guy. After the 1990 season, I also realized that part of that had to do with basic racist attitudes in baseball and on the Mets, but I wasn't mature enough in 1987 to pick that up. I just blamed myself. And Frank Cashen didn't help.

"All of us have personal problems," Frank Cashen said to the papers after Davey fined me for lateness and then doubled it because I wouldn't accept the fine. "But we can't let them interfere with our work or with the team."

And Keith Hernandez, of course, was the voice of authority. "Darryl deserved to be fined," he said. "You can't have one set of rules for twenty players and one set for four." I knew Keith was talking about me. Who the hell were the other three? But still, Keith's point was my point exactly, only we were looking at it from different sides. "Darryl just handled it emotionally and not with tact . . . . Darryl is frustrating to talk to sometimes, but he's got to learn to be on time."

Keith-eith-eith-eith-eith had spoken-oken-oken-oken-oken.

I'd been fined on and off for coming late to practice during spring training, especially on days when I wasn't playing, and fined for coming late to the ballpark in Chicago. I just stopped speaking to Davey Johnson after that. There was nothing more I could say to the man that would have made any sense.

It's opening day for the Mets' 1987 season and I've just hit a towering three-run homer to lead the Mets to a 3-2 victory over the Pittsburgh Pirates. The fans at Shea go crazy. The newspapers run to Mex, who says that he just wishes I'd talk more with the bat and less with the mouth. Thanks, Mex, for those timely words of wisdom.

I got into a lot of fights with teammates during 1987 because I believed I was the only person on the club who cared about winning when the season started. Then, when I stopped caring during the first two months of the season, the whole club turned on me as if I were working for the enemy. That's what happens when you lay yourself out for someone else, realize that you're acting like a fool because the other person doesn't care, pull back, and then take a knock because you refuse to extend yourself any longer. Part of it was racial, I know—I have to have the strongest back on the team so I can carry everyone—but another part of it was the whole nature of being an alcoholic.

Sure there were times when appearances made me look terrible. Take the "virus" incident, for example. I had a chance to cut a rap video on my own time. I'd been looking forward to doing "Chocolate Strawberry" for a long time. But at the same time I really did have a virus and was simply too weak to swing the bat meaningfully for two games against St. Louis at the end of June. Put somebody in who can hit instead of somebody who can't. So while staying away from the game because I was sick, I showed up at a studio to cut this rap track just because I had the chance. I grant you, it looked bad. But because of the double standard on the Mets, even my friends turned on me. Lee Mazzilli accused me of letting the team down. "When you're not one hundred percent," he said, "there are times when you have to dig a little deeper."

Take Wally Backman, Lee said. You take Wally Backman, Lee, because if I take him there'll be some damage done. Backman played with injuries. So did I, during the 1985 season, and no one cared. And team "captain" Keith Hernandez played after having given depositions in a divorce case for two days. Woo, woo, these guys are all-American heroes. Then Hernandez pipes up and says that Maz was speaking for a lot of guys on the team. I confronted Maz in the clubhouse after he gave his little sermon on a pregame show and let him know there were five reasons he should keep his mouth shut—the five reasons attached to my fingers that would make themselves felt.

Then Backman piped up to say that "Nobody gets sick twenty-five times a year." That really pissed me off. "I'll bust Wally in the face, that little redneck," I was quoted as saying. And I meant every word of it, too. And where was Davey? Where was Davey when I could have used some support, some intervention on my behalf? Behind his computer screen, that's where. And he actually managed to find the time to peek up from his keyboard long enough to quiet down the kids in the clubhouse as the team's season spun all the way into dreadful.

There was a double standard on the Mets; that's for sure. The Mets were resting on their laurels and still recovering from the intensity of the previous year; that's also true. But I know that if I could have only looked at my behavior in 1987 with the eyes I have in 1991, I would have seen just how destructive my alcoholism was and what the earthly spirits that were holding me down were doing to my career and my relationships with the other players.

I said it back then that those guys were a bunch of asses who would really miss me once I was gone. I didn't realize at the time, of course, that Frank Cashen would actually manage to trade most of them away before I became a free agent. But I really didn't want to play on a team of backstabbers and mean-spirited individuals who sniped at one another and at the only person who was winning games for them. I felt like I was a horse pulling the entire partying Mets team behind me on a cart, and if I paused to rest my back for a second or to get a drink of water, they'd scream that I was dropping them off a cliff. I was bitter, hateful, loathsome, angry, and mostly drunk.

It took my receiving a painful injury on the field to convince the Mets that I was serious about playing and about winning, but it came too late in the season to do anything for them. After I pounded a two-run homer off the Expos in Montreal in mid-September in the first inning, Expos pitcher Joe Hesketh bounced a fastball off my ribs in the next inning. That was one way to get me out of the game. They X-rayed me, of course, but when they found no fracture, I showed up ready to play the next night, bruised ribs and all. No yapping from Wally Backman that night when I got a base hit. A few days later I stole my thirtieth base for the season and then brought my post–All-Star break batting average to over .300.

The end of the season was as frustrating as the beginning. During that bleak September of 1987, no matter what I did to keep Mets drives going, our defense and offense conspired to lose the games. There were five times during the last month or so of the season when I drove in first-inning runs only to have the rest of the team sit back and do nothing. When I opened my mouth to the press, like Mex, all I got was grief. The press only wanted to hear that Strawberry was a bad influence, had a bad attitude, and only wanted to stir up bad feelings on the team.

So now it's the end of the Mets' 1987 season and I've hit 39 home runs and stolen 36 bases. I'm in the 30-30 club for the first time in my career. I have a .284 batting average—my best year for average in the majors—and 104 RBIs. Mex is strangely quiet.

But what about the team? We drifted around in the first division for most of the season while winning 92 games and losing 70. Not bad, of course, but nothing like the numbers of the previous year. Still there is not one word of acknowledgment for the real-life Darryl Strawberry, the person who is not the media-created "monster of the Mets" who has to put his life in order. That person feels pain, gets hung over, still wants desperately to have a family, and would have truly appreciated some personal support from someone on the Mets. But there was none. You put your bat down at the end of the season and head west for five months of domestic warfare before you head back to Florida to pick up where you left off. The only breaks came at night when I'd nod off to sleep after drinking rum until there was no more pain.

By October 1987, the real-life Darryl Strawberry had disappeared. I felt as if I'd been smothered under an avalanche of press clippings and empties, but in reality I had become fully invisible. I was only a reflection of the press I was getting (including the few favorable interviews I was able to get) and of the things that were said about me in court. There was a voice inside of me that let this all happen. I know that. I know that I let them turn me into a villain when I never was. I was listening for what I thought they wanted to hear and I gave it to them. But I was also playing the role they laid out for me because I was drinking and dependent on whatever voices I was hearing—positive and negative. Unfortunately, there were too few positive voices in my life.

So I became a reflection of what the press said while the demons continued to tear at my soul for the next two years. I was at times ungrateful, insolent, lazy, a malingerer, and a guy with a bad attitude. When I succeeded for the team, the press translated it into my succeeding for myself. When I was not successful, I was not living up to my potential as a player. Even my friend Doc Gooden was astonished to see how much negative press I was getting. He would stop me in the clubhouse and ask me how I was able to take it all. I just shook my head.

I was an emotional cripple as the season ended for us in ashes. Not only had it been a bad year for the team, but it was a year during which I had lost myself completely. I had no wife, no child, and a career as a professional villain. My own son asked me why I couldn't go back to California to live with the family, why I had to stay in New York, why I couldn't see Mommy anymore. Did my father have the same feelings in his heart when he was parted from his family as I was having over Christmas, 1987? Would my son have challenged me when Lisa and I fought the way I stood alongside my brothers and challenged my father? Would Darryl, Jr., feel the same way about his father as Darryl, Sr., felt about his?

The thought was too frightening to consider. I had fallen into the same patterns as my own father, as if I hadn't had a choice. Now, everything about me was in ruins. I needed a miracle. I needed a path out. But as the new year came and I looked forward to flying south to Florida, all I could see ahead of me was despair. Maybe 1988 would be a better year, but for the life of me, I couldn't see how.

13

ALMOST DOESN'T COUNT

August 1, 1991:

"Doc?"

"Yeah?"

"Straw!"

"Yeah!"

"What's goin' on there?"

"Oh man, these guys. They don't want to win!"

"I hear ya, Doc. I hear ya!"

But the more things change, the saying goes, the more they stay the same. If you had called me in spring training camp at Port St. Lucie in March 1988, I would have said the same thing. These guys, they just don't want to win.

When I got to camp in February, I was still bitter about the Mets after what had happened during our 1987 season. I'd had the highest stats of my career, but the rest of the Mets had seemed determined to rest on their 1986 championship and let the 1987 season slip by them. When we totaled up the 1987 numbers they showed that after I was switched to the cleanup position, where I carried the offense, my average skied to .303 for those sixty or so games in the latter third of the year. But I couldn't carry an offense of one person. So I was bitter and wanted to turn things around this year. I would do it with my bat, I said, and my mouth. And that's where the trouble began.

My personal life was gradually coming back into perspective. After having spent most of 1987 separated from Lisa and fighting a long war with her lawyer, we finally decided to get back together for a trial test of our relationship. This year was going to be different. Our reconciliation would heal the bitterness of the past. I would, I hoped, make the difference for the coming year.

I wanted to make it work. I didn't want people writing things about my marriage and my kid either. In fact, I threatened to beat the shit out of New York sportswriter Mike Lupica for what I thought he wrote about my marital problems. He didn't and I didn't, so I granted him an interview in March about my frustration over the Mets and the guys who didn't produce in 1987, which appeared in the April issue of *Esquire*.

I told Lupica the same thing that Doc told me over the phone, that the New York Mets suffered from a kind of victim's complex. They had the attitude that they didn't have to win ball games to be the number-one team in baseball. They seemed to think that just by being in New York, showing up at the ballpark every day, and taking a few halfhearted swings at the ball they could earn their salaries. I wanted to be on a winning team. I'd been on a winning team in 1986, and even though I hadn't contributed as much as I'd wanted to, at least not until the seventh game of the World Series, I'd loved the whole thing.

But from 1987 on, the team seemed like it would never get back to its 1986 aggressiveness. There were individuals who, I thought, didn't want to work hard enough to win, but they were angry about losing and blamed every other member of the team. We were a team of complete dissension. First of all, both Keith Hernandez and I were going through divorces. I felt that I contributed to the team eventually despite my problems, but that Keith did not. Keith's head, I said in the interview, wasn't even there half the time, but Davey Johnson cherished him. Keith could do no wrong. I was going through a divorce, too, but if I showed up even a few minutes late to practice, Davey fined my ass right off. He was trying to bury me the whole year. Why? That pissed me off just to remember what had gone on.

I was also mad at Gary Carter. I believed he had slacked off considerably in 1987. In '86 the guy was a nuclear reactor. In '87, it was like somebody had pulled the plug on his spirit completely. During the year, his attitude was like, "Oh, well, I'm having a bad year," and let it go at that. Then I said, "Sometimes I wanted to say to those guys, Come on, Mex. Come on, Kid. Get your head out of your ass, we're in a pennant race." Yet Keith got special attention from Davey while I was blamed every time something went wrong. That's what I said about Keith and Gary in the interview and that's what *Esquire* printed.

Then I piped up in the interview about Wally Backman, Lee Mazzilli, Lenny Dykstra, and others on the Mets who I thought could have produced more but didn't. Yet these guys had criticized the hell out of me during the year for playing hurt when I was leading the team. You can imagine what I said about them. Wally Backman, I said, was having a bad season and getting on my case. I could have stooped to his level and criticized him back during the year, but I didn't. I told Lupica that I could have said, but didn't, "Wally's not doing jackshit for this team this season, who cares what he thinks?" And *Esquire* quoted that. "Wally spends too much time trying to be like Keith," I told Lupica. Dykstra was playing for himself all year, I also said. "As long as he got his hits he was happy. He didn't care about contributing to the team."

You might ask me why I was still so mad going into training camp in 1988 when I should have been happier. After all, you would point out, wasn't your marriage back on track? Weren't you settling in for a good season? Hadn't you proved yourself last year after Davey, whose decisions you said you could not understand, moved you to cleanup? What was eating at you so much that you had to stoke up the fires from last year before this year had even begun?

Well, Dr. Lans asked me the same questions two years later and the only word that ever came to mind was "family." The Mets had gradually become my family since 1980, as I put more and more family responsibilities and obligations into them. It didn't happen all at once. It took place over a period of years, but I didn't see the complete picture until 1990 when

I realized how many things had come to a head in the 1987 season. It was in 1987 when, after years of drinking and fighting with my wife, the Mets almost became the only family I had. My own little marriage was rocked by divorce as I tried to be a father, husband, and baseball player at the same time without ever having seen what a father was supposed to do. Because mine split when I was a kid and he never was around that much when I was younger anyway, if you had asked me what a father does with a kid, I might have said, "He disappears." Only I knew that was wrong.

I grew up in a family of fighting siblings in which all squabbles were settled up at the end of the day. Sure you battled each other for attention and for first place, but then you put everything to rest and stood together as a group against the world. I shifted that family-loyalty attitude to the Mets, and that was a big mistake. I know that now, but didn't understand it then. The Mets were a business, a professional organization. They were not supposed to be a family. They are a business first and a family only because of the closeness of the players and the tight surroundings. That's why I was always going over the top and was always in trouble. I was always saying I had a right to rebel against my family and could expect to be welcomed back into the fold. I didn't think there was a "book of grudges" being kept. I never realized that at a certain point I'd become a "bad investment" in their eyes. A family is always a good investment no matter what happens. Not so in business. I treated the guys on the Mets like blood. They weren't blood. They were friends—a close friend in the case of Doc Gooden, who came closest to family—and, mostly, professional colleagues.

I joined the Mets' organization right out of high school and without ever having been away from my family before. I gave the Mets the status of family and the responsibility to take care of me, to put up with me, to provide the nest that I would leave from. You can't do that. You can't pick an organization and say, "You're my family." It's unfair to them, completely unworkable, and your need to have a surrogate family will never, ever, be satisfied.

With all of my frustration from the previous year and my misguided family expectations still building up, I burst into spring training camp like a person who was possessed. I wanted to hit every ball out of the park, steal every base that wasn't covered, and catch every fly to the outfield no matter where it was. Just like when I was a kid in Crenshaw and played baseball to escape the pain of not having a family, I wanted to do that again now. My *real* family had broken up; my *replacement* baseball family on the Mets had to take its place. I tried like hell to make that happen, but I only dug myself deeper into a hole. The harder I played in spring training, the more I raised expectations on the Mets that I was going to carry the team. They didn't care about family. They cared about Darryl pulling the entire team along. I didn't want to raise anyone's expectations, as I had done the year before—Darryl will do more this year than last—I was simply looking for a release from the misery of the off-season. But it backfired, and I was in the same rut again as I'd been in in '87. Worse, I was looking at the same tired faces that had been carried off the field last year. I went absolutely nuts.

It was that frustration that was behind my going on the record for *Esquire* to talk about my feelings concerning the 1987 Mets. I also did it partially to get my conflicted feelings for Davey Johnson into print. I believed that because of the pressure on him to perform in 1987, he singled me out as the reason the team was having problems. He didn't complain about Keith—who had spent part of the last inning of game six of the '86 World Series drinking a beer in Davey's office and watching us on Davey's TV—no, he singled me out. Gary Carter had given up on the year, and Davey turned his attention to me even though I was having the best year of my career. So I opened up and said that Davey was trying to "bury me."

The New York press got hold of the interview before it came out and began excerpting it all over the place. As you can imagine, I was not the most popular player in the Mets' Florida clubhouse, especially among the likes of Keith Hernandez, Gary Carter, and Lenny Dykstra. Davey Johnson wasn't particularly happy with what I had to say about him, either.

Reaction to my comments was quick in coming. The newspaper sportswriters jumped all over me, claiming that I was the last person who could complain. "Strawberry doesn't understand the media," they wrote. "Strawberry always complains after he puts his foot in his mouth," they said. I was simply a novice at another man's game, reporters wrote, and shouldn't have made it worse by complaining about the effects of the interview and the reactions of the other players.

I told reporters at the time that my long answers to the magazine's questions were shortened and taken out of context in the article and that my comments about Mex were in the context of our print feud over four years. I was mad, I had told *Esquire,* because Keith had been talking to the press about me since he came to the Mets in 1983. I was the first one to applaud his accomplishments, but he never seemed to return the compliments when I thought I deserved them. Instead, every time he talked about me, it was with the qualification that I was still far from achieving the potential he thought I had. I appreciated his high estimation of my potential, but no matter what he said about me to the eager reporters waiting to tape his golden words, it always turned out negative. I finally got sick and tired of his comments, especially after the 1987 season when I'd been expected to carry the Mets over the finish line. I finally went up to Hernandez and told him that what I said sounded worse in print than it really was, even though I meant it when I said he could have performed more aggressively the year before.

I told *Esquire* that I didn't want the same thing to happen in 1988. But the magazine article seemed more concerned with how many beers I was reaching for during the interview than how many questions I was answering. My comments about Davey Johnson were also taken out of context. I thought Davey had made some bad decisions in 1986 and some even worse decisions the following year. There was no reason on paper we should have lost the division championship in 1987. In 1988, I tried to explain, we should be just as powerful as in 1986. It was up to Davey Johnson to marshal the team's resources to make that really happen.

Then, of course, underlying everything, I was still angry. The wounds had not healed from 1987, and despite trying to be professional about the '88 season, I was still mad at the guys, including Davey, who had made me the scapegoat. My conflicts about the Mets were still unresolved, I felt foolish about investing the Mets with the role of my family, and I had gone through a year of divorce proceedings and finally a reconciliation. Part of me was trying to embrace the world and my new hopes for the future. Part of me was as angry and bitter as hell. And I was still drinking, drinking, drinking, and falling off to sleep in my chair after the sweet bouquet of Remy Martin cognac had deadened all the pain of the day and carried me through the night.

Whatever troubles the interview started seemed to have been put to rest by the end of April 1988, when we waded into a batting and slugging spree with Montreal, the Pirates, and the Phillies. By the middle of April, we were on our way to the lead of the Eastern Division of the National League. By the end of April, we were just about in first place. After we beat the Montreal Expos very early in the season with a volley of home runs, Keith Hernandez told the press that anything that was supposedly stirred up by the *Esquire* article was only in the minds of the press. I know that wasn't true and that there were some true hard feelings for a while, but Keith expressed a desire to put the whole thing behind him and I was more than willing to go along with that. I was also willing to pack into my old kit bag whatever ill feelings I was harboring toward Davey Johnson at the start of the season. Clubhouse feuds benefit very few people except the opposing teams, but as Davey Johnson told the press, we were the kind of team that feuded in the clubhouse and then went out on the field to win games. It seemed as if everyone's desire to get back to what we had in 1986 was making them bury the hatchet and agree to disagree, and not let it get in the way of playing baseball. Okay by me, I thought. Just hope it lasts.

Part of the reason for everyone's good humor was my two opening day home runs on April 4 at Montreal's Olympic Stadium, one of which Wally Backman said had gone 600 feet if it had gone an inch. Expos manager Buck Rodgers said that my shot was the longest he'd ever seen in his thirty-two years of baseball. It was a monster of a hit, to be sure, and I knew it was a flyer as soon as I felt the contact. I couldn't have hit the ball any harder. It just kept on going up and up and up. As I trotted toward first, I saw it on its way toward the roof, but lost it in the lights. It actually hit the lights on the very rim of the roof. The press trotted out some college professor from McGill University who said that he estimated the shot to be 525 feet. But he was too conservative: 600 feet if it went an inch.

By that June we were in first place by four and a half games and it looked like a repeat of the 1986 season. Lisa and I had reconciled, and I told her that I really wanted to stay married after all. I promised her that we would settle down, buy a nice house in California, and honestly try to make a go of it. We were still living in New York at the time. She conceived our second child in the fall of 1987. Right about the time she was giving birth, however, we were beginning to lose our grip on first place after a loss to Pittsburgh in a game that we shouldn't have blown. Davey closed the clubhouse doors to all reporters —he should have kept them closed right through 1990—and we had a meeting at which he lectured us on coming together as a team instead of playing as a bunch of individuals. All of us came in for some criticism, but it was honest, and I was criticized along with everybody else. Davey then excused me from the game that night because Lisa had gone into labor, and I took off from Pittsburgh for New York.

Lisa gave birth to our little girl the following morning. I was a father again. When you have a new little baby it's as if the whole world starts all over again. It's as if your marriage starts all over again and you get another chance to do it right. I saw my baby, all kicking and squirming in her hospital bassinet, and actually felt a burst of, well, "responsibility." She was precious, as precious as a diamond. And that's what we named her, Diamond Nicole.

I felt charged up with a new power. I was "Super D." Nothing's too hard for me. Yes, I want to stay with Lisa and Diamond Nicole. But we were fighting a war out there and I was going into battle. Yes! So even though Davey had excused me from the next game, I wanted to get back into the action and hit me a few baseballs. Bring 'em on. I'm a daddy again. I'll show 'em.

I flew back to Pittsburgh that afternoon, where, in honor of my new daughter, I put the ball out of the park and we beat the Pirates 5-2. We beat them again the next night and went back to Shea with a nice five-and-a-half-game cushion in first. That was the shift into high gear that we needed to let us cruise along in first place for the rest of the season.

I told the press in June, when they were actually praising me for returning to the team to win the game for them the day my daughter was born, that it was my reconciliation with Lisa that was making the difference. In 1987, I was bitter and hateful because I was going through a divorce. In 1988, although I was still drinking I had tried to put my domestic problems behind me. As a result, I was better able to focus on baseball. I was also staying out of fights with other guys on the team. Hell, I was even agreeing with what Davey had to say. Had I gone completely crazy or was my domestic situation the root of all my problems? I'm afraid that I was a lot more vulnerable to my family situation than I thought I was, especially because I was drinking so much. It wasn't until 1990 that I would realize that my drinking was the most serious problem I had.

My returning to Pittsburgh on the day Diamond Nicole was born also made a few guys on the team sit up and take notice of the change in me. Mookie Wilson told the press that he was impressed that I had finally seemed to mature into the role on the Mets that I had been expected to fill for years. I told Mookie that at the end of the last season, I woke up one morning thinking I was eighteen but realizing I was twenty-five. I was still acting like I was eighteen, though, and that was the problem. Once I acknowledged that, once I said, Darryl, you jerk, you're not a teenager anymore; you're a grown adult who's just acting like a teenager, then things began to change. I said to myself, did I want to be the badass of the Mets, the rebel who'd as soon show up late to the ballpark as not show up at all? Did I want to be going through this divorce when it was just my stupidity and ego that was causing it? What right did I have walking around sullen and unhappy and blaming my troubles on the rest of the world? So I snapped myself out of it, for the present, and said that I was going to make the effort to mature.

It paid off when I reconciled with my wife. It paid off when I returned to the team and people said to me they noticed a difference. I felt better about myself and my situation. That translated into a more focused attitude at the plate and an ability to channel the anger I always felt. When I started hitting the ball and getting some tremendous home runs, I knew I was on the right track. Then the Mets began winning streak after winning streak. It got so that everybody was contributing and our pitching was dominating the entire league. It looked like the team had the spirit and the attitude of two years earlier. It looked like a team that would go all the way to the World Series, not like the team that had folded the year before.

When the season ended, we led the Eastern Division by fifteen games and moved into the National League Championship Series against the Los Angeles Dodgers. But these playoffs once again set the team at odds with itself, and that proved to be our undoing. Maybe we believed in our own press in October 1988. Everybody had been telling us all year that the pennant was ours to lose because there was no team in the West stronger than the Mets. We looked the Dodgers over and agreed. After all, we'd won ten of the eleven regular-season games we'd played against them that year. I, of course, knew the Dodgers better than anybody on the team. I was a Dodgers fan and I looked forward to playing games at Dodger Stadium in front of my friends and family. I had a set of high expectations for the series, not only for myself but for the Mets as well. I wanted us to win.

Most of the Mets saw our playoffs against the Dodgers coming in as a replay of our 1986 League Championship Series against the Houston Astros. It wasn't. This time the Dodgers had the drive we should have had. The Dodgers' Orel Hershiser was relentless in the first game. They scored a run off Doc in the bottom of the first and another in the seventh, while Orel made us chase balls all over the strike zone and then some for eight full innings. Even the hometown fans were beginning to yawn. Nothing we could do would start a rally. Then came the ninth inning. With one out and Gregg Jefferies on second, I powered a double into the gap that scored one run. At that point, Jay Howell came in for Hershiser. He walked McReynolds, to put men on first and second, and then struck out HoJo for the second out. Gary Carter chose that moment to come alive with a sinking blooper to John Shelby out in center. The sportswriters like to call these shots "tweeners" because they're too far out for the second baseman or shortstop and too far in for the center fielder. Shelby—I know because I was on base at the time—thought he had a play on the ball as he charged in from center. From my angle, I knew he had no play. Shelby flew in and stretched himself flat out to catch Carter's blooper, but it dropped in front of him as he fell flat on his face. By the time he recovered, two runs had scored and we were up on the Dodgers 3-2. We closed them down in their ninth and that was game one for the Mets.

I will probably go to my grave with one nagging doubt: we might have won the 1988 National League playoffs (and we would have beat the stuffing out of Oakland) had we not made one tiny mistake after the first game. *We shot off our mouths!* It wasn't just Dave Cone's fault, but he got the blame for it. It was all our faults. We were feeling so good, so powerful, so damn "Metted" up that we started blowing our own horn. The reporters were saying to us, "Hey, that was some lucky shot that Carter got," or, "You guys been lucky all year. What's your secret?" or, "Poor Shelby fell flat on his face. Good luck for you." We should have just nodded and said, "Yeah, yeah, that's baseball." But no, we started goofing on them in general, saying it wasn't luck it was skill. They knew we were kidding around and laughing about it until Dave Cone made it *personal*. He said that it wasn't luck, it was just good play. Okay, so far, but then Dave said, "Hershiser was lucky, Doc was good." Uh-oh! He made a personal comment about another player in that player's hometown.

Take it back, Dave.

Apologize now, Dave.

Don't bad-mouth a Dodger in L.A., Dave. That just makes 'em mad.

Dave! Dave! You really shouldn't have done that, Dave.

The *Los Angeles Times* served us up like barbecue after Dave's ill-advised comments. The Dodgers were so fired up that the momentum we should have had going into game two shifted over to Tommy Lasorda's team. Word to the wise: don't get Tommy Lasorda mad, especially when you have to pitch against his team the next day.

Game two, which should have been ours, was a Dodgers' rumble. Their pitcher, Timmy Belcher, spread our three runs over nine innings while L.A. kicked Dave Cone's ass right out of the stadium and across Route 101. He's lucky they didn't put the ball down his throat, they were so mad. Orel came back in game seven to shut us down and out, and that's why I think the entire series was lost on the night after the first game. We were just a bunch of assholes.

Game three, now in New York, was the pine tar game. Using pine tar is technically not the same thing as roughing up a ball or razoring its skin, but it can get your butt kicked out of a game. You can say about game three that what Dave Cone gave to Tommy Lasorda, Jay Howell gave back to Davey Johnson. It brought back memories of the Mike Scott "scuffing affair" after game four against the Astros in '86, except this time the ruling was in our favor.

The pine tar question actually came up much earlier in the

year. Davey Johnson had intimated that he thought there was something odd about the way Jay Howell's pitches broke. They consistently broke too hard to be normal pitches. Howell, he thought, was putting something on the ball. Pine tar was the obvious substance, because pitchers had been using it since the turn of the century. So Davey put the word out to watch Howell's hands and glove, especially when he put them behind his back. Our first-base coach, Bill Robinson, said he saw Jay Howell pulling at the leather strings on the back of his glove during game three. Other players noticed that Howell's glove strings looked a "leeetle too dark" to be on the up-and-up. It looked like pine tar to them.

So Bill Robinson gives Davey the high sign. But Davey holds his cards. He wants to use the edge he thinks he has when it can have the most dramatic effect. He plays it cool and waits for his numbers, waits until Howell has a full count on Kevin McReynolds leading off the bottom of the eighth with the Dodgers ahead 4-3. On this cold, damp afternoon at Shea, the tension is good and high. Then Davey struts onto the field and motions for the home-plate ump, Joe West. "Look it over, ump," he says. West and crew chief Harry Wendelstedt give the ball a onceover. Wendelstedt tosses Jay Howell out of the game and hands Howell's glove to National League president Bart Giamatti. Meanwhile the Dodgers number one reliever is out of the game and there's still a 3-2 count on McReynolds. The Mets fans at Shea start to scream "Cheaters!" at the Dodgers in the outfield. Hey, it's better than booing me. When Pena comes in, he walks Kevin, and the Mets start a five-run rally that I cap with a two-run single. We win 8-4 and have the momentum back along with a two-games-to-one lead.

Putting aside Dave Cone's stupid remarks, speaking in purely baseball terms, the Dodgers turned the whole playoffs series around for themselves in game four when they came from behind to tie it up in the top of the ninth, 4-4, and finished us off with another run in the twelfth. That was what the Mets would have done in 1986. Game four was a particularly frustrating game for me. If I could have bent down, picked the entire team up on my back, and carried them around the bases, I would have. But even that would have won the game for us. I could actually see the other Mets folding under the Dodger pressure in game four and I could see Davey letting the

momentum slip away again. I hit a home run, and tried to get
the other guys to join in offensively as well as defensively, but
the Dodgers wanted it more than we did.

The Dodgers started off the game by taking a two-run lead
in the top of the first. We had a big three-run fourth inning in
which both McReynolds and I homered. That should have
been enough to finish off the Dodgers, especially after game
three, when we pine tarred and feathered them by finessing
their top reliever out of the game. And we still weren't finished. In the sixth inning, McReynolds led off with a double
into center and was immediately driven home by a Gary
Carter triple, giving us a 4-2 lead. I smelled trouble, however,
when Timmy Teufel then struck out with Gary on third.
Timmy should have brought Gary home. Kevin Elster was intentionally walked, and Doc wasn't looking over his pitches
when he hit into a double play that ended the inning. There
were butterflies in my stomach. You don't leave a runner on
third with none out, even when you're up by two, and expect
to win playoff games. I was proven right in the top of the ninth
when a Mike Scioscia two-run homer tied the score. The score
stayed even until Kirk Gibson homered off McDowell in the
twelfth to break the tie. We couldn't do diddly in our twelfth
and the Dodgers had tied us at two games apiece. We were
sinking.

Timmy Belcher all but shut me down in game five the next
night at Shea when the Dodgers beat us 7-4 by simply over-
powering us. We were hardly in the game. We never led and,
frankly, never had a chance at leading. Gloom had begun to
settle over our dugout at Shea because we knew we were being
outhustled by the Dodgers. Tommy had his team whipped up
while Davey seemed to be letting his numbers work for him.
This is no joke, Davey, I kept telling him. These guys are
outplaying us. You can see it. But Davey said that we were in it
in every game and that because we were the stronger team, we
should be beating them.

In game five, I only got a lousy single. But, hey, I was only
one guy. What about my hitting in game one? What about my
three RBIs in game three? What about my home run in game
four? Whadaboutit, whadaboutit?

"You hit, we win, Straw."

So, back in L.A. for game six, I hit, sort of. I got a single. I
might have hit more, but Tim Leary kept walking me. Kevin

McReynolds came alive for us that night with a home run, and the Dodgers made two errors, and we beat them 5-1 to tie the playoffs at three apiece.

Knowing what you know now, you wouldn't think we'd have been confident facing Orel Hershiser in game seven. You wouldn't think that at all. But we'd done all right against him in game three and believed that we'd hit his best stuff. But, you see, Orel had a score to settle. Remember that Dave Cone, who had since come back to win against the Dodgers in this series, had said that Orel was lucky. Orel was offended. Orel is a technician. Orel is a stone killer when he's on. And boy, was he ever on.

For nine innings on the night of October 12, Orel Hershiser was the toughest pitcher I had ever seen in my life. He seemed to draw a power from somewhere—now I *know* where—and frustrated us completely. He never gave our hitters a chance to show how much power we had. The few times we connected with the ball, it went right where he wanted it to, as if it were drawn by magnets. Davey Johnson just sat there in the dugout dumbfounded. He knew Hershiser was good, he just didn't know he was *this* good. I had to tip my hat to the Dodgers and the L.A. fans after Orel struck me out in the sixth inning. It was all I could do. My friends were in the stands. My family was in the stands. Everybody I knew was rooting for the Dodgers and rooting for me at the same time.

I wanted us to win so badly, but Hershiser made us look like a bunch of amateurs. After the game, I sat down in front of my locker and cried like a baby. Nothing anybody could say could ease my feelings of failure at having lost the National League championship right in front of my own mother, brothers, and sisters.

I knew that on paper the Mets were far stronger than the Dodgers, and we could have beaten Oakland or any other American League team. But it struck me during the series that no matter how hard I tried, the Dodgers as a team were more committed to winning than the Mets. That really shook me. The Dodgers were so driven, so pushed, so focused on winning that they simply took away from the overconfident Mets what rightfully should have been their National League championship. That's why I was crying.

I knew we should have won that series. I knew on the night of the first game that the series was ours to lose, not the Dodgers' to win. I *knew* it, but couldn't do anything about it. It was one of the most frustrating series I ever played and it broke the back of the team the following year by weakening our will to win. We were *dominated*, not just beaten. Beaten up, not just beaten. We were outplayed by a team that shouldn't have beaten us but did because their will to win was stronger than ours. Because of how they played, they were better. This was too much for the Mets as a team to handle, and we collapsed. I know that I just wanted to get into bed and not come out of it again, we played so bad.

Have you ever wanted anything so bad it hurt right in the gut to get it? Then when you thought you had it, have you ever had it snatched right away? That's what the 1988 National League playoffs were for me. Worst of all, I didn't want it for the Mets. I know that now. I wanted it for me. Sure the Mets would benefit, but I wanted it just for me. And just for me, I couldn't get it no matter what I or we tried to do. I wept. It was just like hitting a dead end knowing that the following year would be a repeat. I felt like I was being dragged along the bottom.

When you see yourself lose and you know for a fact that your own commitment to winning is not in question, it gives you great pause. For an instant an old, old thought bubbled up in me as the Dodgers outhit and outhustled us: I wanted to be a Dodger. I know, I know. Bring out the pencils and write me up as ungrateful and disloyal, but I have to be honest. It wasn't a new thought. I had wanted to play for the Dodgers as far back as my years at Crenshaw, but the Dodgers didn't have the first-round draft pick that the Mets had. I had hoped from time to time during my minor league playing years that the Mets would trade me over to the Dodger organization so I could stay in Los Angeles, but I also knew that wouldn't happen. So the thought arose in my mind that maybe, seeing as how I only had two years left on my contract with the Mets, I could negotiate my way over to the Dodgers.

It's one thing to think about a future with the Dodgers, but it's another to give voice to that thought. It's even worse to fantasize about how wonderful it would be if you and your childhood friend from L.A., Eric Davis, might actually play on the Dodgers or San Diego together. When I told the *Los Angeles Times* that I had this dream the other night that I might someday play for the Dodgers, the New York press exploded.

You'd think that I'd just handed over military secrets to the Chinese. "Here, Deng or Mao or whoever, help yourself to the locations of all of our guided missiles." And what did I say really? All I hinted at—and it was really only a hint—was that it was getting tougher and tougher to play at Shea Stadium with 50,000 fans booing every time I went into a slump. All batters go into slumps, but when the fans jump on you for being hitless the previous night, it kind of gets to you after a while.

In Los Angeles, however, I got the strange feeling that I might just be playing in front of fans who would actually like my being there. Maybe they wouldn't boo me in my own hometown (so I was wrong). Maybe the fact that I was from here would mean that I could get just a little slack from fans who appreciated me. That was all I said.

"Just another day in paradise," Cashen reportedly said to the papers after the "Darryl wants to play in L.A." story broke. I could never figure out what that meant.

But when the press asked me—always the last person—whether I was seriously thinking about trying to make the switch, I told them "probably not." And at the time I meant every word of it. There's a difference between playing with an idea and just letting an idea play in your mind. But the distinction was lost on anybody I explained it to. It seemed as if wanting to hear what I really had to say was not as important to the press as reporting what they thought I should say. I felt like I was vanishing as a real person, even in my own eyes, in the late fall of 1988 and turning into the creature the press had created. So I continued to drink, letting the human being called Darryl Strawberry become so completely absorbed into what the media were calling Darryl Strawberry that all I had left was the marriage I was trying to put back on its feet and my two little kids.

It was actually kind of dysfunctional when I look back on it because I thought I knew who I was at the time. I kept complaining that everything I was saying was being misinterpreted and misquoted, yet I let it continue. It wasn't as if I especially trusted the press or even cared what they said, it was just that the constant beating I'd been taking from them for the past few years had taken its toll. If they asked me a question, I answered it. If the answer I gave wasn't the answer in the paper the next day, the hell with it. That's how I looked at it.

The more I gave them, the more they wanted. Eventually, they were covering my marriage, my home, my kids, my drinking, my nightclub hopping, you name it. Then they'd ask other guys on the Mets to comment on my life-style until the only feedback I was getting about how I was doing and how I was being perceived by the Mets and my other teammates came from the media. When I wanted a reading on how my marriage was supposedly doing, that, too, came from the media. What do you do when in order to check up on your own life you have to read the morning paper? Kind of strange, don't you think? It wasn't as though I were a movie star who had to read the trades to find out the opening weekend box office of his latest movie. This was my personal life we're talking about here.

I lied to myself by thinking I could turn it around. I was already in too deep because of my drinking and my denying there was even a problem. I couldn't even control the direction my marriage was taking or carry the weight of my family. I didn't even want to think about my tenure in New York—too much pain there! So I went home for my long winter's nap. I would hibernate, I said to myself, enjoy the warm California January and begin again in Florida in February. I would put 1988 all behind me, I said. I had hoped to change things in '88, but all I had seen was that no matter how hard I told myself I tried, things hadn't changed at all. They had only gotten worse. And I was still drinking.

I would turn over a new leaf in '89, I said, always making a new resolution with the new year. But the new season started sooner than I thought it would. And my new agent also had some new ideas about contracts. And suddenly what was supposed to be new was very much like what was old.

14

BLACK ON WHITE AND READ ALL OVER

In early 1989 I began to get a more accurate picture of what had been happening to me on the Mets, and by then it was truly too late. My new agent, Eric Goldschmidt, and I had been talking since the end of 1988 about seeking a contract extension from the Mets to cover 1990, my option year under the free agency rules, and beyond. At first, we were hoping to avoid any end-of-year craziness that sometimes gets in the way of an athlete's performance on the field. It didn't take a rocket scientist to understand what the Los Angeles papers were suggesting about my value to the Mets during our 1988 National League playoff series against the Dodgers. Jim Murray, for example, came right out and said that I was one of the most intimidating players in the National League. The Los Angeles papers respected me and treated me as if I belonged there. And when I expressed my fantasy of playing on the Dodgers, my hometown team, with my long-time friend Eric Davis, the New York papers jumped all over me while the L.A. papers said, "Hey, Straw, that's not a bad idea. C'mon out."

From a purely psychological standpoint, I wanted to avoid the pressure of playing out my option year and going through free agency. I wanted a commitment from the Mets before the 1989 season that I was still wanted in the clubhouse, but I also wanted a contract reflecting what was happening to heavy-hitter contracts in general in baseball. Eric Goldschmidt thought that after our success in 1988, the time was right to open negotiations. We chose early 1989 to make the first approach.

I had learned to take nothing for granted when it came to the press and to assume nothing before it actually appeared in print. The only thing you can bank on is that newspaper reporters want to sell newspapers, and if they can sensationalize something, they will. But even I, hardened as I was, wasn't ready for the press reaction in 1989 and the effects that played out for the rest of the year.

Up until the beginning of spring training camp, the papers had been looking forward to a powerful Mets season. I had been the acknowledged team leader the previous year, the papers said. If the rest of the Mets could only support my hitting and run production, the team would go all the way. The National League playoff loss to the Dodgers in 1988 was the direct result of our team's being outhustled by an inferior ball club. This year, the sportswriters said, the Mets have learned their lessons and if Darryl Strawberry does what he did last year, the conclusion was written in stone. I loved those kinds of predictions because usually they're worth money in the bank. Or so we thought.

Through Eric, I asked the Mets to sweeten the final contract year deal—1989—and my option year deal—1990. I wanted an extension and I wanted a new salary to reflect the role that I was playing on the Mets. This was no longer 1985, we argued, when our last contract was negotiated. Since then, I had contributed to the team's World Series victory and had almost single-handedly carried the Mets to a National League championship the previous year. Even my biggest detractors on the Mets had been saying publicly that there was an entirely new chemistry on the team because of my performance.

Overnight the entire situation changed. The Mets were very reluctant to begin any discussions while the 1989 contract was still in place. The press jumped on me. I was suddenly an ingrate. The entire team seemed to turn on me too. "Who is Darryl Strawberry that he thinks he can renegotiate a contract that's already in force?"

Actually, the situation was far more complicated than just "Darryl wants more money." Of course Darryl wanted more money. Everybody wants more money. That's how America operates: more money, more money, more money, more money. When a bunch of white people float junk bonds around seventeen countries to get more money, people call them geniuses. When a bunch of white guys convince hundreds of savings and loans to invest their money in junk bonds to engineer a buyout of a major corporation, divide that corporation up into tiny pieces, or recombine operations and fire thousands of loyal employees to help the bottom line, and then pocket wads of cash while the people who made the company work wait on unemployment lines, financial analysts call them super-geniuses. When a movie star generates a huge box office and wants to renegotiate the back end on a multipicture deal, people praise that star's agent for being sharp enough to understand the bottom line. But when a black athlete wants more money because his performance on the field increases attendance figures, people turn on him like a villain. "What you need the money for? Ain't you got enough?"

When I saw those fangs come out, the first thing I said to Eric was, "I'm getting outta here." If the Mets and the New York press think that I'm the world's biggest villain for doing what New York is known for, then I simply don't belong in New York. Tell them, I said to Eric, that I'm gonna play out my 1989 year in New York and hope the Mets don't pick up my option year in 1990, and then I'm going into the free agency market to play for the highest bidder. They sell stocks to the highest bidder, don't they? Fine, I'll rely on the open market to determine the value of my contract and I'll abide by the rules of supply and demand: there's only one Darryl Strawberry who led the league in home runs, and there are twenty-six baseball teams. It's the American way.

Actually, though, I was ambivalent about the whole thing. Part of me wanted just to get the hell out. Part of me wanted to stay because part of me still believed I was in the Mets' family and that I would be deserting them if I left. When you can't treat your professional career with a professional cold-bloodedness—which I couldn't do at that time—the press and the fans pick up on your ambivalence. I was vulnerable and I let people know it by vacillating about my plans and my feelings. I know now that it's better to be more focused on what you want professionally and not let personal feelings get in the way. If they do, admit that they're personal feelings, indulge them, and then put them aside. I would have had a much cleaner exit from New York had I done that.

Eric went into talks with Frank Cashen and Al Harazin right at the beginning of training camp. The newspapers had gotten hold of the story and tied it to my quotes the year before about wanting to play in Los Angeles. Suddenly, the press began talking about a grand design, a strategy for forcing the Mets to pay big bucks to keep me in New York when my heart was really in Los Angeles. Now I truly became the villain. Not only did I want to move from the city that had adopted me with "open arms" to la-la land, but I was using my option year on the Mets as a lever. How underhanded can a person be?

The whole situation erupted at a team picture session at Port St. Lucie in March. Here's what happened. For weeks before "the fight," Keith Hernandez and Gary Carter had been riding me about my wanting to reopen my contract. All of this was kind of a tit for tat after my comments about them in *Esquire* the year before. They began saying that Strawberry was a crybaby for wanting to open his contract now and for sulking around the clubhouse while Cashen & Co. was deciding what to do. Then on March 1, I told some reporters at the camp that if the Mets didn't give Eric Goldschmidt the consideration of sitting down and talking with him about extending my current contract, I was going to walk out of camp. If I couldn't have the courtesy of the kind of treatment I thought I deserved, then I didn't want to be a part of the Mets. Period.

The next day, we were supposed to pose for a team picture session. Keith and Gary had been having a high old time telling reporters that they thought I was a baby and going on about my need for the additional money. Right before the picture session, I walked up to Hernandez and Carter and told them that I didn't comment on their contracts and I didn't interfere with their negotiations with the Mets. So what the hell were they doing getting in the way of *my* money? Contract talks are one of the truly private issues that players have with their teams. What gave Carter and Hernandez the right to intervene in my contract talks and to breach what everybody considers to be a private issue? I told them that I was sick and tired of being treated like a second-class citizen on the Mets by people who should be supporting me instead of sniping at me.

"We're all tired of this baby stuff," they said.

Screw you, baby stuff. It's my money.

That's when I lost my temper and before anyone realized it, Keith and I were swinging at each other. Our teammates got between us and pulled me away, all to the delight of the assembled cameramen who were rolling, rolling, rolling away their videotape and film. And they kept on rolling as I stormed off the field.

Keith called this a "family dispute" afterward and said it was resolved. Maybe it was. I apologized to Keith afterward. Keith and I had learned to tolerate each other over the years. He'd criticize me to the press; I'd criticize him, too, and sometimes we'd have public fights. This one got physical because I lost my temper at his and Carter's attitude. I got mad at Keith because he was discussing my contract negotiations in public. I didn't discuss Keith's contract negotiations in public. I didn't ask him to feed my family. If he didn't have to feed my family, he didn't have the right to discuss my financial situation in public.

I asked the reporters who had such a great time with the story how each of them would feel if one of their colleagues in the newsroom began commenting for attribution about the status of their contract negotiations and the validity of their salary demands? Wouldn't they see it as an invasion of privacy? Shouldn't I have seen it as an invasion of my privacy? Did I have any privacy? I was beginning to doubt that I did, because it was so obvious, even to me at this point, that I was simply a second-class citizen on the Mets.

Part of me said that I was like the Rodney Dangerfield character who gets no respect. But it wasn't funny. I wasn't getting any respect and it was translating into money issues. I also felt, as I looked around the locker room and saw only a couple of other black players, that there were racial issues at work here. The Mets put black ballplayers in a second-class role, paid them second-class salaries, and weren't about to negotiate contracts at the top levels of the league. The Mets might also just be cheap. Whatever it was, it was eating at me and affecting my desire to contribute because I was feeling like a fool. I decided I'd had enough.

I walked out of camp the next day and was promptly fined $750. I told Davey that I'd be back the next day and would play out my option year, but enough was enough. I was leaving after 1990 because I had had it with the crummy treatment I had gotten from the Mets.

The next day we had an exhibition game against the Dodgers, who were the world champions and who had beaten us in 1988 for the National League championship. As I ran out onto the field, the fans booed me something fierce. That hurt. They weren't booing me for not getting a hit or for dropping a ball. They were booing me for standing up for myself. This had become a personal issue. Worse, I truly was being treated as if I had no rights whatsoever in this case. This was a labor negotiation. Why was I the bad guy when all I did was ask for a raise? Whatsamatter, blacks can't ask for raises from their bosses? There's a law against that these days? A black guy tries to get a better deal from his boss, gets criticized by his teammates, stands up to them, and gets booed for it? You think that's fair? I didn't! And I got mad about it.

When I heard the boos coming down upon me, I realized I had to do something about it fast. So I tipped my hat to the stands, ran past first base, hugged Keith, and gave him the biggest, wettest Roger Rabbity kiss I could.

SMAAAACK!

I slobbered all over the son of a bitch. The fans loved it. The papers photographed it! Keith tensed in terror. Darryl Strawberry, Mistuh Show Biz! When it was my turn to pick up the bat, I belted a home run off Tim Belcher that traveled so far, they saw it flying over Cuba.

"He wiped the slate clean with one swing," Davey Johnson said to reporters afterward. And that summed up my relationship with the New York Mets. As long as I was hitting home runs, driving base runners home, and giving the fans a show, I was entitled to my share of the accolades, but just as soon as I stepped out of line, I was no good. I got what Dr. Lans would later call "conditional approval" when I wanted "unconditional approval." Because I really wanted the unconditional approval and affection that you could only get from a family, I didn't feel I had to toe the line to get it. But because I know my father didn't give me unconditional approval and affection,

I was especially needy for it. So whenever I thought I was in a familylike situation, I immediately went after unconditional approval. You can't get it in a business, and I couldn't get it from the Mets. Whatever warm feelings they gave me were absolutely based on my performance. It was driving me crazy because I wanted so much more and because I began to see the whole thing was arbitrary.

I began to think that all of my real emotional hang-ups were made even worse because I was a black player on the Mets at a time when they weren't especially sensitive to black players' issues, let alone my own personal needs. I looked around me on the Mets and I saw black players come and go and I noticed that all of them had problems. Nobody was talking about Keith's acknowledgment of his drug problems back in St. Louis, but they sure were talking about Mookie's "attitude problems," Doc's recovery program at Smithers, and "Darryl's drinking." White players like Gary Carter were allowed to shrug off their bad seasons, but the black players, it seemed, were "problems."

It was a double standard. I don't have any animosity in my heart toward Gary Carter today. We're teammates, we've both been born again as Christians, and I love Gary as a brother. But *at that time* I couldn't help but see the double standard in place, and it made me mad. Then I thought, how could I be foolish enough to want to be in their "family." I felt ashamed of myself for being so naive, for having been tricked. These were old, old childhood feelings that were stirred up in me, and they made me feel and act irrationally. I had no way of coping with them except to think about my father and drink.

I took a good, hard look at the Mets after I began seeing the world in terms of black and white. I compared the Mets to the Yankees and saw that despite George Steinbrenner's public brouhahas with Reggie Jackson and Dave Winfield, he would still field five to seven regular black ballplayers during the season while the Mets had only Doc and myself on a regular basis. Sure we had Mookie, but they blamed Mookie's troubles on me and traded him away. When you're black in this sport, you begin to hear rumors about how you have to be better than the white players on your team just to get the same kind of contract, and you hear that managers don't like to play their black players too much because then they have to give them more money. Most players dismiss these as rumors because they don't want to think that after all these years and after twenty years of the civil rights movement and other advances, you're still being judged on your color. But then one day you look around you and you begin to place some credence in these "rumors," and you begin to have a different outlook on the team you're playing for.

It seemed to me that the Mets had fewer blacks on their team than most of the other Major League teams and that they had signed precious few black players. Was I so much trouble to the Mets that they didn't want to deal with other blacks because of the example I was setting? But what was I doing? I had carried the Mets back in 1988, leading the team in home runs and RBIs. I tried to be a leader and resolve my own immaturity, but the moment that I talked about money with management, that's when they turned. They decided they were not going to pay Darryl Strawberry one thin dime more than he had agreed to for his final year and his option year. But I was convinced that if I had been a different color, it would have all been different.

The Mets didn't want to look bad in the public eye, so they portrayed themselves as the injured party in the newspapers. Now I was public enemy number one when it was the Mets were the ones who had refused when we asked them to negotiate. They made it seem as if I were the person responsible for the breakdown in communications. I knew that whatever the Mets were doing, the way they were characterizing me was aimed at me personally and went beyond the bounds of a professional relationship. This created such hard feelings in me that it was almost impossible for me to overcome them as the 1989 season got under way. I was placed under the microscope to see whether I would fink out on the Mets, but it had been they, unfortunately, who had finked out on me.

Another part of the power that management was able to bring to bear on me, and I'm sure on other black players, was the power of the media. When you look around the clubhouse or the press box and see who's holding the microphones in your face, setting up the cameras, and asking you the questions, you see that all the faces are white. It's intimidating. I would have loved to have been able to sit down with a black sportswriter and simply unburden my mind. I would have felt that he would have understood what I was upset about, because the troubles I had were the troubles that he might have encountered in his own life. We would have shared the one common bond that unites most black professionals in America: there are very few of us and no one understands that we bring to our jobs a unique background and set of perceptions.

White reporters become defensive when they deal with black athletes. If you don't jump where they want you to jump and say what they want you to say, they get angry in very subtle ways and recharacterize you according to their own image of what they want you to be. That's how they make you disappear. I can guarantee you that you have never seen the real Darryl Strawberry in print. If the real Darryl Strawberry ever turned up in black and white, I might not even recognize him because I have only seen re-creations of him based on what some reporter wanted him to look like. He's gone. That's why I can't relate to what I read about myself.

If white reporters think you're not forthcoming enough, they say you're moody or that you have an attitude problem. If you feel funny about answering a certain question, a reporter, trying, I'm sure, to be a friendly and ingratiating "blood," will say, "C'mon, Straw, don't cop no 'tude with me." That's bull! I'm not copping any attitudes, I simply don't want to be the recipient of his hostility in the next day's column. However, if you give the white reporters what they ask for, then they abuse you right down to your spiked baseball shoes. I've been called everything since I arrived in New York. I was a crybaby. I was a spoiled brat. I was a pampered bonus baby. I was an unruly child. I've been called things that would be considered demeaning, insulting, and downright abusive by white ballplayers.

Some guys, like Joe Durso and Danny Castellano, are genuinely nice guys. They went out of their way to find out what I was really thinking and feeling. They didn't write "pro-Darryl" material; far from it. But they gave me the impression that they understood that I had feelings. They took the time to find out what I was thinking about something before they went ahead and said "Darryl thinks this" or "Darryl says that." I really respect anyone who can sit down and accurately represent what you think and feel and make sure that what he says about you is true, and not a media creation. There were very few other writers who took the time to do that.

If Frank Cashen had once taken the time to sit down with me, either in 1989 or in 1990, to explain why he was not going to renegotiate my contract, I would have understood. If he would have only said *once* that he wanted me to remain with the Mets, but that renegotiating my contract would have meant renegotiating all the contracts, I would have understood that too. Had I been in his position, dealing with a player like me who had shown so much immaturity in the past, I would have taken the time to let that player know how much he meant to the organization, but how much the organization had to adhere to certain bargaining principles with all players, regardless of their race or background. I would have bought that hook, line, and sinker, because I was *looking* for that kind of communication. I needed the support of the Mets family; I craved it. I wanted to stay on the Mets. If they had stepped forward and said the magic words, "Darryl, we want you, we love you, you're one of us, you belong here, but we can't pay you the dough you want. Work with us and help us find a solution, because we're all together in this," I probably would have started crying like a little kid just because I thought I'd found the approval I was looking for. But the Mets taught me a hard lesson: business is business, and emotions play no role. It was a bitter, bitter pill for me to swallow, and I didn't digest it for another eighteen months. But at that time in 1989, they put out all the signals to me that they didn't want me to stay on the team, and that's still the hardest thing in the world for me to accept.

After all the trials of spring training in 1989, we blasted St. Louis 8-4 to open the season. But after two weeks we'd lost six out of eight, had chalked up only three wins since opening day, and were dead last. The press hooted and we were thoroughly embarrassed because we'd been the first place team in the East the year before. Davey Johnson issued an ultimatum in the clubhouse. "You cut out playing cards," he said. "And no more golf games. You guys are playing lackluster ball. You're the best team in the East. Start playing like it!"

Then Davey gave a clubhouse press conference and said he wasn't going to stand in place while the players goofed off until they decided they were champion baseball players. "If I'm going to take the heat, I'm going to pass it down," he said. The team hadn't been overestimated. It was a championship team, but it was going nowhere but deeper into the cellar because the players weren't living up to their billing. "This is serious business," he said, obviously feeling pressure from the big boys upstairs. "And we all get paid very well to do what we're doing." Ominous-sounding words from a man whose team should have won the World Series the year before but never even made it out of the National League championships.

I hit two homers in a single game against the Cards on April 16, but the team still lost. Then the press gathered around me in the locker room. Take a number, fellas; this is gonna be a goodie. "We stink," I told them. "It's not a pleasant moment around this club. We have to work for it. We can't go through the motions anymore." But those were hollow words in the artificial pressure cooker of a division race. Even I wasn't playing well, and I knew it.

Everybody was trying to rush things on the Mets that spring. I was rushing my spring, trying to kill the ball every time I was up; Gary and Keith were off as well. Then to add injury to insult, I got hurt in April when I overswung on a Steve Ontiveros change-up during a game with the Phillies on a cold, damp evening. I hit the pitch, but in grounding out I tore some of the muscle fibers in my shoulder and strained the tendon. The Mets trainers taped it up and gave me medication for the pain, but the medication made me groggy and I stiffened up. I tried to come back against the Chicago Cubs, but I could barely lift the bat. I was laid up for five games.

I managed to pull my average up to .288 by May, but I still wasn't hitting nearly as well as I should have, and the rest of the team could sense that. I was too anxious. Too angry. Too intent on batting my way to an impressive year that would prove to the front office that they should negotiate the extension we wanted in 1989 instead of waiting until 1990. The Mets gradually climbed into a tie for first in the East by the week of May 4, but then barely played .500 ball against Cincinnati, the Astros, and then the Reds again.

We went from bad to worse. Just as my right shoulder began to act up again and keep me from taking my full swing, Gary Carter's troubled knee filled up with fluid and he could barely walk, let alone play. They put him on the fifteen-day disabled list, but when we looked at the way he was suffering we knew that he might well be out for longer than fifteen days. Then when I began to accept that the pain in my shoulder might be season long, my back began tightening up. I knew that was happening because I was shifting my weight to adjust to the pain in my shoulder, putting added stress on my back muscles.

At the same time when I was barely able to play, Timmy Teufel had popped his ankle out while jogging. So we lost two heartbreakers to the Dodgers around the middle of May. These were games I had wanted to win because of our loss to them in the playoffs the year before. And to make matters even worse, while we were fighting tooth and nail to maintain our slim lead in the Eastern Division, Keith Hernandez crashed into Dodger shortstop Dave Anderson while breaking up a double play. He broke the play up all right, but also broke up his right kneecap and had to be sidelined. Now we'd lost both Carter and Hernandez, and I was playing hurt.

Things were looking mighty grim because the bulk of the responsibility was being carried by younger players who had little experience and were playing more like guys on a college team than professionals. Davey was becoming more frustrated with each passing day. He tried to light a fire under the guys, but as he said, "You can't light fires when there ain't no fuel."

Right around the middle of May, I was blindsided by my wife, Lisa. I guess she was tired of being alone during the season, and probably tired of a lot more. She filed for divorce in Los Angeles. Our marriage had been a roller coaster since 1985, even though I was sincerely trying to make the relationship work. I hadn't yet faced my drinking problems head-on, nor had I come to the understanding I would eventually reach regarding my relationship with the Mets and my problems with "family" in general. I was too focused on baseball, the eroding 1989 season, and my contract problems to think about anything else. That was a mistake.

Could things have gotten worse? Sure they could, and did. Gary had to have surgery on his right knee and was lost to us for most of the rest of the season. Davey Johnson pulled up with two ruptured disks in his back and was hobbling around the clubhouse trying to postpone the surgery that would have laid him up for the rest of the season, too. Joe Durso wrote in *The New York Times* that "pain poured over the Mets in waves."

Ronnie Darling began piping up to the press, pounding his fist in frustration as he saw the stats build up against us. We could feel his frustration roll through the clubhouse whenever he walked in and looked around. "The computers say we're the best-hitting team in the league," he said. "We should be right up there, but look around. Computers don't hit." Then HoJo spoke to the press about his frustrations. Makes no sense, he said. "You got a team that scores a lot of runs one year and then doesn't." He was right, it made no sense. But then it made more sense when you realized that I was almost doubled up with back pain, Gary was flat on his back in the hospital, Timmy Teufel was gingerly hobbling around on a very weak ankle that sounded like Jell-O sloshing in a bowl whenever he put stress on it, and Keith had a busted knee.

"We've got the blahs," HoJo told the papers. "Maybe we're spoiled by the success of the last five years, and we expect too much."

"Strawberry's not producing," Davey Johnson chimed in. "He's only hitting .200 with runners in scoring position. We have some of the finest hitters in the league, but if they don't hit, the team will suffer."

I couldn't say much to defend myself. Mad as I was at the situation and pissed off that nobody was bringing up the injuries affecting my play, I knew that I had to do something to help the team get going. I was letting myself get sucked into this "family in need" thing again and taking the burden upon myself when I knew logically that it wasn't mine to shoulder.

I told one reporter, "If Hernandez were here, he'd be the man making things happen. He's not, so I have to."

With the season gradually slipping out of our grasp, with my shoulder and back healing then hurting, and with the divorce proceedings going forward without my being there to do anything to stop them, I knew I had to take some action to try to break this downward spiral. I was afraid about winding up alone without my family and afraid that I might let myself get into a position where I would let them down even though I didn't want to. The more I thought about that, the more I thought about my own father.

I had to open a dialogue. I had to find some little piece of meaning in everything that was swirling around me, especially in the failure of my own marriage. I tried to rationalize away my feelings of hostility toward him at first. I said you can't carry around grudges forever. You have to look at the realities of your own family. My father was still my father no matter what, and part of him was a part of me, no matter how bitter I was. I had to face that anger full on. I had to see what was behind the curtain that I'd been setting up since I was thirteen. I was feeling bad enough about life already, I might as well punch through the wall. That's when I picked up the phone and called him.

I just said hello and grunted politely a few times. I think he was more surprised at hearing from me than I was at my calling him. Then I called him again. I asked him how things were going, how he was getting along in life, how he was coping with things. We didn't talk about his divorce or about mine. He'd ask me how the shoulder was and whether the Mets would pull out. We avoided the big elephant standing between us of what happened on the night he left the family. We just left it there, right in the room, and made believe we didn't see it. Sure it was awkward at first, but we found ways around it and learned to duck the hard questions, like, *Why did you never say a single word to me in fifteen years?*

He must have realized that his children were good kids who had turned out good. He must have seen that we weren't a pack of losers or anything. Well, maybe he'll see it someday. Maybe he'll say something—one word, even—that will let me know that I'm in a family. Maybe. We keep on talking, but the elephant ain't moving.

On June 5, the Mets were butchered by the Cubs 15-3. Starting pitcher Dave Cone was knocked out so hard and so fast that he never even had time to warm up his arm. He spent most of his two innings on the mound ducking and watching balls sail into the outfield. The next day the Cubs knocked Bobby O flat on his backside, 8-4. We won the third game 10-5, but the Cubs took the final game of the series 5-4, and we knew that we needed triage. That was before Pittsburgh beat us two out of three games.

We had spurts of winning, but nothing changed. Then the front office shook up the lineup by trading our platooned center fielder, Lenny Dykstra, and relief pitcher Roger McDowell to the Phillies for Juan Samuel. Juan, Roger, and I are currently on the Dodgers together. I like Juan, but I felt that giving up Lenny *and* Roger, mainstays of the 1986 championship team, was a mistake. In 1990, Lenny turned out to be one of the league's leading hitters with the Phillies, where he was playing every day, and Roger McDowell was a fire-stopper for them.

We slipped into third place in June, only three or so games

back, but we couldn't put together that burst of runs and pitching—a winning streak—that would launch us into first. We'd been able to do it in '86 and again in '88, and would do it in '90, too, but in '89 we were flat. Then in a game against the Montreal Expos, pitcher Kevin Gross threw a ball that hit my foot and broke my right toe. It was more pain, more frustration, and more time on the bench instead of on the field. Then, just as I was trying to come back, Doc Gooden complained of sharp pains in his right side when he pitched and the doctors diagnosed that as a small muscle tear. Doc was out of the lineup.

I decided not to play in the 1989 All-Star game because of my injuries. I looked at our lineup, the walking wounded who were barely able to get together for a game, and decided that I was better off playing healthy during the second half of the season than playing in the All-Star game and risking injury. It was a wise decision, because just before the All-Star break, I went wild and got my seventeenth home run of the year against Pete Rose's Reds in a game that was marked by fights and the threat of a real rumble.

We beat the Reds that night on my two-run homer and two other hits. Late in the game pitcher Rob Dibble hit Timmy Teufel with a pitch. Teufel charged the mound, and Juan Samuel came tearing out of the dugout to get into the ensuing fight. Juan was showing all of us that he was anxious to shed some blood for the Mets. That's good. That's aggressive baseball and the way new players can prove themselves. Very macho. Anyway, Juan stirs up some bad blood over on the Reds' side of the field and tempers are seething.

Well, everyone figured that Dibble had thrown at Teufel because Teufel had gone four-for-four in the game. But not Pete Rose, who, after the game, claimed that if he'd been going to throw at anyone it would have been someone like Howard Johnson, who had stolen bases when the Mets had a big lead (a well-known way of making the other team mad). "If they're going to run like that," Rose said, "they shouldn't be so surprised if someone gets knocked on their butt."

Okay, Pete, you're my hero and all, and that's fair enough. But answer this. Why didn't Dibble drill the guy who stole the base, instead of Timmy, who had nothing to do with it?

So Pete makes his statement and things seem quiet until Reds pitcher Norm Charlton calls the Mets' clubhouse looking for Samuel. I picked up the phone and told Charlton to come on over and not to forget his ass because I was gonna kick the shit out of it. Norm Charlton, get a load of this guy, a rookie pitcher with the *guts* to call our clubhouse to start a fight with a bunch of winners who had been there before and knew what it was all about. What a fool! A fight is a fight. You mix it up on the field and then you leave it there and go about your business. The fans like to see the dust fly and tempers explode. You get tossed out of the game, but you're pros and don't want to see another guy get hurt. And you never call a clubhouse looking for someone.

We had to teach Charlton a lesson he wouldn't soon forget. Dis ain't ya night, Charlton.

Charlton, Danny Jackson, and Tom Browning, the word came down, were moseying over to our clubhouse for a little postgame show. If they were looking for trouble, I was there to make sure it found them first. A few of us Mets set out under the stands to get the drop on them. I didn't grow up in the shadow of Interstate 10 for nothing.

However, security guards headed us off at the pass and kept the two groups apart. The next day we did it our way by beating the Reds 6-3, with Juan Samuel getting a home run off Dibble pitching in relief. Juan said afterward that that evened things up in his mind. I myself hit a double and drove in a run, and that put an end to it. Then the word came down from the National League prexy's office that if there was any more violence, we could expect some suspensions and heavy fines. Hey, don't look at me, prez, I didn't start nuthin'.

In early July, Hernandez started coming back from rehab, playing on our minor league A team down in Florida, and the Mets pulled up to within two and a half games of Montreal. Then HoJo signed a $6 million plus contract to keep him out of free agency. Hey, that looked good to me—not the money, but the fact that the Mets wanted to keep him from filing for free agency at the end of the season. Maybe a sign of things to come?

By the end of July, even with Gary Carter and Mex Hernandez back in the lineup, we were slipping. We were in third place, behind the Cubs, and five games in back of the first-place Expos, and not playing intensely at all. We had a three-game series with the Cubs coming up that I thought would be a real dogfight, the kind of scrappers' game in which the guys left standing would be the ones to take on the Expos for the division championship. I believed we were ready.

Meanwhile, Keith's interview in the September issue of *Playboy* turned up on the newsstands, in which he said that he had a special attachment to me and that he understood the "intense, immense pressure" put on me from the day I was drafted by the Mets. Wow! I opened up to him when I read that. I knew that he and I had similar personalities, and that sometimes we rubbed each other the wrong way. There'd be days when I'd want to send him into a wall—I took a swing at him in the beginning of the season—and that there were days when I knew he wanted to kick my can right out of Shea. But there were other times when I looked up to him with respect and admiration. And reading the *Playboy* interview on that day, I think I actually wanted to plant another kiss on the big stupid lug.

Didn't help us against Chi, though. The Cubs creamed our asses to plunge us down to fourth place. Then we picked up Cy Young Award winner Frank Viola to toughen up the pitching rotation now that Doc would be out healing for a stretch of time. Then we gave up Mookie for Toronto Blue Jays pitcher Jeff Musselman. The whole team seemed in transition, as if Cashen were determined to build a new club before the end of the year. Then there were rumors that Davey was going to go, too. He had dinner with Frank one night and said afterward that he felt like it was his last meal. But Davey survived.

The team managed to lurch forward at the end of August into second place, two and a half games behind the Cubs, tied with the Cardinals, and a half up on the Expos. Despite the disasters that had befallen us during the season, we were still in it. But the papers were quick to point out that when the Mets won the East in the past, they had done it by fifteen and twenty games. When they had just been in contention, they had always lost. It's a pattern, the papers said, so don't hold your breath, Mets fans.

Almost on cue, we went into a September slump that put us six or so games out by the twentieth. During the slump, Davey gamely tried to rouse us with locker-room speeches and by meeting with us one-on-one. His conversation with me was especially frank because somehow we both knew that our days in Mets uniforms were numbered. That's exactly how it turned out by the end of the following year. Davey said that although it seemed at times that he was laying the blame for the team's failure at my feet, he didn't mean to be cruel. "You don't realize it," he said, "and a part of you doesn't even want to accept it. But you do occupy a leadership position on the team where your performance is concerned. When the guys see someone with your talent blast the ball out of the park or even hit consistently in tight situations, they get inspired and come around on pitches they would normally miss. That's how you lead, by example."

I was moved by what he said, not because I hadn't heard it before, but because Davey was taking the time to bring me into his camp. He needed me. When I feel needed, I do tend to respond. Maybe that's unhealthy in some situations, but in team situations, I want to participate. Then Davey said that he'd been with me since I was in the minors. "Eight years is a long time," he said. "But I've never seen you as low as you are right now."

I told him how the divorce had gotten me down even worse than my problems with Lisa in 1987. He said that he understood how personal problems can choke you up so you can't see which way is up. "Funny thing is," he said, sounding more like an uncle than a club manager, "all the worrying you're doing won't actually solve your problems. You'll eventually resolve all of them one way or another. Or the pain will subside so you won't feel so bad. But all of that will happen *after* the season. All you're doing right now is clogging your mind so you can't accomplish anything. You have to unclog your mind, free it of all your worries because you won't solve them anyway, and try to play baseball with a clear head. It isn't easy, but it's the only path you have."

There was never even a hint of unfriendliness in his words. He sounded as concerned as any friend could be for another. He said it made him sad, personally sad, to see me looking so glum. "You were always the guy with spirit," he kept on telling me. "It's sad to see someone you knew as a kid with all that energy and fire so burdened down by the worries of being an adult."

In those moments, Davey sounded like family. It was one of the very few times after 1986 that he did. You see, Davey and I were at odds so often because what we really wanted from each other pulled us in different directions. And when we did communicate it was more an accident after bumping into each other and realizing we were both human beings in an impossible situation. But once in a while, his voice could become one of the few voices of sanity I'd ever hear.

That afternoon, Davey spoke right to the part of me that felt like the Mets were my family and that I should make whatever sacrifices were necessary to stay on the club. I'd be lying if I said I wasn't moved by what he said. If anything, he stirred up my conflicts about being a Met or going the route of free agency. His advice about worrying and clearing your head made sense, however, and I tried to follow it as much as possible. I would get up in the mornings and tell myself that today was going to be a different day. Today I'd put everything right on the shelf except for baseball. But after the game, when I'd be alone and thinking to myself about Lisa and the kids and all the hostility the divorce was stirring up, I'd want to go out for a few drinks with friends. Then I'd drink. Then I'd go to bed sad and lonely again. I was depressed. But I didn't know until I was in Smithers that it was the drinking that was depressing me the most.

During the last week of the season, when we knew that it was over for us and that we were simply trying to cross the finish line so the race would count, all the frustration I felt finally came out in one nasty interview. I said to the reporters that I really wanted to play on the West Coast. Being away from my family was killing me and causing the split-up. "A change of scenery would be good for me," I said. "I'd finally relax and play the way I'm capable of playing. I won't sign a long-term contract here, even if the Mets offer me one." I didn't know what I was saying, because at that very moment, Eric Goldschmidt was holding out the possibility of a four-year contract to the Mets' management. I guess the part of me that was speaking was the guy who couldn't see a future for himself in New York. The Met who'd come up from high school and loved this team more than himself, even, was frustrated beyond endurance.

"It really bothers me," I continued, "the way the fans turn on you, the way the media always has its knives out for you. I'm the man who always gets the blame."

Some of the local New York papers rallied to my support after that interview. *The Village Voice*—the *Voice*, can you imagine that?—said that I was the best player in New York since Mickey Mantle but that because of everything that had happened, I'd "jumped from a confident future to a disappointing past without ever basking in the present. He's not having fun, and neither are we."

I was moved by those comments because they were so painfully true. Not even letters of encouragement from ex-President Richard Nixon could help me out. That's right, Richard Nixon, and make no mistake about it. He's a big sports fan and he's written to me over the years telling me not to worry about the media and to have courage in the face of adversity. He once told me that reporters are going to write what they want to write no matter what you say or do. He ought to know because he's been there in the thick of it and still walked away to tell about it. Took a licking and kept on ticking. He has told me in his letters that he thinks I'm a great baseball player and not to let the fans or the press get to me. I call his notes "cheer-up letters" because they arrive when I'm down and always perk me up a little. He wishes me luck and tells me that he's one hundred percent behind me.

I wish someone could have told me what to do about my family. My divorce proceedings had so screwed up my head that no matter what I tried to do on the field, I couldn't get the cobwebs out long enough to make a real contribution. I missed my kids so badly that it was like a piece of me was missing.

I talked to my son, who always seemed very wise for his age, as if he knew much more than he would ever say. Darryl asked me why I couldn't come home. Standard question in families where parents are divorcing, I know, but it always seems like a new question when it comes out of your own kid's mouth.

Why didn't it ever come out of mine?

"I want you to come home to California," Darryl, Jr., said. "Why do you have to stay in New York when we're in Los Angeles?"

How can you answer your kid when he asks that? How could my father have answered that for me? Even I can see there are problems here. Meanwhile, however, I still had to spend the last part of the season with little Darryl's questions in my head as I tried to hit a baseball that looked like an aspirin tablet, it was so small as it flew across the plate.

With the onset of winter in California, Lisa and I made an attempt to reconcile again and I moved back to the house in Encino that I had bought for the family the year before. But we only began fighting more. Then the judge handed down his decision in the St. Louis paternity suit filed by Lisa Clayton and I was publicly humiliated. I was mad that the Mets hadn't given me the support I felt I was entitled to and mad that I was walking into the 1990 season completely unsupported. I was also seething with anger because of what I'd come to understand about my position on the Mets and what I believed the Mets were trying to do to me. I knew I had a hard year ahead of me.

Christmas and New Year's were tense times for me because of what I was trying to beat down inside my spirit. There were the old demons at work again, bubbling up inside me like an active volcano. The more I tried to quiet myself with thoughts of the coming spring, the angrier I got. The more I tried to medicate myself with booze, the more unsettled I got when the booze wore off and the headaches set in.

I had continued speaking to my father, more at my brothers' urging than my own initiative, but we were still estranged. I couldn't get his problems out of my mind and I couldn't get him to understand my problems with him or with my own kids. We were like two people trying to talk to each other from behind two glass bubbles, yet I wanted desperately to communicate with him. He had the answers. He *has* the answers.

I knew that I began taking it out on Lisa again. Maybe she began trying to spend as much time as possible out of the house to avoid me. Maybe that's why she didn't come home early the way she said she would on January 26, 1990. I had been sitting up waiting for her. Lisa's mother was up from Altadena and was staying in the house to watch the kids. She'd put Darryl, Jr., and Diamond Nicole to bed hours earlier. She was avoiding me, too. I was left to my own devices. I was brooding. Lisa was late. It was after midnight. I drank and tried to doze off, but I couldn't. I was too angry. Then it was two in the morning and she still wasn't home. I was starting to think dark and ugly thoughts. I was feeling abandoned and angry. The demons were dancing through the fires of my mind. I heard a car pull into the driveway. The automatic garage door opened. I heard the sound of the BMW engine reverberating in the garage. Then the automatic garage door closed with a growl. Then I heard the slam of the Beamer's door.

It was three A.M. I got out of my chair. Lisa came through the door. Was she smiling?

15

AMAZIN' GRACE: 1991

When January and February come to Los Angeles, with the warm rains that smell very sweet in the early morning, the desert drought of November and December is washed away. The ground softens and a damp west wind seems to inspire a complete rebirth. The year is bright and new, fresh blades of grass and shoots of tropical plants are popping up everywhere, and everything seems possible.

When people wake up on New Year's Day, they think about the promises they've made to themselves and broken and the resolutions they intend to keep for the coming year. Some people make new pledges to their families; others, especially in California, and I don't know why, say they want to travel to seek new experiences; and others want to renew their spiritual vows. Some people, like me in early 1991, have achieved a complete break with the past and look forward to embarking on an entirely new future.

In January 1991, I began practicing at Dodger Stadium in

my new uniform with my new number. I was no longer number 18 on the New York Mets, but number 44 on the Los Angeles Dodgers. On the sunny days, when the grass was soft and warm, I was impressed again with the greenness of baseball, the freshness of it all, and the way that even in the most hopeless of situations one hit, one stolen base, one wild pitch can change everything around. So as I swung away at the balls that seemed to be hanging in the strike zone just above home plate, waiting to be hit, I promised myself that this would be a year of changes.

Despite everything I said I wanted for myself during 1990 after I was released from Smithers, I had slipped right back into too many old, familiar patterns. I had let the pressure of my negotiations with the Mets get to me and sour the decade I spent in their organization with bad feelings. I had let the anger of my family situation again spill over into my professional life, and clearly I had not learned everything I told myself I would learn. I had been thoroughly psychoanalyzed that final year on the Mets, but despite the intellectual understandings I had come to, I was still being emotionally jerked around by forces outside of my control. I had no structure to my life. There was still a deep pit where I knew that other people had an understanding and a sense of self. I was walking through life under a "cloud of unknowing" that prevented me from breaking through to the truth about myself.

I remembered the story from Sunday school about the merchant who spent his entire life bargaining and bargaining until the process itself became the point. There were no longer any goods to bargain for, but the merchant kept at it. He kept going until he saw something that was of greater value than everything he had bargained for and made him want to sell all that he had in order to obtain it. Was I like that merchant? If so, I had not found what I was looking for.

I knew that much of what was going on inside of me, and had been going on for years, had to do with that terrible night my father left the family. Despite our conversations since that time, we never had what you would call a reconciliation. I believed he still felt something warm for his family, but the years had seemed to cover it over with a kind of scar tissue. They had done the same for me. Desperately I wanted to break through this tough callused skin and bridge the gap between my father and me, but I didn't have the language. How can you reach out when there is nothing to reach out with? How do you forgive when you don't know that you should be the one doing the forgiving? Who can give you the answers? I was blind, I knew, but had to find a way to see the truth.

I was looking toward February and the opening of Dodgertown, in Vero Beach, Florida, where the team would gather and we'd start playing old rivals in the Grapefruit League. The Mets were on our schedule and I knew I'd be facing them and my friend Dwight Gooden. But I still had to find a way to rekindle my spirit, which was flickering after all the bitterness and bad feeling that had built up over the years.

My wife and I had become estranged again. You'd be estranged from your family, too, if you had threatened to kill your spouse with a handgun because of the rift between you. I felt that the house I had bought had become filled with, to use a convenient term, evil spirits. I mean that quite literally, too. You look at a window, a dresser, a chair, a furniture arrangement in a room and it brings to mind a set of feelings that have to do with evil and violence. I could relate unhappiness to every corner of the house. I was filled with remorse. Maybe, I thought, Lisa and I could find an answer to our troubles together and do things differently in the future. I didn't know how we'd manage this, but anything was possible.

Lisa's uncle, Bill Payne, a former Marine and retired LAPD officer, had a suggestion. "Why don't you take a few days to think about things at the Morris Cerullo Convention Center out in Anaheim," he said. I'd heard of it before; most Christians in Los Angeles were very familiar with the evangelical meetings where Morris Cerullo officiated and preached and with the ways he would heal people's spirits right up there on the podium. "You'll learn a lot about what you've been going through and maybe get a chance to talk to people who are looking around for answers the way you are."

It was kind of an informal thing. You didn't have to make any commitments or anything, and Bill Payne knew that I was in a lot of difficulty with my life. He suggested that anything I did to put myself into the right groove would help me out starting the new season. No sense, he said, falling right back into old habits once you're on the Dodgers. Wipe the entire slate clean, he suggested, change the way you're thinking, maybe.

I took him up on it and we made our own kind of pilgrimage

to Anaheim, where, it seemed, people from every county in California had come to find answers, to heal spiritually, or even just to give thanks for having been helped when they were sick. There were fathers bringing their children to hear a spiritual message; young women who, like me, had been around the bases more than a few times; a few cops from different jurisdictions who were coming to renew whatever it was they were afraid of losing; business people and athletes; older people; and large groups of middle-aged women who looked like they were carrying their share of troubles.

Partly, the spiritual convention had the air of a carnival at first. People were greeting friends they knew and making contact over great distances. Partly, there was serious business to attend to, Uncle Bill told me, the saving of souls. Bill was in dead earnest about what was going to take place. "You will learn things about yourself you never dreamed of. You will see yourself in a different way. If you are blessed at the end of this, you will see what it's all about."

Maybe, and I was hoping against hope, I would eventually "get it." Maybe I would see a greater point to all of this and be able to make the breakthrough I'd been trying to make since last season when I came out of Smithers. Professionally, I was in a different place now, I told myself. Wouldn't it be wonderful if I could get myself—or if something could get me—to a different place spiritually?

My mother and my sister had become born-again Christians, but as much as I had claimed to understand the same spiritual truths that had been revealed to them, I was still blind. Maybe now I'd see. There were evil demons, I believed, that were still running through my soul, turning my life inside out. Perhaps here was a way I would find a release.

Could I be saved?

I spent the first few days in a series of classes. Uncle Bill had warned me about this, but I was still a little taken aback at how serious all this was. There was no partying here, and the gatherings weren't social. The people doing the talking, Morris Cerullo and all of the people helping him, were talking as if they believed they were carrying a special kind of knowledge that had to be revealed instead of taught. All they could do was prepare us for the revelation so it would have an impact and not fall on a closed heart. I understood that. How many times had I sought for understanding only to believe that it had passed me by because I wasn't ready to accept it.

Now, I knew, I was being given the chance to recapture some of the understanding that previously I could only hold on to by the edges in hotel rooms after games. In the morning the insights I had come to the night before would be gone. I knew there was a deeper purpose to all that was going on around me. We were taught about how spirits of the earth corrupt the soul. We were taught about how there really were evil spirits that surrounded us, invaded our thoughts, and made us do things we consciously would never want to do.

They taught us how to find those spirits within our thoughts and how to recognize them for the evil that they performed. We were taught to isolate the feelings of wrath, avarice, sloth, pride, lust, envy, and gluttony. They were all around us, we learned, and we became accustomed to living in these sins from the time we were children. To purify ourselves, we had to purify our way of looking at life.

All of this made sense to me, even if I didn't have a method of putting any of it into practice. I could recognize the kind of person I had been. I could see how year after year I was slipping lower and lower into a prideful state. I could also see how much pain I had felt and continued to feel. I even recognized guilt—whether it was legitimate or not—and felt the need to make amends. But there was no closure to any of these feelings. I had no sense of personal power or legitimacy. I could play baseball, and I was looking forward to playing it in Los Angeles, but beyond that there was nothing else.

During the course of the next few days at the convention in Anaheim, I found myself becoming more open to what was going on. I tried to approach the whole thing with an open mind instead of my typical "this is all bull" attitude that I had approached so many things with in the past. I tried to act like the adult I knew I had to be to survive in this environment. I can honestly say that I felt myself begin to change. I was able to pinpoint the aspects of my life that were negative, and even more important, the people talking to me showed me a positive side to myself.

I know what you're thinking. Of course there was a positive side to myself—I am a pro ballplayer, I make lots of money, I lead a glamorous life, and so forth. But that's not what I'm talking about. The trappings of my professional life are just like clothes. Great clothes, but clothes that, when you're going to your grave, simply get stripped off. You go in without any trappings, and you go forward to your final rewards entirely equal to every other person in all respects except one: how you lived your life. Good deeds! If you lived it morally and tried to avoid sin, you're better than if you lived the high life and were the tool of the spirits of the world. So I had to see what about my life stood up to analysis when you took away the trappings and looked at it for what it really was.

Once I understood this, I could look back on all the people I had known in baseball and in the world of celebrities and pick out people who were too much in the world and those who were seeking to avoid the pull of earthly spirits. This was one of the assignments we had during our few days of classes. When I looked around me, it was almost as if I could pick out the uniforms of people who were and who were not in the world. I saw myself in relation to people, how I'd been used and how I'd used others.

I saw it all, and it was almost like a dream: people marching through the world in various states of disillusionment and corruption; people looking for answers. I could see all the different professions and how they tried to use one another and use people, consuming them for their own ends. I saw the role that I played in that too. I saw people who were "winners" in a spiritual sense. These were people who worked honestly at what they did and preserved their own lives and the lives of their families. These winners were individuals who understood how to turn what they earned into acts of charity for other people. Then I saw the "wasters" of the world, people who consumed and consumed without any thought about the needs of others. Wasters saw the world as their domain to use up and befoul. The world was a battle between winners and wasters, and I wanted to be on the side of the winners.

I saw how my alcoholism and abuse, my sexual promiscuity, and my unsympathetic attitudes toward people had created innocent victims. I had to make amends for what I had done. I saw how if I kept living in the world from day to day and believing in the lies of the world how much further away from a state of grace I would actually be. I resolved to try to find my way toward grace logically, but it wasn't easy. You can't apply logic to this kind of situation. I really was on a kind of pilgrimage, I understood, a pilgrimage from a state of confusion and doubt to a state of revelation and enlightenment.

As the week went on, I began to get intimidated by what I was trying to grasp. I was not going to live forever. My life was finite. Actually, life is very short, but the craft of living properly takes a long time to learn. And when you realize that all you occupy in your life is a tiny little spot of earth, you understand your limitations. I became truly weary as I spiritually wandered from place to place in every different session we had. When would the insight come? When would I be able to say about myself that I had been graced with a revelation about my own existence? But it still eluded me.

My uncle Bill told me to be patient, that at the end, everything would be clear. But I had begun to doubt even him. "Why did you bring me to a place where all I could see was the evil things that I had done?" I felt like Scrooge after the visits of the three ghosts. All I could see were the evils of the world without the understanding of the good of the world. Where was it? Who represented it?

Then on a Sunday morning we gathered for a "meeting," or mass, in the large auditorium. We were asked to think about the insights we had come to during the previous week and the work we had done on analyzing our own spirits. All of the new visitors, myself included, were asked if they were ready to receive the Holy Spirit. I looked at my uncle and he simply nodded. "But how do I know if I'm ready?" I asked him.

"I know you're ready," he said. That was all.

How did he know if I didn't? But at his urging, pushing actually, and he's a pretty strong guy, I went out into the aisle and filed up with the line toward the podium. I was kind of embarrassed and, along with the others, just slouched toward what everybody was calling the New Jerusalem. Finally I arrived at the podium and I was led to a spot right before the minister.

He put his hands on my head and prayed that I would find salvation and that the power of the Holy Spirit would enter into me. As he prayed, I felt a tingling sensation that I had never felt before. I truly didn't know what it was. Then he gripped me tight and called upon the power of revelation to enlighten me right NOW!

And I was suddenly struck as blind as blind could be. I couldn't hear, I didn't know where I was for a second, and the force that hit me literally knocked me right off my feet. When I was able to open my eyes and get up, I was welcomed into the world as a new person.

When I opened my eyes I could see as I had never seen before. It was as if I had truly been blind for all my years but now had been granted the power of sight. But it was a special kind of sight, insight, a power to see through the trappings of the world and deep into the essences of things and people. It wasn't like X-ray vision or anything—don't get me wrong—it was just an ability not to lie to yourself about what you were seeing. I was able to tell the truth to myself for the very first time in my life since I was a teenager.

I was aware of a sensation of happiness and peace. I had found it, I told myself, and Uncle Bill agreed with me.

"You have indeed found it," he said. "You have done well. And now you must do better and share your insight with others."

So I began to share it with others. I began talking about the revelation I had had and it started to put people off, but I didn't care. I'd found it! I was too happy. I was too sure of what had happened to me to be thrown off. Besides, there were many other people I was speaking to, people like Gary Carter, who had already found what I knew I had found.

"You're going to lose your edge," I was warned.

"Finding spiritual peace is the death of long-ball hitters," other people said to me.

"Prepare for a disastrous year in L.A.," someone else predicted to me. "Athletes who become born-again Christians are notorious for performing badly during their first few seasons."

But none of those comments bothered me because I understood more about myself than at any time in my life. I knew that it would affect my game and the way I hit the ball. I said if that's the case, so be it. I am the same baseball player, but a different human being. The Dodgers actually got more than they bargained for, Bill Payne laughed. They bought a long-ball hitter, but they wound up with a long-distance runner as well.

I still don't know all the answers, still don't even know many of the questions. I only know that I have indeed been like the merchant who spent his whole life making bargains. Then one day I found this wonderful pearl. It was so valuable, because it represented truth, and so completely without flaws, I was willing to give up everything I owned just to own it.

Maybe the pearl represents salvation, maybe it represents the power of the Holy Spirit, maybe it represents a level of enlightenment I have now that I didn't have before. Maybe. But it also represents a certain understanding that existence can be flawless if you know what flaws go along with being human and what flaws are almost voluntarily made. I think I can see that now, although I still have a lot to learn.

Maybe all of this will make me a better baseball player, too. I hope so. Baseball is the easy part. Living is the hard part.

16

A STRAW IN THE WIND

What could be better than watching an exciting game seven of the World Series on a nice warm evening in Los Angeles? *Playing* in the World Series on a chilly hostile evening in Minneapolis–St. Paul. That's what's better. I could've been there. I coulda been a contenda. I had a seven—count 'em, seven—RBI game at home against the San Diego Padres on August 21 in our end-of-season drive to finish first in the National League West. I hit grand slams. I hit everything. But instead of playing, I'm just another guy watching this thing on TV. If we hadn't lost that first series in the middle of September to Atlanta, and blown a couple of those games against the Giants in October, we could've been there. We could've beaten the Pirates and won the pennant. Then we would've beaten Minnesota.

Hmm, interesting the way Lonnie Smith takes that big lead off first like he's going on a hit and run. He better keep his eye on his third base coach a little more if he's gonna break for second on the swing. That's one of the secrets of good base running, especially at the end of a tie game like this. Atlanta's trying to play Billyball—or Bobbyball, I guess. But this should have been the Dodgers playing Tommyball. Only if we were there, there wouldn't have been a seventh game because we would have taken 'em in five. Six at most.

In my opinion, if you were to sit down and compare the rosters of the 1991 Dodgers and Braves, you'd see that the Dodgers were stronger on paper. Maybe not by much, but enough to have won the National League West. And that was what kept us going through the 1991 season. We spent most of our time in first place in the National League West because we believed we were supposed to. But you've got to give credit where credit's due. Atlanta fielded not only a powerful team, but a team that was really a "family," a team with the drive to win.

For the Dodgers, the 1991 season was a "might have been" year. I hope it will become for us what 1985 was for the New York Mets: the kind of year that shows you what you can really do if you play together as a team instead of as a bunch of individuals. In 1985, the Mets had the talent and the power. The disappointment at the end of the season forged us into a real team, and that made it possible for us to do the impossible in 1986. I hope 1991 does the same thing for the Los Angeles Dodgers.

We began the '91 run for the flag by getting into a quick dogfight with the San Diego Padres for the lead in the West. Things didn't look too good early in the season. By the middle of April, when I was still sweating out my swing and only hitting .179, we were 0-3 against the first-place Padres and hanging on by our fingernails, one and a half games behind. Every game was a must just to stay at .500. By the end of April, we were still a game and a half out of first, but now we were in third place, behind San Diego and Cincinatti. Atlanta was a game behind us. There were some wild, high-scoring games in the beginning of the season before the pitchers settled down, but Orel Hershiser was on the mend and showing some of the brilliance and dominance he had shown in years past. We promised ourselves we would make our move in May and leave the other teams in the dust. We hadn't yet figured on the Braves. It was still early.

When veterans like Brett Butler, Gary Carter, and I come into a clubhouse on a new team for a first season together, there's bound to be a little bit of feeling out at first. Do you come on strong and really show who you are right away? Do you try to start out as the leader? Do you try to bring to your team a piece of what you had on another team or look at it as a totally new beginning? With a leader like Tommy Lasorda, we took our cues from the way he handles things. Brett and I each decided on our own to hang back at the beginning of the year and not come on too strong until we spent a year in the clubhouse. We also felt we didn't have to be leaders because Tommy Lasorda's style in the dugout is so aggressive. I had seen it before I came to the Dodgers, now I was witnessing it firsthand.

Tommy is an important presence on the Dodgers. He gets involved. He's not a laid-back manager. When Tommy wants you to do something or stop doing something, he tells you. You know exactly where you stand with Tommy Lasorda and I like that. When you're on deck with the tying and leading runs already on base and he says to you, "Straw, you better hit that ball like there's no tomorrow," you know you'll be a lot happier when you walk back into that dugout if you've cleared those bases.

Tommy had said to me at Vero Beach during the preseason that he didn't want me to feel as if I had the responsibility to carry the entire team. "It's not your show," he'd say over and over again when I'd talk about what had happened on the Mets and my feelings that if I didn't produce, the team would fail.

"That's not how it's going to go on the Dodgers," Tommy would say. If baseball's just a job, he'd say, then there's no point in playing it. "It's not like punching a time clock," he told me once down in Florida. "You have to treat it like a game and you'll excel at it. Treat it like working the night shift someplace and it'll become a chore." That's just what I wanted to hear, and I set out to have a fun season.

So I took my cue from Tommy and didn't press the leadership issue. I stepped into the batter's box with the idea that I wanted to produce, I wanted to get in the neighborhood of 100 RBIs and 30-something home runs, and I wanted to get about 30 stolen bases for the year. These weren't "musts," but they were goals that would assure me I hadn't lost any ground since coming from New York. But about leadership, I figured, "Hey,

I busted my brains over that issue on the Mets; I'm not going to press it now."

Another issue that involved Brett and me, as well as Gary Carter and Orel Hershiser, was our spiritual brotherhood. I didn't consider myself to be an evangelist or a minister, just a believer. I knew about the Baseball Chapel—a ministry of Christians in baseball that's been in operation for about eighteen years now. There are a lot of guys I know and used to play with who are members of the Chapel, including "Junkman" Bob Knepper, Howard Johnson from the Mets, the former San Francisco Giants' pitcher Dave Dravecky, and Sid Bream down in Atlanta. With the support of Orel, Brett, and Gary, I joined the Chapel too.

Orel's faith was an inspiration all season. I first saw the intensity of his commitment back in 1988 when the Mets played the Dodgers. Orel didn't get angry when Dave Cone joked about his good luck. He didn't get frustrated when things didn't go his way. But Orel had a way of bearing down on you when you faced him. He came back from his injury during the off-season this past year with a real energy. There wasn't a single negative thought in his spirit. Everyone said that coming back would be a nearly impossible task—everyone but Orel. He "knew." He "had it." He understood that it was his mission to get himself back into shape, not just to win games but to set an example for millions of people watching him pitch. He had to show that his faith and his belief would get him there. And they did!

It was painful watching Orel work himself into shape during the early part of the year. I just stood aside and watched him apply the power of his spirit and his belief to the techniques of pitching. He'd make a little adjustment here, a small change of position there, or a shift in his stance. With every pitch you'd see him get just a touch stronger. "The power's there," he'd keep saying. "Control will surely follow." And for those of us who know him, we felt every criticism from the press or the fans along with him. But we also knew that Orel would triumph because he was blessed with revelation and insight.

People were also criticizing Gary Carter for being too old to take the banging around that catchers get. I knew Gary better than anyone from butting heads with him during my years on the Mets and I knew that you never *ever* count out Kid Carter. He's the most intense ballplayer I know. He can beat you on spirit alone. So can Orel Hershiser. That's enough to stop half the teams in the National League West. Then you add Brett Butler.

Brett realizes that because of his public commitment to Christianity, he's become a role model to people watching him on television. He's been quoted as saying that "some people won't see the gospel of God except by me, according to me. It's my responsibility for the kingdom of God to play center field and live my life to the utmost." That's a heavy challenge, and when you undertake it, you've got to be prepared to go all the way. Brett is, and that's what makes him so dangerous on the ball field. With his play in the outfield and his .285 lifetime batting average, he's the kind of guy you think twice about when you see him staring at you from the batter's box.

People got on me too, early in the year, because they thought I had lost my "edge." They didn't realize that I was still as hyper as ever. I still fought with myself over how angry I should get at opposing pitchers and batters and how much I should push myself. I still doubted my ability to lead and worried about my responsibilities to the rest of the team. I knew I still had problems chasing bad pitches. But I also had a feeling that these were problems I would solve. Maybe it would take me a year to work myself into playing at home in Los Angeles, but I would do it. Still, I was pretty frustrated.

I was swinging too high and too low. I was going after pitches that Little Leaguers would have watched bounce over the plate. I was too worried about showing the hometown fans that Darryl was back and worth every dime of the $20 million they were paying him. I wasn't having fun; I was too busy proving my worth. It was the wrong attitude and Tommy Lasorda was the first to straighten me out.

"I don't care if you don't get a hit the whole first half of the season," he said. "Take your time. You're gonna be here for a while. No one's rushing you to hit back-to-back grand slams."

Then Brett Butler came up with a few suggestions. "You're a natural player," he said. "You'll work everything out you have to work out. Just don't listen to what people say about you. Listen only to the one voice you know is true." He added that I shouldn't be afraid to focus my anger at opposing pitchers and hitters. "It's righteous anger. It's competitive anger. It's what you're supposed to do," he said. That helped me a lot.

Toward the middle of May, we clawed our way past the

Padres into first. San Diego quickly dropped into third and then fourth, and we found ourselves in a struggle with Cincinnati for the lead in the West. I still didn't have my swing down right and the fans were hooting that I didn't have the fire in my belly to get the job done. I had the fire all right, I just didn't have the "firewater" in my belly that suckered me into shooting off my mouth the first chance I got at the end of every game. I just decided to play it cool, work the rust out of my swing, and get used to my new life-style. I was playing ball for the rest of my life, I told myself, not just for this game or this season.

Then the collision happened. I was running like all getout after a line drive on a Wednesday night when I hit the right field wall. I was really shaken for a moment and then I felt a blaze of pain. They got me to the hospital where the doctors X-rayed my separated left shoulder. Great! That's my power shoulder. They wanted to put me right on the disabled list, assuming I wouldn't be ready for weeks, but I fooled 'em. I was in the starting lineup just two days later. My faith helped me overcome the pain of the separation, but the shoulder was still weak. I had to sit out a few games and couldn't contribute as much as I wanted to.

By early June we were in first, two and a half games over the Braves and nine games over .500, but I still wasn't hitting. We were being carried by our pitching staff. Morgan seemed to have reached an early peak and John Candelaria was coming on strong in relief. In fact, Candy hadn't allowed a run since April. The team was confident. In fact, people were saying that we would be eight or nine games ahead of the second-place team by the time the regular season ended. Part of me said, "Man, does it get any easier?" but another part of me said, "Watch out. This ain't over yet."

I was in and out of the lineup, worried about my shoulder and worried that I wasn't getting my hits. It seemed that every time I tried to settle down, I wasn't able to get the strength in my shoulder that I needed. That's when Tommy Lasorda and the trainers stepped in. It was June 2 and the shoulder was still sore from the May injury. "Get him out of the lineup," they said. "Let the shoulder rest once and for all so it's strong when we need it." Tommy said that the real pressure would come after the All-Star Game on July 9. He said that's when we'd see some superhuman baseball out there, and he wanted me to be ready for it. "Sit it out, Straw," he said. "Look, we're still in first place on our pitching and on Samuel's, Lenny Harris's, and Murray's hitting. When you're back in the lineup, we'll blow the other teams off the field."

On Monday, June 10, one week after Tommy pulled me from the starting lineup, I woke up in the hotel in Chicago where we had an away game against the Cubs and tried to move my sore shoulder. No pain! I worked it around to see if I could get a twinge out of the muscle, but it seemed okay. So I phoned my coach Bill Russell and said, "Look, I don't care what Tommy said, my shoulder's fine and I want to be in tonight's lineup. I can't wait until the break."

"We need the hitting, Straw," Bill said, and phoned Tommy Lasorda to tell him that he thought I might be ready. Tommy gave the green light and I was in the lineup.

What a game we had in Chicago that night. We beat the fourth-place Cubs 13-5 on 16 hits. Even Tommy was amazed that I played and that we did so much damage to Chicago. Fans told me afterward that it was my presence back in the lineup that got the other players to hit. I felt that might have been true, and for the first time in my career, that feeling didn't frighten me the way it used to on the Mets. Here on the Dodgers, I didn't mind picking up the burden of leadership. It was a good feeling, and I was enjoying the sense of camaraderie among the Dodgers.

On June 12 we suffered a tough loss to our first-place rivals in the East, the Pittsburgh Pirates, and dropped to two games in front of Atlanta. The Braves seemed to match us step for step. I was confident, but still went hitless in Pittsburgh, striking out with the bases loaded in the third inning. The big play was when Eddie Murray missed a stop sign by the third base coach and went chugging ahead for the plate on a Kal Daniels line drive. He was easily tagged out. It was a game we could have won and should have won. The Pirates were trying to show us why they were in first place and we were trying to show them why we were in first place. They showed us better than we showed them.

On the same night, Steve Avery was on the mound for the Braves making the New York Mets look bad. Not only did Avery spread five hits over nine innings, he also went four for four at the plate and tripled in a run. We'd better have a nice safe lead, I thought to myself. These weren't the old Braves. Things to come. Things to come.

On and on we dueled through June, like a couple of heavyweights banging our way into the late rounds. My shoulder was acting up again. Tommy told me to chill out for a couple of weeks while the rest of the team slugged it out, so on June 18, I went on the disabled list. Then Atlanta faltered. Cincinnati took over second place. The Dodgers began to win again.

July 3, my first day off the disabled list: Maybe the world didn't see the throw I made from right field to nail San Diego's Fred McGriff at home and stifle a Padres rally. I scooped up Benito Santiago's single on one bounce, saw that McGriff was headed home, and whipped a line drive from the middle of right field to Kid Carter who was blocking the plate. McGriff tried to knock the ball away from Carter and felt the effects of that collision for the rest of the season. Now I was feeling my oats. I knew my shoulder was back. The next night I belted my first home run since coming back from the disabled list. We ratcheted ourselves up to five games over the Reds and eight and a half games ahead of Atlanta. It looked like there was no way we could be stopped. The division championship and the pennant were ours for the taking. By the All-Star Game, we owned this league.

I was looking forward to the All-Star break. It had always been a turning point for me in previous years. I had been named to All-Star teams every year since 1984, and I was in 1991 too. But this year I decided to sit out the All-Star Game. Winning the pennant meant more than beating the American League. I took the time to make sure the shoulder was healed and would come back strong.

We emerged from the All-Star break smoking, nine and a half games over the third-place Braves and five over Cincinnati. Mike Scioscia was still hurt, but Gary Carter, who took his place, had had a thirteen-game hitting streak. I was only hitting .188 with runners in scoring position, but I knew my time was coming. We were cruising. So somebody asked Mike Scioscia in the clubhouse, "Hey, Mike, what's the secret of the team's success this year? You guys gonna go all the way?"

"The only way we'll lose this thing," Mike Scioscia answered, "is if some other team gets flat-out hot, plays .650 ball, and beats us. Because injuries don't seem to affect us. And slumps don't seem to affect us."

Uh-oh, Mike. Statements like that have a terrible way of coming back to haunt you when you least expect them to. I know.

And the tomahawks go chop, chop, chop, chop, chop.

The second half of our season began in Montreal on July 11, and we played, said Bill Plaschke of the *Los Angeles Times*, "as if suddenly cursed." He was right. Nothing Bobby Ojeda did, not even his home run with a runner on, could save us from ourselves. Tommy Lasorda was cool about it—"They tried to give us the game" he said, "and we wouldn't take it." Still, nothing he said made the loss any easier to bear. Montreal was a spoiler in the National League. They shouldn't have beaten us. We should have taken them far more seriously than we did. I still believe that it was the Montreal series starting off the second half of the season and the way they were able to shut down our hitters—including myself—that began our unraveling.

We lost to the Expos the next night in Montreal too. Is Olympic Stadium tilted or something? We couldn't do anything right there. The Braves picked up two games on us. July 12 and they were seven and a half out.

Chop, chop, chop.

Almost two weeks later and we'd lost about eight of our last ten games. The Braves were just two and a half behind us. Was somebody keeping an eye on these Braves? Did anybody notice that they were winning all these games without Sid Bream and Dave Justice? These guys were hurt, sitting on the bench. What was gonna happen when they got well? I didn't like the look of things at all.

I had begun a long hitting streak, but it wasn't doing us any good because we were losing games, and the Braves had moved up to three and a half games out of first. Our position had seemed so comfortable in the middle of July, but by the end of the month the season had turned into a battle. Then we hosted Montreal and faced Mark Gardner, who would have one of the great nights of his career. Gardner pitched nine innings of hitless ball. He threw dazzling stuff, nothing that smoked by you, but beautiful off-speed curves that were unhittable. Lenny Harris said it best when he told reporters afterward that Gardner had kept the entire Dodgers batting order off balance the whole night. We couldn't get an angle on anything he was throwing. Fortunately, Orel Hershiser and Kevin Gross kept the Expos scoreless also, and we went into the tenth tied 0-0. Then Lenny just barely beat out a slow infield grounder to scratch out a single in the bottom of the tenth.

You could see Gardner get shaky after that. He'd lost his no-hitter and now the game was in jeopardy. Everybody knew it. It was like a change in the air. He gave up a single to Eddie Murray that moved Lenny into scoring position at third. They pulled Gardner's butt out of the game and brought in Jeff Fassero. But Fassero got behind me on the first pitch, and I knew I could end it right there. He was afraid to pitch to me, taking no chances on giving me anything close to the plate. I didn't have to do anything fancy because there were no outs, and Lenny could score from third on anything that I hit to the outfield, he's that fast a runner. I just had to not go after stupid pitches. Then Fassero threw another ball and put himself in the hole, 2-0. Now he had to either pitch to me or walk me and load the bases. He should have walked me, buying himself some time to get settled in. His next pitch was low and outside again, where I knew he was gonna throw it, and I just stepped in and scooped the ball over the shortstop's head for a base hit that scored Lenny Harris and won us the game.

Mark Gardner had pitched his heart out. Everybody on our team thought so. Our pitchers were even laughing about it. Jay Howell called it one of the strangest games he ever won, because how can you win a game against a pitcher who throws a no-hitter? The Dodgers' fans gave Gardner a standing ovation when the Expos pulled him out in the tenth. Even Tommy Lasorda said he pitched "a helluva game," and Tommy's pretty close to the vest when it comes to complimenting another team's pitchers. Maybe he'll give the nod to Doc Gooden or Nolan Ryan, but that's it.

The press and the fans celebrated our victory, but Tommy didn't like it. We had to work too hard for it, he said. Gardner was good, but our hitting was off. No one should be shutting down the meat of the first-place team's batting order for so many innings. "You got a nice piece of the ball, Straw," he said. "But it could have been too little too late." We've got to bear down, he told us, if we're going to win this division. We'd pulled ahead of Atlanta a little more, but if a team like Montreal could shut us down, we'd soon lose our edge again. We responded, and the next night *we* shut Montreal down completely behind Bobby O. Things were looking up. My average was around .245, and Atlanta had lost to the Cubs. Maybe we'd coast into August after all. Then the bottom fell out.

We were set to face Dennis Martinez in the final game of the Expos series and I took my thirteen-game hitting streak over to Dodger Stadium. I told myself I was going to hit a towering home run. Well, instead, Dennis Martinez ended my hitting streak by pitching the Expos' first perfect game. We were in the record books, but on the wrong side of the ledger.

I sighed as I watched my streak end. I'd had them before and I knew I would have them again. The year before I'd hit in seventeen or so straight games before the streak came to an end when the Mets broke off negotiations. I'd felt completely deflated and useless when that happened and it showed in my play. The trick with hitting streaks is not to worry about failing. Look up, not down, and don't let your mistakes keep tripping you up. When you've got the likes of a Dwight Gooden throwing 96-mile-per-hour pitches that break inside or outside just as they cross the plate, you don't have time to worry about hitting streaks. You have to stay on top of what the pitcher's doing so you can stay ahead on the count. Instead of worrying about it when the streak comes to an end, you have to pick yourself up again and start a new one. That was the kind of thinking that helped me after Dennis Martinez shut me and the rest of the Dodgers down on July 28. Then we rolled into August and our fall from the top.

The New York Mets were pulling into town. They were not the same Mets who had tossed their hats into the Shea Stadium stands six years ago. Most of those players had long since been traded. Gary, Bobby O, and I are on the Dodgers. Lenny Dykstra is a Philly. Keith Hernandez, Mookie Wilson, Wally Backman, Roger McDowell, and Ron Darling are all gone away. Juan Samuel was there for a while in 1989, and now he's on the Dodgers with Gary, Bobby, and me. Only Doc and Howard Johnson and a few others remained on this very different Mets ball club.

Hojo's in the spotlight now that I'm gone, the papers said. "Since Strawberry's no longer casting his long shadow across the Mets from right field, Howard Johnson has emerged as the team's most visible player." Buddy Harrelson, for the time that he was there in '91, exhibited his usual class when he explained that HoJo was more of a leader than I was. "Not with his mouth," Buddy explained to the press, "by the way he plays, hard and hurt." Laughs rumbled across the clubhouse as Buddy continued, "He's twice gone through a full season without ever saying he couldn't play, then had shoulder surgery when it was over."

As the '91 Mets rumbled up the Hollywood Freeway and into Dodger Stadium, fresh from losing to the Padres, there were old scores to settle, old wounds that take years to heal. There were memories of triumph in two of the greatest baseball games ever played and of frustration over what might have been in the years after 1986. There were emotional scars as well, among the players who had moved from coast to coast, from team to team, on the red-eye. Just as the cities of Los Angeles and New York are always in competition, so are their National League baseball teams. The Dodgers and Mets slug it out for no other reason than to slug it out.

The Mets were struggling along the West Coast in worse shape than they'd been in years. Wrecked by poor trades, they were trying to rebuild around a shaky core. A lot of what they said about HoJo was true. He was holding down a tough spot and performed consistently better than I did in my final years with the team. He may not hit the scoreboards too often, but he hits home runs with the best of them. Still, the Mets were wobbling under Buddy Harrelson in his second and final year as manager. Dave Cone told the press that the team was troubled. They were about five games behind Pittsburgh and had to sizzle like they hadn't sizzled in the past two years to catch the Pirates. Even HoJo told the press that the Pirates were better prepared to win ball games than the Mets. "We have some bad attitudes here," he said. My old teammate Dave Magadan, who had made so much of a difference with his bat the year before, said that some of the Mets were acting as if they were already out of contention.

There were other signs of cracking in the Mets facade. Buddy Harrelson's decisions were being questioned again, and when he had called an optional batting practice before a recent game, only a few players showed up. Players were starting to show signs of temper at Buddy and at the coaching staff.

Team members were angry at one another, accusing one another of giving up before the season went into its final month. And now they were moaning about losing the group that had put them over the top in '86.

But these same Mets came into town and beat us two out of three. Our bats were still silent and the fans let us know that they weren't happy. It was humiliating. It was something we didn't want to go through ever again. It's one thing to lose to a powerful Mets team that can do no wrong. But it's another thing to lose to a messed-up Mets team that had just been shut down cold by a second-division ball club. The fans were getting anxious.

Somehow the games of August all seem to blend together. We didn't play all that badly, but the Braves just kept on winning, and by August 31 they were in first place, a game ahead of us. In the early days of September, we were neck and neck with Atlanta. When we met the Houston Astros on September 12, it was a grudge game for me because I was responding to a challenge thrown down by the Astros' rookie relief pitcher Al Osuna. Osuna had pitched well against us early in the season and had bragged that he was shutting me down. I was mad at that remark. I always get mad when someone says something personal about me. I had shoulder problems and Osuna got lucky. Fine, live with it, but don't throw it back at a guy who can hardly pick up his bat. Osuna was pissed that I told him to wait until I was up to speed, that then he'd see a different Darryl Strawberry. Osuna said that I'd see what he could throw the next time we met. I took that personally as well.

Osuna entered the game in the eighth inning and threw three straight balls that I thought were aimed right at my head. I didn't like that. I never like it when someone comes in tight at me after challenging me. I waggled my bat right at him and yelled at him to watch out. Then he blew another high pitch by my head and walked me. I glared. Next time, Al. Next time.

In the tenth inning, with the score tied at two, Osuna walked Brett Butler and hit Lenny Harris on the hand. Up to your old tricks, eh, Al? Now it's my turn. I raised my bat at Osuna. Then he threw a fastball low and tight that I was able

to scoop out of the bottom of the strike zone and send deep
into the right field stands, about 400 feet away. Lots of oohs
and aahs. I had had the last laugh on Osuna, and we went on
to win the game.

Everyone saw our two series against Atlanta—first there,
beginning September 13, then back in L.A., beginning September 20—as the most exciting games in the National League
during that month. It was all coming down to the wire, down
to the head-to-head clashes between the two teams. Who
would give in first? Who would slack off at the end of a game
so that the season would end and we could all go home? I kept
telling myself it wouldn't be the Dodgers.

In Atlanta on September 13, we began a three-game series
against the division-leading Braves. Fulton County Stadium
was hot and crowded. As we were warming up, I could see
little kids in the stands, barely old enough to walk, chopping
those tomahawks down at me. Chop, chop, chop. Then the
game started and the fans started their *Darr-rryl* chants. They
were so loud and so long I thought I was back at Shea. Well,
they paid for their tickets, so let them make noise and chop as
much as they want. I was there on business, National League
business, and they'd soon see what I meant.

With the *Darryl* chants ringing in my ears in my first at-bat,
I pounded a single to score Brett Butler. When I came up again
five innings later the fans were still on me. Okay. I took Tom
Glavine hard and deep for a home run to right that tied the
game at 2-2. I singled again later, and then again for my fourth
hit of the night, and we beat the Braves 5-2 and were back in
first.

But the next night, the Braves beat us, then again on the
final day of the series. Now we were one and a half out with
only eighteen games remaining. A few days later Atlanta paid
a three-game visit to Dodger Stadium and this time we won
the series and went into the latter part of September with a
one and a half game lead, which we quickly stretched to two
when the Braves split a doubleheader with the Reds.

The trick was for us to win all our games at home because
we seemed to run into lots of trouble on the road. On September 25, for example, in a game that should have been a
walkaway for us at Jack Murphy Stadium in San Diego, we
made three errors and blew the game 8-2, while Atlanta was
losing the second game of that doubleheader with the Reds.

We could have gone two and a half up on the Braves that night, and it probably would have made all the difference in the world with nine games remaining on the schedule. But with the three errors—by Juan Samuel, Lenny Harris, and Mike Sharperson—we looked like we were playing on a golf course with divots and holes instead of on a baseball diamond. This was a game that we should have won, but didn't. It was not the way to get into the playoffs, and we knew it. Meanwhile, Atlanta still chopped along behind us, waiting for us to stumble so they could snatch it all away.

I sank into an eleven-game slump in the latter weeks of September. I was trying to keep us alive, but the weight of the season had begun to drag on all of us. We were playing as individuals now, not as a team. On those few occasions when we came together as a team, we enjoyed the spirit. But it wasn't natural. Maybe there were too many of us from other organizations in our first years on the Dodgers. Maybe we weren't arrogant enough or weren't ready to speak up to the other teams. Maybe we were just too low-key when we should have been hot-blooded and ready to fight for the pennant with our bare knuckles if we had to. When we displayed some team spirit and fire, it made a difference. When we played the Giants in our final home game against them during the season, for example, it looked as though we would blow the game and sink into a tie with the Braves, who had come from five runs behind to beat Houston 6-5 that afternoon.

The Giants were leading 2-1 as we went into the ninth inning three outs away from losing it. The team's spirits were down. Whose spirits wouldn't be down after seeing Atlanta come back against Houston the way they did? That was an example of kick-ass baseball, and we knew that we'd have to play at that level to win the division. Eddie Murray knew that as he watched the scoreboard and understood what we were up against. He looked around the dugout at all the players who were no longer in the game. He saw guys wearing ice packs, guys half dressed, and guys just sitting there as if they were in a stupor. He whipped them up, got them to the edge of the dugout where they could be part of the game. He got them involved as teammates instead of as spectators. It worked. With a pair of outs against us in the ninth, I hit a single that scored Brett Butler with the winning run. We stayed a game up

on Atlanta and moved toward a final showdown with the
other West Coast teams.

I have to say that as excited as I was about the run I drove
across and about breaking out of my slump, I was nervous
about Atlanta. The Dodgers were just hanging on by their
fingernails. Atlanta was doing much more. Sure, both teams
had been in and out of first place in September. But the difference was that the Atlanta players were operating as a team,
not just as a bunch of professional jocks with gym bags who
showed up to play, shook hands, and then went home. I was
miffed because I was seeing my teammates as my family again
—the way I had on the '86 Mets, when everybody was into
winning—and I saw that they weren't coming together as a
family. That was when I promised myself that I was going to
make a change the following year. You don't see a team like
Atlanta down by five runs come from behind to win a crucial
game and not feel as though you learned something from the
experience.

After our win against the Giants, we won the next two over
the Padres. We had won eleven of our last fourteen games, but
our lead over the Braves was still just one game, so when we
lost our last home game of the regular season to the Padres,
9-4, and the Braves won their sixth straight, beating the Reds,
they tied us for first place. We would play our final three games
against our long-standing rivals, the Giants, at Candlestick
Park, while the Braves would finish up with the last-place Astros at home in Atlanta.

It seemed as if the Giants wanted to beat us more than the
Astros wanted to beat the Braves. On Friday night, October 4,
Steve Avery of the Braves no-hit Houston for almost seven
innings and the Braves coasted to a 5-2 win. The game was
completed even before ours with the Giants started. Giants
pitchers Bud Black and Jeff Brantley shut us down that night
and we lost 4-1. Now we were a game behind with only two to
play.

The next day, our offense never could get it going. Trevor
Wilson shut us out on two hits and we lost 4-0. The Braves
went on and clinched the division by beating the Astros again
5-2. Down the stretch, Atlanta won eight straight crucial
games.

Atlanta went on to play the Pittsburgh Pirates for the National League pennant. The Pirates had led the National

League East for most of the year and were waiting for their chance to win the pennant they had lost to the underdog Cincinnati Reds in 1990. The 1991 National League Championship Series went to seven games, with the Braves managing to pull out the final two in Pittsburgh for the victory.

When our season ended in October, Brett Butler and I talked about what we would do the following year. We knew, even as we watched the Braves in the playoffs, that we had the better team. But we knew that the Braves knew how to play better than we did. We went public. No need to hide our feelings. Next year we would be back. Next year we would exert leadership. Next year.

World Series, game seven: *Crack!!* Lonnie Smith seems to jump at the sound of the bat. He puts his head down and takes off for second as the ball flies into the outfield. Look up, Lonnie! There's his third base coach waving him on. But when Lonnie picks his head up he starts looking around. Where's the ball? Don't look for the ball, Lonnie, look at your coach. Lonnie thinks he sees Minnesota second baseman Chuck Knoblauch and shortstop Greg Gagne throwing and catching a ball. Duhhh. "I got it," somebody in a Twins uniform yells right in front of him, and instinctively Lonnie slows down to look. "Forget about 'em, Lonnie," his third base coach, Jimy Williams, yells, now waving him on frantically. "Get on home." But it's too late. Lonnie held up long enough for the Twins outfielder to get the ball and throw it in. He makes it to third and that's all.

Gagne and Knoblauch have just faked poor Lonnie out of a run. It could have been a key run, because if Atlanta had carried it through the ninth inning, they would have won the game and the Series. This time it was the Braves' turn not to have it go their way. It should have been us in the Series. I still say, the season had been ours to lose, not the Braves' to win. Maybe next year.

Brett and I will be back next year. There'll be some new faces on the Dodgers and maybe a few old faces will be gone, but Brett and I, and now my old friend Eric Davis, will be there. I've waited years to play on the same team with Davis and now it's going to happen. With both of us in the outfield along with Brett Butler, the Dodgers will be unbeatable.

Brett, Eric, and I will try to instill the sense of family that I thought was lacking this year. We will try to show our leadership on the field. We will try to be the glue that keeps the team together in tight situations. Compare the '92 Dodgers with the '91 Dodgers. You'll see a team that won't give up on itself and that won't have to rely only on its key players all the time. You'll see togetherness and team spirit in the dugout. You'll see a *team* and not individual guys playing their game and leaving the stadium to go home to the news at eleven to see their pictures on the videotape.

The New York Mets also have a reason to look forward to what they're going to do next year. Just five days after signing Eddie Murray from the Dodgers, the Mets signed Bobby Bonilla to the most expensive contract in baseball. And they signed him for a full five years, too. I figure that now, after one year, 84 losses, and almost twice what I was asking for, the Mets have finally got around to replacing me. All it took was two quality players and close to a cool $40 million. But it wasn't about money. It was never about money—not for me and not for them. You can't spend that much money in a lifetime. I believe now that our negotiations were all about power and ego and who was going to do what for whom. The Mets let me go because they wanted to let me go, not because they didn't want to spend the money. Throughout the '91 season, I believe the Mets were still looking for someone to put up the numbers that I did. No matter what, I always put up the numbers. Now I'm doing it in L.A.

So we close the book on 1991. It would have been a lot easier for the Mets to have simply offered me that fifth year. It would only have cost them about half as much as they're paying now. But they haven't really replaced me. Now Eric is back in Los Angeles. Now Brett and I are going to make a spiritual difference on the Dodgers. Now things are going to happen that will really make 1992 a year of fireworks all over the National League wherever the Dodgers play. No, the Mets ain't seen nothin' yet.

I'd like to believe that after all my years on the Mets and my one year on the Dodgers I've come to know a secret about how baseball's supposed to be played. I've come to see that, like Doc Gooden said, it's like life. You can't hang back and wait

for what you want to come along. Just like you can't hang back
in baseball and wait for someone to tell you that it's okay to
hit, okay to get mad at a pitcher, okay to exert your leadership
on a team. Now I know, after all these years, that you've got to
go in on your own say-so. I know that it's not going to happen
unless you make it happen. Sounds pretty basic, but when you
hang back most of your life and follow someone else's lead, it's
what you do as an adult. Now my days of hanging back are
over. I've made too many mistakes that way and let too many
people down. You want to see a leader? Just watch us play next
year.

There's a long winter ahead of us, a long time to think about
what's going to happen next season. But as someone once
wrote, When winter comes, can spring training be far behind?

THE BIGGEST...THE MOST...THE BEST...THE WORST...

THE ULTIMATE BOOK OF SPORTS LISTS

Andrew Postman
and Larry Stone

- *19 Dramatic Turnarounds and Comebacks*
- *8 Most Offensive Nicknames*
- *10 Ugliest Sports Moments*
- *25 Classiest Sports Moments*
- *11 Commonly Flouted Baseball Rules*
- *3 Stupidest Sports Questions*
- *6 Snappiest Answers to Stupid Questions*
- *17 Most Appropriately Named Sports Figures*
- *12 Los Angeles Dodgers Who Appeared on Sixties Sitcoms*
- *15 Famous Ex-Cheerleaders*
- *9 Most Boring Events and Teams*
- *13 Greatest Upsets*
- AND MUCH MORE!

"Historically informative and very, very funny."
—Tim McCarver, *CBS baseball commentator*